*About the book —*

**Putting Minds to Work** is an introductory text which identifies basic skills necessary for professional competence in teaching. Teacher-pupil relationships are shown to be more significant than subject matter in the classroom but, at the level of training in the elementary skills underlying the management of such relationships, they are shown to be more easily developed through communication about subject matter in a special approach to lesson planning.

This lesson planning is presented as a prestructuring of the framework of verbal exchanges. It is developed through the use of three main features: (1) a topic analysis discipline; (2) a behavioural objectives continuum; and (3) episodes, the basic units of the lesson.

The book extends the ideas of self and the structure of subjects at the centre of contemporary thinking in the teaching profession. It examines and explains educational principles in depth. Practising teachers will find it helps them to crystallise their ideas, and beginning teachers will find it gives them security yet promotes professional autonomy through the skills and strategy options it specifies.

This is a most useful book for all those involved in the training and retraining of teachers and of staff in industry and social service organisations.

*About the author —*

**Douglas W. F. Brown** is a Senior Lecturer in Education, Secondary Division, at Christchurch Teachers' College, a position he has held since 1963.

He has a total of 16 years' experience in primary and secondary schools, teaching not only average children but pursuing a special interest in under-achievement as seen in reluctant learners and children of high and low intelligence. Mr. Brown has spent three years in special work with children of high intelligence and 10 years teaching Maori and European children with the special problems of remote areas.

In addition to his classroom experience, Mr. Brown has lectured, tutored and acted as a teaching assistant at the University of Canterbury, and has devoted a large amount of time to outside work in refresher and in-service courses for educational and social service organisations.

## *Putting Minds to Work*

An Introduction to Modern Pedagogy

# *Putting Minds to Work*

## An Introduction to Modern Pedagogy

### D. W. F. BROWN

*Education Department*
*Christchurch Teachers' College*

JOHN WILEY & SONS AUSTRALASIA PTY LTD

SYDNEY    NEW YORK    LONDON    TORONTO

370.994
B 812 P

PRINTED IN AUSTRALIA BY HALSTEAD PRESS, SYDNEY

*To Avril, Michael, Ralph, Jenny, Katherine and Matthew*

# Table of Contents

# *List of Illustrations*

Figure
No.                                                                    Page

# *Preface*

The teacher is a "significant ego" in the classroom, for *his* needs so often influence the outcome of his teaching. Many teachers fail because satisfaction of their needs is imperative. Their pupils fail too. From the viewpoint of professional competence, feelings of *professional* inadequacy are all too frequently at the heart of the matter—even for teachers of many years' experience. This book results from the expressed need of teachers in many refresher and in-service courses for a systematic exposition of principles of method and an outline of skills which could enable them to achieve a more soundly-based competence in the areas giving them cause for greatest disquiet.

A generally acceptable and comprehensive list of basic professional skills is not possible with present understanding of teaching and learning processes. However, given awareness of modern developments, teachers would be likely to agree that mastery of the complex skills of planning and management should be the focus of professional preparation. This introductory text is concerned more particularly with the planning aspect, on the premise that mastery of critical skills underlying effective management can be achieved most economically through planning exercises.

The organisation of the text to emphasise the two themes *planning* and *management* is for convenience of exposition, based on the proposition that the complex nature of teaching makes it essential for some skills to be developed in relative isolation. Planning is here conceived as the anticipation of verbal contingencies to create a framework for the verbal exchanges necessary for mastery of the more complex ideas of a topic. (As such it ignores such housekeeping matters as the issue of books, ventilation, and movement to groups.) This prestructuring involves a number of skills which are subject-centred and so are relatively uncomplicated by matters of personal relationships which loom so large for the novice in the management of the lesson. If, for instance, the novice teacher starts his lesson with an intimate knowledge of his topic organised to be consistent with pupil readiness, is clear as to goals, and has statements and questions that are likely to promote thinking on significant ideas of the topic, he is more free to cope with the complex affective and social factors in management. He is more likely to succeed because he is prepared: not just because he knows his topic but because *he will be familiar with the complexities of its communication.*

At first sight the planning advocated is intimidatingly complex and rigorous—and even abhorrent to those committed to "soul" in teaching. Critics contend, for instance, that the planning exercises put the student teacher in a strait jacket: they become like those generals who have been known to fight a set-piece battle and have been defeated because of inflexibility. On the contrary, it is found that such planning *increases* the likelihood of flexible management through its required anticipation of contingencies. Some insecure student teachers do hold rigidly to a plan, but this is indicative of failure in *management* skills, not of planning.

---

The planning exercises contained within this text are far more comprehensive than is contemplated for use in schools. The point is that they are exercises designed for the development of skills which will finally make such detailed preparatory work unnecessary.

---

But while the main emphasis for the practical purposes of an introductory text is upon planning, the primary concern is with the quality of classroom management. The basic theme here is that when teaching is characterised by those skills which it should have in common with other professions rendering a *personal* service, teachers meet one of the most significant conditions for successful teaching.

Complementing the above is a firm belief, gained from general classroom teaching of children of low intelligence and special work teaching children of very high intelligence, that many children under-achieve because teachers do not know how to *put their minds to work*. If his parents throw Ken into the water he may well swim and, in the course of time, become quite competent. However we would be incredulous if we later heard that Ken had become an Olympic swimmer *without any systematic instruction and intensive training*. Yet in the development of *intellectual* ability this is largely what we do expect. Pupils are presented with the information (knowledge) in a more or less systematic way but it is assumed that they, unaided, will be able to develop the more sophisticated skills needed to process that information. When, then, a pupil fails it is readily assumed that he is lacking in intelligence or that he comes from a background providing inadequate motivation for schooling. The extent of failure is highlighted by Holt:

> Most children in school fail. For a great many, this failure is absolute. Close to forty per cent of those who begin high school drop out before they finish. For college the figure is one in three.[1]

While we do not know enough of teaching and learning processes for certainty, a profitable source of insight, from a pragmatic viewpoint, has proved to be the more elementary cognitive processes involved in concept formation and communications. These are treated as major sources of ideas on the conditions needed for learning and hence on teaching method.

Good teachers are confident they already do much that is advocated in this introductory work, and this is a necessary measure of its validity.

[1] J. C. HOLT, *How Children Fail,* Pitman, London, 1964, p. xiii.

However these same teachers usually feel, and this is important from the standpoint of improving professional competence, that they have done so largely unconscious of principle. So it is that perhaps the most significant feature of this text is the attempt to communicate explicitly the nature of principles considered to underlie the expertise of the classroom teacher. The theory may at times be strange but teachers should find it helpful when communicating insights gained from their own experience.

In conclusion, if the style is at times dogmatic, I hope it is for the sake of clarity: if there are assumptions made without due reverence for academic niceties, it is because pedagogy is closer to the firing line: we cannot always wait for a directive from the general who commands from the rear.

DOUGLAS BROWN

*Christchurch,*
*New Zealand.*
*November, 1971*

# *Acknowledgments*

The development of this book has been supported and enriched by many friends and acquaintances in the teaching profession who over the years have been ready to share and explore new ideas bearing on the nature of professional competence.

I am deeply indebted to the members of the Teaching Skills Project of the Secondary Division of the Christchurch Teachers' College for providing a lively testing ground for ideas and for encouragement and, at times, much needed support.

I owe special thanks to the following staff: to Neil Paget for informed criticisim, concrete suggestions, and painstaking work towards preparation of the final draft, and for proof-reading of the manuscript; to Frances Forster and John Macaulay for assistance with the chemistry and geography illustrations respectively of Chapter 13; and to Bevan Werry for the major contribution to the mathematics illustration of Chapter 14.

Finally, to my wife, who knows how to listen.

D.W.F.B.

# CHAPTER 1

# *Introduction*

*Putting Minds to Work*, as an introduction to pedagogy, is intended to help with the professional training of teachers in the area of teaching method—pedagogy being defined as the art or science of teaching; *especially instruction in teaching method.*[1] It is intended for use in association with a comprehensive text in educational psychology[2] and regular periods of supervised teaching practice. As an introductory text it has to be selective; but as I happen to espouse the cause of *systematic* training of professional skills, it is also strongly biased. Perhaps insight into the cause of my aberration and its professional context may serve to enlist the sympathies of the reader.

## ORIGINS OF BIAS

My first appointment as a class teacher was in the Chatham Islands in the South Pacific about 500 miles east of Christchurch, New Zealand, where my pupils were greatly in need of a skilled teacher. Unfortunately for them I was, it turned out, a teacher in little more than name. I could recognise some of the more significant features of the serious scholastic under-achievement that confronted me, but was quite unable to do much about it. I failed: and miserably. With the realisation of failure I began a search for professional competence.

Many post-mortems, theory books and discussions with more successful teachers later, the realisation came that teaching as a profession was long on theory but short on the ability to communicate the "know-how" of real professional skill. I also became firmly convinced that the teachers' colleges were the source of much of the difficulty, if only in the fact that any suggestion for systematic training in skills was regarded as having the flavour of the "subversive"—as an attempt to return to a reactionary authoritarianism. Consequently, members of what was claimed to be a profession had to gain sophisticated skills on a trial and error basis. The shortcomings were all too apparent: wasted time; misdirected effort; unproductive emotional tension; and the loss of teachers who could no longer tolerate their own incompetence. Further, the situation was not greatly relieved by the quality of the in-service and refresher courses where

1

teachers who had become skilled the hard way would attempt to pass on the skill they had acquired. There was little direct and effective help here beyond "I have found this useful"—a *hints for the handyman* approach. Teachers lacked the ability to pass on their skills to the beginner: their skills tended to be intuitively based, and thereby to lack the disciplined grasp of principle which would have made them communicable. But it was quite remarkable how widespread was the personal dissatisfaction of the experienced teachers at these courses: officially they were regarded as competent yet they felt there was good reason for disquiet.

However, when one looks at teachers' college programmes for even the semblance of training in professional skills, it is all too frequently entirely in vain. Colleges still reject anything suspected of association with *pedagogy*, or, alternatively, are dominated by the notion that professional skill is acquired best by doing the job in the classroom—as an apprentice.

## HISTORICAL BACKGROUND

Pedagogy became a "non-person" in the world of teacher training in the period between World Wars I and II as a result of popular reaction to its arid formalism and neglect of the child being taught. Teachers were inspired to discover the child they were teaching. Teachers' colleges featured studies of child development in all its aspects. Philosophies of education appeared to set new goals for teaching. The child-centred movement which developed was soon able to point to many improvements: individual differences in intellect and personality were catered for in various ways, which produced happier classrooms and, given the premises upon which the movement operated, better all-round performance. Perhaps the most characteristic feature of these new classrooms was the recognition that the child had something to *say* and that he should say it if he were to learn as well as he might; and that he learned best by *doing*—in the sense that he had to create his own understanding. Democracy in the classroom. The old pedagogy withered and died in the teachers' colleges, its tenets those of an outmoded, authoritarian era. (It has survived in many secondary schools but is now weakening in the face of rumblings from better educated parents and outraged students.) What, then, has happened in the development of theory and practice to justify rehabilitation of pedagogy?

Unfortunately for the child-centred approach, there was a built-in weakness which was not generally recognised until Sputnik I prompted a frantic reappraisal of the child-centred regime. It was soon acknowledged that the system had gone too far in that it ignored those requirements for intellectual growth which depend upon a disciplinary factor in teaching. The best teachers were well informed on the development of intellect and personality of their pupils but knew very little about how to put the pupils' minds to work in a disciplined way that would promote development of intellectual ability. (The inability of teachers to do much to help those of high or low intelligence is a case in point.) Classroom talk, for instance, was all too often characterised by a formlessness which followed from the teacher's inability to direct thinking in a constructive way.

Pupils in such classes learned to respond with anything they could recall which was in any way relevant to a question (and often not) and these offerings would then dictate the ebb and flow of discussion. This is a far remove from the requirements of disciplined thinking necessary to achieve understanding of complex ideas. The *project*, intended to epitomise the self-directed pupil activity of *learning by doing*, was all too frequently material slavishly copied from an encyclopedia and prettied-up with more expenditure of time and effort. Busywork!

Three educational developments gained prominence during and after the period of reappraisal, possibly because they represented an interest in the *intellectual*, in the sense of content to be mastered and the quality of thinking achieved:

1. *Programmed learning*, which is primarily concerned with the organisation of knowledge into "little bits" under conditions of repetition and confirmation of success that have been empirically found to improve learning best.

2. The study of the behaviour of teachers and pupils in the classroom—what they actually *do* and *say* and *achieve*. (This has been discovered to be a more profitable source of insight into human learning than the study of white rats in university laboratories.)

3. A new conception of intelligence as problem-solving capacity which is considered to be developed to a large extent out of past experience of coping with problems of the environment.

Many insights were gained, but the following appear to be the most significant for our present context:

1. *Teaching as practised is an extraordinarily bumbling process.*

   Present day classroom instruction is an attempt to attain ill-defined objectives through imprecise methods. It amounts to leading others in the pursuit of shadows along an unmarked pathway.[3]

2. *Teaching is a complex interaction process involving feedback of information between teacher and pupil and a complex changing of roles.*

   . . . teaching is fundamentally a social process involving communication and interaction between at least two people, a teacher and a student. It is a kind of dialectic in which both serve as teacher and student at different times and at different levels. A teacher is not only instructing a student, but is also learning about that student, and using what he learns in making decisions about what to do next in the course of his teaching. Similarly, the student is not only learning, but is providing information to the teacher in the on-going interaction.[4]

3. *Teacher actions have enormous influence upon the intellectual growth of their pupils.*

   Classroom learning experiences are not usually designed to provide a cumulative sequence in the maturation of thought which is at once psychologically sound and logically valid. All this has contributed to considerable under-achievement in the mastery of autonomous and disciplined thought processes.[5]

Teaching thus appeared to be in need of more sophisticated and skilled methods, particularly those that would promote the development of intellectual ability. There is, of course, a danger of over-reaction comparable with that against pedagogy earlier. It could so easily happen that the strengths of the child-centred approach were thrown out with the unwanted methodology bathwater. That would be a serious loss: if only for the fact that intellectual performance of most students has so clearly been demonstrated to be dependent upon consideration of affective and social factors, that is, those which arise from a respect for the *individuality* of the learner.

Given the need for more sophisticated method, why an ugly word like pedagogy? Simply because it is distinctive to teaching, and perhaps because its rehabilitation in the teachers' colleges would be taken as a serious attempt to do something about training in professional skills.

## A PRESCRIPTIVE APPROACH

Unfortunately, there is such a state of flux in our knowledge of teaching and learning processes (much of the lore of the white rats is now of doubtful relevance) that it takes a profound arrogance to postulate this principle or that method as fundamental to good teaching. As Adams and Biddle state:

> For over half a century, reviews of teacher-competence research have consistently pointed out that failure of the research to provide any clear, unequivocal evidence to confirm what constitutes good teaching.[6]

To make matters very much worse, the prevailing opinion in research favours *descriptive* studies of what is going on in particular classrooms, whereas the essence of this introduction to modern pedagogy is that it is *prescriptive*: a concern not so much with what *is* going on in particular classrooms, but with what *should* be. If taken at face value this is naïvely arrogant and certainly unfashionable. This I concede, but submit the following in mitigation of the offence:

1. What is presented in this text arises from sixteen years of class teaching in primary and secondary schools and more than twenty years of sifting theory and research and testing methods to develop programmes which would enable the novice teacher to achieve professional competence more rapidly and less painfully than I did.

2. Teachers, lecturers and students, in giving close and continuous scrutiny to this developing work over the years, have led the way to considerable improvements, have provided a safeguard against messianic advocacy, and have provided a degree of objectivity. The test has always been: *will it work for the teacher in the classroom?*

   (a) Teachers on courses and in classrooms have been prepared to share their knowledge and to speak frankly about their difficulties in achieving professional competence once they were aware of the project. The information thus gained (mainly in reaction to communication of developing ideas) played a substantial part in determining priorities and objectives.

(b) Lecturers of the Secondary Division of Christchurch Teachers' College who are voluntary members of the *Teaching Skills Project*, which was organised to test and develop the ideas presented in the text in the training of students in their particular disciplines, have insisted on many changes for the better.

(c) Student teachers in the college have been merciless critics for several years and, more recently, as their objections have been met more successfully, most encouraging colleagues.

*Putting Minds to Work* was chosen as a title because it highlights the underlying theme of the text—that there are identifiable teacher actions which are necessary to start students working and keep them working anywhere near capacity. But students are people with thoughts and feelings of their own and, if one accepts the final goal of putting minds to work to be to promote the development of a student's ability to educate himself, *teacher actions must involve three interdependent domains of human behaviour:* cognitive, affective, and social.

While planning tends to be subject-centred, the explication of the theme *putting minds to work* is not complete without consideration of *management*, wherein the emphasis is on the individuals and groups and the *processes* of teaching and learning. A pedagogy which was primarily cognitive would be ignoring both the general goals of modern education and the established truth that successful teaching depends upon affective and social factors in learning. The general significance in terms of final goals will be apparent in the following description of the ability to educate oneself:

It means that one has both the desire and the capacity to learn for himself, to dig out what he needs to know. It means that one has the capacity to judge what is worth learning. It means, too, that one can think for himself, so that he is dependent on neither the opinions nor the facts of others, and that he uses that capacity to think about his own education, which means to think about his own nature and his place in the universe—about the meaning of life and of knowledge and of the relations between them. "To refuse the effort to understand," Wayne Booth, dean of the College of the University of Chicago, argues, "is to resign from the human race." You cannot distinguish an educated man, he continues, "by whether or not he believes in God, or in UFO's. But you can tell an educated man by the way he takes hold of the question of whether God exists, or whether UFO's are from Mars."

To be educated in this sense means also to know something of the experience of beauty, if not in the sense of creating it or discoursing about it, then at the very least, in the sense of being able to respond to it—to respond, that is to say, both to the beauty of nature and to the beauty of the art made by our fellow men.

To be educated also means to understand something of how to make our intentions effective in the real world, of how to apply knowledge to the life one lives and the society in which one lives it. The aim of education, as Alfred North Whitehead has written, "is the acquisition of the art of the utilisation of knowledge". Indeed, "a merely well-informed man is the most useless bore on God's earth".[7]

A reading of the "Affective Domain" of the *Taxonomy of Educational Objectives*[8] will serve to indicate how critical the affective factors are, quite apart from those social factors which are not implicit to their expression.

Though *Putting Minds to Work* gives high priority to the personal equation in teaching and learning, it has a wider connotation than is usually given that expression. The following brief comments indicate significant features of this wider interpretation.

1. The teacher is a person and one whose ego needs can all too easily be the most significant factor in student failure.

The proposition is that teachers need to be aware of how their own personalities influence the course of interpersonal exchanges and to be trained to manage stress situations which may develop in relations with individuals, groups, or the whole class, in order to increase the probability of a positive outcome for the pupils.

2. Teachers at present are generally equipped with a simplistic notion of personality development and associated behaviour, in which they are led to believe that persistent misbehaviour and poor motivation are manifestations of the neurotic, which can be corrected given a certain range of teacher actions.

No wonder many teachers have problems of control—this conception ignores the condition of failure of socialising processes, which evidence suggests could well account for a substantial amount of the disruptive behaviour experienced in the classroom! The point is that this condition, as displayed in character defects, is not amenable to management on the basis of insights into the nature of the neurotic. In fact some teacher actions based on this misconception directly exacerbate and even provoke the disruptive behaviour!

3. A class is not just a collection of individuals; it is also a community comprising many kinds of groups.

Much that is held up as desirable practice is based on invalid generalisation from the nature of individuals: what is good for the individual is good for the group! Unfortunately this so often ignores the idiosyncratic features of *group* learning.

Bearing in mind this background to modern pedagogy and the nature of the bias peculiar to this text, let us proceed to a fuller investigation of the domain of pedagogy.

## REFERENCES

[1] Webster's *New Twentieth Century Dictionary*, World Publishing Co., Cleveland, 2nd Edition, 1963, p. 1320.
[2] E.g., D. P. AUSUBEL and F. G. ROBINSON, *School Learning*, Holt, Rinehart and Winston, New York, 1969.

³ B. Y. KERSH, "Programmed Classroom Instruction", in R. GLASER (Ed.), *Teaching Machines and Programmed Learning II: Data and Directions*, Department of Audio Visual Instruction, National Education Association, Washington, 1965, pp. 321-68.
⁴ L. STOLUROW and K. PAHEL, "Letter to the Editor", *Harvard Educational Review*, Summer 1963, **33**, p. 384.
⁵ H. TABA and FREEMAN F. ELZEY, "Teaching Strategies and Thought Processes", *Teachers' College Record*, 1964, **65**, pp. 524-34.
⁶ R. S. ADAMS and B. J. BIDDLE, *Realities of Teaching*, Holt, Rinehart and Winston, New York, 1970, p. 82.
⁷ C. E. SILBERMAN, "Murder in the Schoolroom: Part I", *The Atlantic*, June 1970, p. 84. Copyright © 1970, by Charles E. Silberman.
⁸ D. R. KRATHWOHL *et al.*, *Taxonomy of Educational Objectives—The Classification of Educational Goals, Handbook II: Affective Domain*, David McKay, New York, 1964.

## RECOMMENDED READING

*Understanding pre-Sputnik Methodology*

COUNTS, G. S., *Dare the School Build a New Social Order?*, John Day Co., New York, 1932.
DEWEY, J., *Democracy and Education*, Macmillan, New York, 1916.
DEWEY, J., *Experience and Education*, Macmillan, New York, 1938.
KILPATRICK, W. H., *Foundations of Method*, Macmillan, New York, 1925.

*Understanding Contemporary Descriptive Studies*

ADAMS, R. S. and BIDDLE, B. J., *Realities of Teaching: Explorations with Videotape*, Holt, Rinehart and Winston, New York, 1970.
AMIDON, E. and HUNTER, E., *Improving Teaching*, Holt, Rinehart and Winston, New York, 1966.
GORDON, I. J., *Studying the Child in School*, John Wiley & Sons, New York, 1966.
SMITH, L. M. and GEOFFREY, W., *The Complexities of an Urban Classroom*, Holt, Rinehart and Winston, New York, 1968.

### PART I

# The Domain of Pedagogy

# CHAPTER 2

# *Everyone Knows About Teaching*

Teaching is not restricted to teachers. People of all ages and vocations have occasion to exchange information in dialogues in which they seek to bring about a permanent change in the capability of the other party. Thus playmates, parents, bosses, workmates, supervisors, youth leaders, in this common-sense vein, all *teach*.

Learning is something everyone has done, is doing, or will be doing—intentionally or unintentionally.

Not surprisingly, on the grounds of experience, everyone can claim at least some degree of ability to evaluate teaching. Thus, you may know quite a lot about pedagogy even though you know nothing of its jargon. The following transcription and commentary assumes this *readiness* on your part and is in the form of an exercise designed to prepare you for a formal discussion of the domain of pedagogy.

---

The transcript of a lesson is on the left-hand side of the pairs of facing pages which follow. On the right-hand side are the remarks of three student teachers who are in the process of deciding on the merits of the lesson. (None of the students is a geographer.)

After consideration of the lesson transcript, you will be asked to identify the opinion closest to your own.

---

*From the teacher's Lesson Plan:*

*Topic: Japan as a Trading Nation.* This is the second lesson on Japan
—one of a series of six. This is a double period lesson. Class
Grade 8.

Class had previously studied Great Britain and has an elementary
understanding of the concepts of population density, resources,
imports and exports and standards of living as they apply in
that country.

The first of this series on Japan was on *Family Life in Japan.*
The following were noted: food preferences, high value placed
on education, wide range of vocations available.

*Main Idea of the Lesson*

Though Japan as a trading nation has many features in common
with Great Britain, its most significant difference is in the
dependence of the economy upon the importance of raw
materials, and efficient processing for re-export.

## TRANSCRIPT OF THE LESSON

$$T = \text{teacher} \qquad P = \text{pupil}$$

*T*1      Today we are going to continue with our study of Japan along
the lines we planned following our evaluation of our study
of Great Britain.

*T*2      You will recall that we agreed that this topic should be
*Japan as a Trading Nation* . . . and this is what we are going to
do today. (Title put on blackboard)

*T*3      Now, remember that we decided on Japan because it appeared
to have some features which would perhaps make it easier to
understand than other countries of the Orient following on
our study of Great Britain.

## STUDENT COMMENT

*Mike*       Knows what he's about. List of concepts looks good . . .
             though I'm no geographer. I like that main idea.

*Lynda*      Well, frankly I'm doubtful. What he calls his main idea is
             impressive but he'll need to be good to get that across.

*Shirley*    I like it.

*Mike*       A good introduction. Look how he makes a link with previous
             work and he's done some planning with the class.

*Lynda*      It's far too formal. Lacks interest. I doubt very much that he
             allowed the class very much say in that planning. With an
             introduction like that, he just doesn't seem that sort of person.
             But he does relate this lesson to previous work.

*Shirley*    I like it. He means well even if he's a bit formal.

*T4*      First, let's check we know what we are talking about. Joan, what *is* the Orient?

    *P1*    Please sir, the countries of the East.

*T5*      Such as?

    *P2*    China. Vietnam.

    *P3*    Indonesia.

*T6*      And? Come on, it's obvious!

    *P4*    Japan!

*T7*      Gary, name a country that is NOT in the Orient.

    *P5*    Great Britain!

*T8*      Is he right? (Class chorus of YES)

    (Teacher now points to all major Pacific countries on map asking class to call names. If not known, immediately tells. Having done this he asks class to say whether or not each belongs to the Orient. Class participation is good.)

*T9*      Now what were the features we noted about Japan that made it appear possibly like Great Britain as a trading nation? Let's see if we were right.

    *P6*    It's in the same place.

*T10*    Don't be silly, Jennifer. It can't be in the same place. What do you really mean?

    *P7*    Oh! It's in the same . . . but I really mean on the other side of the map. No, that's wrong. What I mean . . .

    *P8*    She means that it's in approximately the same latitude, probably that it's a small country, and that it's near a continental land mass.

*T11*    Is that what you meant, Jennifer?

    *P9*    I suppose so.

    (Blackboard note on location and size, under heading: Common Features of Japan and Great Britain.)

*Mike*      Good. He's businesslike. Makes sure they know an important concept.

*Lynda*     Too much fuss over very little. I don't like this. Too much teacher talk for a relatively unimportant idea in this lesson.

*Shirley*   Well I think it's good. He takes the Orient idea and goes to some trouble to make sure they know it. And he's not satisfied with them saying they know it . . . he tests them with some countries that are not in the Orient.

*Lynda*     This is an example of what I meant earlier. The man is arrogant and singularly unperceptive—Jennifer had a good idea there. Did Jennifer or anyone else but the teacher and *P8* understand? The lesson really fails here. He's rejected Jennifer and he's got no idea of how to go about getting understanding.

*Shirley*   I think he handled that well. Look how *P8* volunteered to help. He must have good relations with the class. And he is considerate—look how he has referred back to Jennifer (*T11*), even if she was a bit surly.

*Mike*      Fair enough—Jennifer's not too bright—he gave her a pretty fair go.

*P*10   Please sir, what about population?

*T*12        What do you mean, "population"?

*P*11   I mean that there is a lot of people for not much land.

*T*13        So?

*P*12   Like Britain there would not be much food.

*P*13   You can't be sure of that. You mean *you* think so! (Speaking to *P*12.)

*T*14        Is there anything we know at present that would support Gavin's idea?

*P*14   We sell them mutton.

*P*15   My father was in Japan after the war and he wasn't allowed to eat their vegetables because the farmers use human manure to grow them in and you get hookworm. . . . (Class giggles.)

*T*15        Right! That's enough of that! (Loudly and firmly.) Trust you, Donald, to come out with something like that. Now I've said that's enough and I mean it. (Silence. Loud snort from Donald. Donald ordered to leave room. Pained silence.)

*T*16        Now let us get some more ideas on the board. (Firmly.) Let me remind you of our purpose, to remember the features we thought made it like Great Britain, and see if we were in fact correct.

*T*17        We shall start by getting our basic facts. Let's start with population which you considered so important. What is Japan's population?

*P*16   About 100,000,000.

*T*18        I think at this point we need more information. Here is a summary of basic information on population, land, resources, imports and exports.

*Mike*        He's got his feet on the ground—no nonsense from Donald—
obviously a troublemaker.

*Shirley*      A teacher's got to have control. If you haven't, how can you
teach?

*Lynda*       What I said before. He just cannot see a good idea when he
meets one. What an unnecessary fuss—couldn't he just *accept*
their feelings?

*Mike*        I like this. Firm control established. Tells class what is going
to happen and gives them the facts. Well prepared.

*Shirley*      Very good.

*Lynda*       Has some good points—trying to get the class settled to the
topic. Obviously he's done some planning—more than I can
say for most of the teachers I saw.

C

(Teacher reveals simplified tables on blackboard, and conducts a brief quiz to ensure class can *read* them. Explains where necessary.)

*T*19    Earlier we were on population. What can you say about the population of Japan?

*P*17    That it's about 93,000,000.

*P*18    That it increased very rapidly earlier but not so much now.

*T*20    What evidence have you for "but not so much now"?

*P*19    My father said so last night.

*P*20    It's in that table.

*P*21    No it isn't—that table only goes to 1965—this is 1968.

*P*22    Yes it is. You can tell from the table.

*P*23    How?
(Pupil goes to blackboard without asking permission and points to table. . . .)

*P*24    These numbers are not getting bigger as fast as these are here. Population growth is slowing down. It won't change suddenly so it will be like that now.

*T*21    Yes, very good, Chris. Do you all see that? (Pause—class nods.) But to understand what size of population really means in Japan we need to know something more than its size. Look at the table . . . look at the table where it refers to the land. Now think of Britain.

*Shirley*    This is a good teacher. Look how he has the tables prepared to produce them at the right time, and then he makes sure the class can interpret them. I wish my teacher had done that.

*Lynda*    Good points—especially (*T*20) where he wants them to be sure that it is understood. Pity he didn't do this more frequently.

*Mike*    Like I said before he's good—doesn't let them get away with anything—(I mean in *T*20).

*Lynda*    One of the brighter parts of the lesson. Real pupil participation. Cross talk. He's forgotten to be bossy.

*Mike*    He's slipped here; I wouldn't allow those pupils to talk like that—could lose control.

*Shirley*    Like I said. He means well. This is where he really brings it off —though I'm not sure about that bit where the pupil goes to the blackboard without permission. That doesn't seem right to me. What would happen if they all did?

*P25*   It's really like Britain—only worse—a larger population and a small amount of land.

*T22*    Yes, that's right.

*T23*    Let's take this further though—what kind of land is it that matters most when we talk of population?

*P26*   Land for growing food.

*T24*    Look at the map on page 36 of your books.

*T25*    What are you puzzled about, Mary? Use your head, girl, and look at the title.

*T26*    Well, then, Mary, what does it tell you about land and food?

*P27*   I don't know sir.

*T27*    Come on, girl, what does a relief map tell you?

*P28*   I don't know sir.

*T28*    Hmm. Well let's see. Can you sum up, Ralph?

*P29*   Population him too big; land him too small, sir. (Laughter.)

*T29*    Hmm. Always the funny man!

No comment.

| | |
|---|---|
| *Lynda* | I strongly object to this sort of thing. This is an attack on the person. The man's a blundering fool—I'll grant you he probably means well. |
| *Mike* | Trials of a teacher! |
| *Shirley* | I'm glad he asked Mary but he shouldn't have spoken like that to her. |
| *Lynda* | This man's self-importance is unbearable—why can't he just join in the fun? |
| *Mike* | Good control. That Ralph needs firm handling. *T29* is a good-humoured way of putting him in his place. |

*T*30     However, it's right as far as it goes—but, Joan, what hasn't he said?

*P*30   That they won't be able to grow enough food.

*P*31   You can't be sure of that. Japanese eat rice and eat less than we do.

*P*32   Maybe not, but look at the tables of imports anyway—and I know we export food to Japan—mutton for instance.

*T*31     Well our position seems to be that we think there is insufficient land to grow enough food and our tables seem to confirm this.

*P*33   I don't think so sir. Japanese eat a lot of fish and the food on that table is mainly luxury food for Japanese.

*T*32     Well, Frank, I think this would be as good a place as any to tell us about that article you showed me the other day.

*P*34   (Frank outlines an article on Japanese food productivity, Japanese food preferences, diet, and importation of food exported by New Zealand. Teacher makes notes on blackboard.)

*T*33     Thank you, Frank—that sums up the position very nicely.

Lynda    Cross talk again. But I just don't believe that the class would be up with him at *T*31.

Mike    Not sure of this—it's what I think is called cross talk—it looks good but I don't think the class would all get as far as the teacher thought. You know I'm getting rather doubtful about this lesson.

Shirley    He's let them talk and then he has summed up their thoughts. That's good.

Lynda    He has planned for this. The blackboard summary would be a good idea but I wonder how much the class would understand? He did nothing to see they *did* understand.

Mike    I like the blackboard notes. Something for them to put in their books.

Shirley    Good planning and something for their books.

T34        Could we turn now to Japan as an importer and exporter of goods? Look at these two tables—compare them. Can you see any significant relationships between the two? (Import and Export tables.)

(Class silent)

T35        What is being imported in large quantities here?

   P35  Iron ore, sir.

T36        And what is being exported in large quantities here?

   P36  Goods made from iron and steel.

T37        Well?

   P37  Japan imports a lot of ore and makes it into steel goods for export.

T38        Now what about Great Britain. Does Great Britain import ore and manufacture it into steel goods and export those? Look at the tables.

   P38  Yes she does.

   P39  That's true—but there's a very big difference.

T39        Yes—but what *is* that difference?

   P40  Japan does it much more than Great Britain.

*Shirley*    I've always liked teachers who have charts and tables. It means you get something useful in your books.

*Lynda*    The class silence is significant. I think he had lost them. He had probably forgotten that they need help in reading tables.

*Mike*    On the ball here . . . takes them firmly through a prepared table. But how sound is his knowledge of this topic?

*T*40        I want you now to go into your groups and spend some time comparing the tables on the blackboard on Japan and the others in our books on Great Britain, in the light of what we have decided and then do the following:

1. *Answer the question:* Are Japan and Great Britain as alike as trading nations as we thought they might be?

2. *Prepare a statement* to describe Japan as a trading nation in comparison with Great Britain.

(Class in six groups for 20 minutes, followed by reporting back and blackboard listing of findings, most of which favour that they are very alike but two emphasising the degree of difference in the matter of importation of raw materials and processing for re-export.)

*T*41        Joan's group seems to sum up the thinking of four groups: *Japan and Great Britain are more alike than different as trading nations.*

Bill's group seems to express better the thinking of the opposition: *Japan depends very much more than Great Britain on the importation of raw materials and so must be very different.*

*T*42        Bill's group has come very close to the idea I had about this problem when we started this lesson.
(Blackboard note of main idea of lesson.)

(Lesson concludes with class taking notes which teacher compiles from pupil responses already listed on blackboard, coupled with relevant tables.)

*Mike*      Nicely rounded-off lesson. I'm not sure about it all though. I can see myself in that class—I'm beginning to suspect why I did not like certain subjects at high school.

*Lynda*     I don't think they got anywhere near *understanding* the idea stated in the teacher's plan—in spite of his statement to the class in *T*42. There is a very big gap indeed and I don't think the lesson did much to bridge it. I'll bet he *told* them all the other ideas—*or perhaps he didn't really know his topic.*

*Shirley*   Quite a good ending with something to write in the books. I think Bill's group did well to get so close to the idea the teacher wanted.

SUMMARIES

*Mike*      Firm control; seemed to have some very good features in planning; I'm unsure about effectiveness of lesson as a whole— probably not as much achieved as the teacher thought.

*Lynda*     An unsuccessful attempt at planning; poor personal relationships—I suspect a good class is going to be ruined—too much ineffective teacher talk—little real understanding achieved by class—and I'm doubtful about the teacher's understanding of the topic.

*Shirley*   Quite a good lesson. Planned. He keeps them busy and they get something in their books. Does not do so well on control.

---

Which of the above views comes closest to your own?

---

DISCUSSION

The following is a brief analysis of the comments of each of the students and also gives the salient features of their first teaching practice. Keeping in mind the summary you chose as being closest to your own view, to what extent is the corresponding analysis below likely to be a description of *you*?

*Mike*:    identifies with the teacher as a figure of authority. There is relatively little awareness of the significance of the pupils' thoughts and feelings. Significantly he interprets the teacher's question "What evidence have you for '*but not so much now*'?" (*T*20) as the exercise of authority. Mike, it will be remembered, commented that the teacher "doesn't let them get away with anything"—which implies a disciplinary role.
           There is some awareness of inadequacies in the teacher's grasp of the subject and of the possibility that the pupils may not have achieved as much as the teacher assumed.

---

On his first teaching practice session Mike was primarily concerned with control. Although he was well prepared, he dominated his class and talked excessively so there was little pupil contribution.

---

*Lynda*:   identifies with the needs of the pupil but is also conscious of possible deficiencies in the teacher's grasp of the topic. She is preoccupied with the feelings of the pupils and the ways in which the teacher must act to promote understanding. Central to her thinking is the idea that the pupil's feelings as a person must be considered and the teacher must allow the opportunity for pupils to express their thoughts. Lynda, unlike Mike, thought *T*20 gave such an opportunity.

> On her first teaching practice session Lynda established excellent rapport but was unable to exploit this because she could not manage the discussion methods she favoured and because she had difficulty establishing class routines.

*Shirley*: identifies with the teacher and his purposes. Thus she is impressed by his good intentions and his concern to see that his pupils have something systematic in their note books. On the other hand she appears relatively insensitive to the feelings of the pupils, tending to see a threat in what is not in accord with the teacher's expectations. Compare, for instance, Shirley's comment on the Jennifer episode (*T9-P9*), where Jennifer is regarded as surly, with Lynda's comment that the teacher had *rejected* Jennifer.

> On her first teaching practice session Shirley gave copious notes for copying into books, or talked *at* the class. She justified her deficiencies in terms of her good intentions and was strongly resistant to any appraisal of her performance.

## CONCLUSION

While, then, everyone knows about teaching, he does not necessarily know about it in ways which best favour the interests of those being taught. Our ways of relating to things and people predispose us to structure classroom experience, and our role in it, to meet our own needs. Further, as in the case of Lynda, we may simply lack the skill to act on our good intentions.

### A Teaching Problem

Given the teacher and pupil exchanges (*P10-P15*) above to where Donald informs the class:

> My father was in Japan after the war and he wasn't allowed to eat their vegetables because the farmers use human manure to grow them in and you get hookworm. . . . (Class giggles.)

What would *you* say to the class in order to accept Donald's idea yet cope with the feelings of the class? (A model answer is on page 35.)

# CHAPTER 3

# *Who is Professional?*

The ILO-UNESCO definition of teaching as a profession states:

> We must accept that teaching is an occupation wherein the practi-
> tioners, possessing high moral principles and a deep sense of social
> responsibility, *render a personal service* based on the possession of
> a body of knowledge particular to the calling and *a set of specialised*
> *skills gained initially through rigorous education and training* de-
> manding high intellectual attributes and reinforced from time to
> time in service, wherein the practitioners individually endeavour to
> fulfil scrupulously all their obligations and wherein they collectively
> either determine or strongly influence and safeguard standards of
> conduct and performance.[1]   (My italics)

The nature and development of this *set of specialised skills* is central to
a course in pedagogy. What are these skills? How are they developed?

This chapter discusses these questions from the viewpoint that while
intuitive understanding of teaching processes often displays considerable
insight, its unpredictability (as between one individual and another)
means that a pedagogy course can take little for granted either of understanding or skills. To highlight areas in particular need of systematic
training, the focus of interest will be on areas where lack of knowledge
or skill seem most likely to have seriously detrimental effects upon learning.

The discussion takes the form of an outline of the more important
features of the domain of pedagogy as illustrated in Figure 3.1.
From Figure 3.1 we see the ten areas which must encompass the "set of
specialised skills" referred to as the basis of professionalism in teaching.
These ten areas, each of which will be elaborated to point up the basic
skills for planning and management, are:

1. "Self" of teacher and pupils;
2. Communication;
3. Knowledge;
4. Cognitive skills;
5. Affective and social skills;
6. Psycho-motor skills;

7. Readiness;
8. Goals;
9. Conditions of learning; and
10. Strategies.

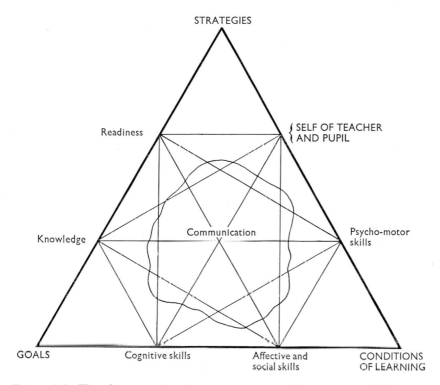

Figure 3.1: The domain of pedagogy: in terms of categories of planning and management

## "SELF" OF TEACHER AND PUPILS: THEY ARE PEOPLE

### THE TEACHER

The mere fact that teaching involves interpersonal exchange implies that both positive and negative qualities of a teacher's personality can have a considerable influence upon events in the classroom. Given, for instance, that a teacher should promote independent thinking in his classroom, he will only be able to do so to the extent that he can tolerate the uncertainty of outcome that must characterise activities directed at such a goal. Then, too, if he feels sufficiently secure in himself he will be able to accept the negative thoughts, feelings and even behaviour of his pupils as they become genuinely involved in these activities with him. He will have bridged a credibility gap, let alone a generation gap, to a meeting of minds. As Allport says:

Elsewhere I have argued that in teaching values and attitudes it is not the deliberately adopted curriculum that is effective. It is rather the *obiter dicta*, the parenthetical remark, the "little true things" and above all the example of the teacher that count.[2]

On the other hand, a teacher who is primarily concerned with himself, who cannot, for instance, tolerate uncertainty of outcome of free discussion and who feels the negative thoughts, feelings and behaviour of others as a personal attack, denies independence and demands conformity.

While teachers will readily concede the above in principle, in practice it seems they all too frequently act as though unaware of how powerfully they, themselves, can influence the pupils of their classes. However, it is the practical experience of those who give training in counselling that people who at heart would prefer to express a greater concern for others *are* capable of quite remarkable adaptations of attitude and behaviour *as they become aware of themselves as others experience them.*

In Figure 3.2 a man is informing his companion of a situation involving his companion's girlfriend. If you were in the position of being told this, how would *you* answer?

Figure 3.2: An exercise

Three answers to the above problem were:

1. That's all right. Have a good time!
2. Oh hell!
3. A fine one she's turned out to be!

Assuming each person has a "stable personality", i.e., he is capable of coping over a period of time with a job and family responsibilities, it is reasonable to expect some consistency of behaviour in the face of such crises. Thus, for the sake of illustration, each of the responses can be taken as indicative of three distinct orientations or outlooks on life.

The first person can be said to be self-punishing (he was extremely so in fact), the second to be openly expressive of his true feelings of hurt, and the third desirous of punishing someone else—in this case the girlfriend. Obviously the consequences of each of these responses are likely to be markedly different. For example, assuming the original comment was in the tone of voice of someone *obligated* to inform his companion to avoid his being hurt by some third party, the first response might pass muster for diplomacy, the second generate feelings of guilt and the third antagonism. It is not surprising then that a teacher who is predisposed to interpret incidents as a threat to self will tend to generate negative feelings in his pupils. On the other hand, when a teacher's feelings are concerned about the *self* of his pupils, a positive outcome is more likely.

So it was that in Chapter 2 Mike saw the episode with Donald in one way and Lynda another. Donald had volunteered the information that human wastes were used to manure the ground in which vegetables were grown and that New Zealand soldiers were consequently not allowed to eat them. The class was "disturbed" as a result and Donald was ordered out of the room. Mike saw this as a situation indicating a need for control and approved the "firm" handling. Lynda, on the other hand, saw a need to accept Donald's idea and the feelings of the class. Here Mike was more concerned with *himself*—Lynda more with the class.

The implication seems clear—a teacher needs to "make himself over" in those areas where his habitual behaviour is antithetical to this role as one performing a *personal service*.

## THE PUPIL

That the pupil is a person whose thoughts are important and who must be given the opportunity to *do* things rather than merely to hear about them is a proposition common to the educational psychology texts of the thirties inspired by the New Educational Fellowship. They emphasise, too, that because he will have a conception of himself as a person his experience of success and failure, praise and criticism are recognised as highly significant factors in his past, present and future learning.

Unfortunately, while various studies have indicated the differential effects of various degrees of success or failure, praise or criticism upon pupils with different *degrees of anxiety*, few have drawn adequate attention to the very different psychological reality these categories of experience have for some. For example, for a pupil who is predisposed to identify emotionally with the teacher, these experiences have the intended psychological reality, and the pupil responds along the lines of the conventional expectation limited by the degree of his anxiety about achievement. But a pupil who does not identify with his teacher emotionally, and who is compulsively anxious about achievement, tends to interpret praise and criticism merely as objective indications of success or failure, and to react to success with inflated ambitions and to failure with such heightened anxiety as to perform even more inadequately.[3] Further, there are those who in their state of alienation define their world, or more narrowly their school experience, as one in which they are the helpless pawns of an unfeeling environment. Success, failure, praise and criticism for these individuals are merely the good or bad fortune that it is their lot to endure.[4] Not surprisingly such pupils are not responsive to the usual prescription

D

of massive doses of success and praise—for it appears they do not believe that these could be consequences of any actions of theirs. Obviously a teacher needs to be very much more sensitive to how the individual *pupil* feels.

Significantly none of the student comments in the transcription of Chapter 2 differentiated between ways in which pupils responded—even Lynda, who was most strongly oriented to the pupils' needs, *assumed the teacher's actions had the same psychological reality for each pupil as they had for her.*

From consideration of the above it is proposed that not only does the teacher need a knowledge of child development as is usually developed in educational psychology texts, but also a knowledge of the different ways in which *pupils* typically define the more significant aspects of the school experience. Further, this knowledge needs to be supported by the ability to *recognise* such differences in orientation to school experiences and by the ability to set up both general conditions in the classroom which promote learning for all and conditions which are tailored to meet the needs of the special, individual case.

---

*Areas of specialised skills highlighted by the discussion so far are implicit to the following abilities:*
1. To communicate concern for others that transcends concern for self.
2. To discriminate between different pupil orientations to school experience and to create appropriate conditions for learning.

---

## PROFESSIONAL COMPETENCE

Given the need to play such roles in relations with pupils, it will be apparent that professional competence depends upon the acquisition of complex skills. However, it will be obvious that to achieve these skills the teacher needs a self-assurance in teaching situations which will permit him to have a concern for his pupils which is greater than his concern for himself. The implication is clear—a teacher's professional preparation should include a practical programme of training similar to that usually considered necessary for counsellors in training.

While a text such as this cannot develop this area of knowledge and skills development, the priority it should receive in a pedagogy course would appear self-evident.

## COMMUNICATION

### LISTENING AND RESPONDING

To render a personal service a teacher must be able to communicate with his pupils—an ability which requires a reciprocity of listening and responding. Considering the teacher's part in communication, he must not only listen to what is said but to what the pupil is trying to say, and he must respond appropriately. The significance accorded to appropriateness of response follows from the nature of mental processes and from the need for the pupil to create his own understanding.[5] Thus, to achieve understanding, a pupil frequently has to grope for words and ideas to express what may be imperfectly perceived in terms of what is as yet imperfectly understood. He "fumbles" for words and ideas. If a teacher is oriented to listen and to respond appropriately to that "fumble", he can increase the likelihood of a successful outcome—not only for the individual pupil, but also for the class use of the contribution.

---

*Exercise*
T  Why do we have policemen?
P  Burglars come at night to steal—there was this TV programme...
T  (cutting in firmly) Yes, that's right. The police are there to protect everyone.

The above is a good example of listening and responding.

Yes ☐          No ☐

---

In this example the teacher *is* listening, but more for a cue to indicate a train of thought approximating his own so he can continue as planned. If he had continued to listen to the pupil it would have become apparent that the pupil may have been responding at the level of *association* with a recent experience—and was not *explaining*. Further, the pupil's answer in no way conveyed his understanding of the function of *protection* the teacher had in mind. The teacher was only waiting for the chance to speak again, having gone through the *motions* of "class discussion"! He was focused on himself—in keeping to a plan—not on the understanding of his pupils. No; a *very poor example*.

The episode with Donald cited above illustrated another facet of listening and responding: that of listening for feeling, and of responding appropriately. The perceptive teacher would note the class behaviour as indicative of embarrassment and deal with this in a constructive way as in the model answer given here.

---

*Model Answer To Problem Page 29.*
Yes, we tend to be embarrassed by this kind of talk but there is an important idea in what Donald has said so let's explore this further.

---

## KNOWLEDGE

The development of intellectual ability has long been hallowed as a goal of education. Intellectual ability is considered here as being the result of *cognitive* (*thinking*) *skills* operating on *knowledge* as the material of thought: the more sophisticated the cognitive skills and knowledge, the greater the intellectual ability.[6]

However, it is only in recent decades that there has been systematic investigation of the ways in which this goal might be better realised in the classroom. For example, we are indebted to:

1. *Bloom et al.*[7] for a delineation of a hierarchy of sub-goals for the development of intellectual ability.
2. *Bruner*[8] for popularising the notion that in the context of teaching, knowledge should be considered as having a *structure*.
3. *Gagné*[9] for an analysis of the conditions of learning necessary to achieve knowledge of different categories of complexity.
4. *Piaget*[10] for establishing that the quality of intelligence (and hence of cognitive skills) is dependent upon the kinds and range of experience *directly* through manipulating the environment and *indirectly* through mental representations.

## A DEFINITION OF KNOWLEDGE

Bloom *et al.*[7] defined knowledge in terms of what is remembered either by recognition or recall.

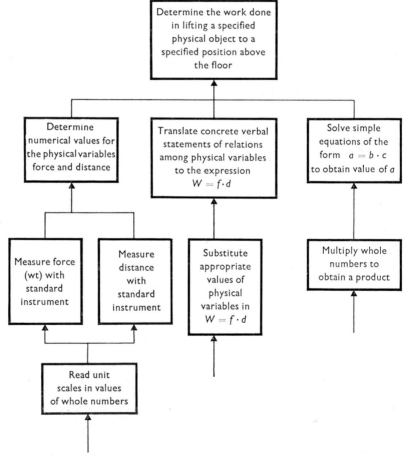

Figure 3.3: Solving physical work problems; a learning hierarchy pertaining to a science topic (from Gagné[11])

Bloom's viewpoint results from the evaluation of examination questions to discover the mental operations they invoke; hence the nomination of *remembering* as the differentiating characteristic of questions which are designed to test knowledge. However, from the viewpoint of the teacher who is seeking to *develop* knowledge, it is more profitable to consider it as a *store of information* from which the efficiency of retrieval will depend critically upon the quality and the organisation of the items stored.

In solving problems (situations whose meaning is obscure on presentation) we depend upon what is often a very complex retrieval of information in a succession of attempts to impose meaning on the situation. In this context of value in problem solving, Bruner has proposed the notion of "generic ideas", i.e., those which have such generality that they can be used to give meaning to a wide range of experience, i.e., they have *transfer* value. He has proposed, simply, that some ideas are so very much more important than others that they should be given high priority in school syllabuses when teachers seek to develop *quality* in the store of information.[8]

What is proposed is that ideas in the various subjects can be organised as in Figure 3.3 as learning structures, and that these would be most profitably organised under "generic" ideas.

Structures such as those in Figure 3.3 indicate inclusiveness and hence, following Gagné,[12] the *sequence* in which ideas should be met. There is, however, a serious flaw if such structures are used as the basis of lesson planning or to prepare a learning programme: *they do not make explicit the interrelationships between ideas.* Teaching which aims at pupil understanding must necessarily focus on *relationships* between ideas as the basis for sound generalisation. Therefore *sequence* is not enough (see Chapter 4). If a teacher does not face the discipline of making the interrelationships between ideas explicit, he will not be equipped to organise and manage pupils' exploration of a set of ideas from which they will generalise the new idea. A much more rigorous discipline is needed—one which requires not only that a topic be structured (in the sense of inclusiveness) but that the interrelationships between the ideas be made explicit. This will be called the *topic analysis discipline.*

However, while a *structured* organisation of the general ideas of a syllabus, or more particularly of a topic, is well established in modern curriculum development and in some classrooms, it has some inadequacies. For instance, its inappropriate application to some subjects and lesson topics (such as in English and aesthetics) has thrown doubt on its value, thus restricting its use in the very subjects in need of its implicit rigour of thinking.

The difficulty is that the meaning of a notion, proposed essentially to indicate priorities in a disciplined statement of the ideas of syllabuses and topics, has been extended to imply that *all* subjects would benefit from the use of methods successful for those subjects most amenable to structuring.

But teaching depends critically upon communication, so that if the ideas of a topic are not rigorously definable, the methods used to make the communication effective must be chosen in recognition of this fact.

It seems, then, that teachers should differentiate between topics in terms of *the communicability of their inherent ideas,* and they should adopt teaching strategies designed to cope with the communication problem. To do otherwise is to assume that the only reality we can know is that which is amenable to scientific rigour. Bunkum!

---

*Areas of specialised skills highlighted by the discussion are implicit to the following:*

1. A topic analysis discipline.
2. The ability:
   (a) to differentiate between topics in terms of the communicability of inherent ideas, and
   (b) to adopt appropriate strategies.

---

## COGNITIVE SKILLS

In the past, teachers in general have been satisfied that they have been developing intellectual ability when they have communicated *knowledge,* mastery of which has been demonstrated by the ability to remember without error. However, the twentieth century has seen the evolution of a new conception of teacher adequacy in this area. Major features of a generally held contemporary view would be:

1. The transformation of the concept of knowledge to emphasise *quality.* This is perceived in terms of
   (a) ideas which have transfer value and so will save learning in related ideas,[13] and
   (b) the *application* of knowledge to problem solving as a more significant test of mastery than remembering.
2. The development of such knowledge and the ability to apply it (i.e., intellectual ability) is seen as dependent upon the development of various cognitive skills.
3. The need of the teacher
   (a) to translate ideas so that they are comprehensible to the pupil at *his* stage of cognitive development, and
   (b) to allow the pupil to come to grips with the ideas using the cognitive skills peculiar to his stage of development.

## THE DEVELOPMENT OF COGNITIVE SKILLS AND THE PROBLEM OF CLASS MANAGEMENT

### Piaget's Stages of Development

Piaget has written in considerable detail on the development of cognitive skills, and while many have questioned the specifics of his findings because of difficulties of experimental replication, their broad outline of cognitive development has gained general acceptance.[14] But his work poses a very real problem for the class teacher—that of being able to see the wood for the trees. While, for instance, knowledge of the limitations of a pupil's thinking in mastering a concept in mathematics at a certain age will help with the specifics of a programme in mathematics, it is of little value in the management of a class discussion of a problem in which the class has greater freedom to contribute, as, for instance, in social studies.

In a summary of developments in Piaget's work, Berlyne provides, incidentally, criteria for a rule-of-thumb appraisal of a pupil's style of argument *in problem solving*.[15] The value of this is that identification of the logical pattern of the pupil's "stage" of thinking enables the teacher to select the most appropriate management technique.

### STAGE OF INTUITIVE THOUGHT (4-7 years)
Children at the intuitive-thought stage vary conditions haphazardly and observe what happens in particular cases without deriving any general principle.[16]

This line of thought appears to be governed by accidental association rather than logical inference or causal relationship. Also, as in the stage previous to this (not described), what is perceived is treated as more trustworthy than the product of thinking. Identities may be imposed on a whole situation by virtue of some characteristic of a part or just the outline, the child remaining oblivious to all evidence to the contrary.

### STAGE OF CONCRETE OPERATIONS (7-11 years)
At the concrete-operations stage, one factor at a time is varied, and its effects are duly noted.[16]

This line of thought is characterised by the ability to analyse the problem, but with an inability to handle the problem of integration. The whole tends to remain unorganised because of a preoccupation with the parts. Thus at this stage a pupil may have several partial solutions to a problem but cannot take the step of integration which would give the complete answer. Then too, he still has the ability to remain oblivious to the inconvenient facts and thus can demonstrate a spurious confidence in argument.

### STAGE OF FORMAL OPERATIONS (11-15 years)
Not before the formal-operations stage does the child plan purely scientific investigations, varying the factors in all possible combinations and in a systematic order.[16]

This pupil is more cautious: he uses the logical forms which lead to hypotheses. His discussion is of the form:

if . . .          then . . .
but . . .
on the other hand . . .

### TRANSITION STAGES
Transition stages can be distinguished between, for instance, the stages of concrete and formal operations.

A child at this "in-between" stage has begun to manage formal operations to solve simple problems but regresses to the mode of concrete operations when faced with a difficult problem. From the teacher's management viewpoint, there is a special problem: in regressing to, say, the stage of concrete operations, such a pupil frequently demonstrates a quality of thinking inferior to that which was typical when he was *passing through that stage*. He behaves as if his experience with the higher stage has caused a disorientation. Thus a girl aged 13 (who later did well in mathematics and physics) when required to explain a penny sinking to the bottom of a bucket of water, assured the teacher that a penny was heavier than a bucket of water. When asked why she thought this, she replied that she had held them both in her hands and she "just knew". Management of situations like this will obviously require sensitivity of teacher perception and response.

### Progress through the Stages is Uneven

Ausubel and Robinson suggest that an individual's

> overall developmental status may be described . . . on the basis of an estimate of his characteristic or *predominant* mode of cognitive functioning. . . .[17]

They suggest that there is too much unevenness in experience between one subject and another, even one topic and another, for progress from one stage to another to occur *simultaneously* in all areas. Further, when faced with new subject matter, the individual who is predominantly at (say) the stage of formal operations, tends to begin with concrete operations and then to move more rapidly to formal operations than when he was developing through those stages. The teacher, it would appear, has to be aware of his need and create conditions which satisfy and also facilitate the move to adopt operations of the higher stage.

## TEACHING GOALS IN THE COGNITIVE DOMAIN

From an analysis of college-level examinations, Bloom *et al.*[6] have provided teachers with a taxonomy of cognitive skills. The taxonomy has generally been taken to imply that if a teacher gave his pupils appropriate exercises they would develop greater expertise than they would otherwise. Thus Sanders prepared a book on classroom questions in social studies which would help teachers prepare the kind of question which would bring designated cognitive skills into play in solving problems.[18] Then too, the taxonomy has been the springboard for reform of examinations.

There does not appear any real evidence to show that giving practice in answering such questions is the teaching procedure showing greatest profit in terms of development of skills. From the research evidence on the possibility of accelerated progress through Piaget's stages and pragmatic trial in classes of Grades III—XII and college students, it seems that there is more value in an *initial* emphasis on more primitive skills which underlie those of the taxonomy.[19] Further, not only should these skills be developed first but the process should be with a self-conscious awareness of process, as this makes possible the development of a special *evaluation vocabulary designed to facilitate communication on the products of cognition.*

The more primitive cognitive skills proposed as basic for teaching purposes are those which are central to processes of concept formation and communication. Significantly, Ausubel and Robinson find it necessary to postulate an *abstract* logical stage as a necessary condition for the development of Piaget's stage of *formal* operations.[20] They do so on the grounds that Piaget's stages

> are derived from a problem-solving task rather than the context of *acquiring the meaning of concepts or propositions*.[21]

An approach to the development of cognitive skills which seeks to exercise specific skills and to develop an evaluation vocabulary with a concomitant self-conscious awareness of process, carries with it, of course, the possibility that such activities may be incompatible with the pursuit of other, equally worthy goals. The teacher will need to strike a balance between them.

Smith and Smith make the point in a discussion of the need for the human individual to exercise what they call *feedback control* of information. Their remarks are pertinent here:

> With too little guidance, a learner may lose interest by not being able to establish any significant degree of control over a task. On the other hand, too much guidance also deprives him of personal control. The goal is to enable the learner to establish his own patterns of control over tasks, skills and knowledge that have social utility lest he turn his attention to less desirable activities.[22]

---

*Areas of specialised skill highlighted by the above discussion are implicit to the following abilities:*

1. To translate ideas so they are comprehensible at pupil's stage of development.
2. To discriminate between pupil behaviours as indicative of stages of cognitive development, transition state regressions, or temporary regressions because of novelty of a task.
3. To respond appropriately to cognitive behaviour of the different stages.
4. To plan the development of basic cognitive skills and manage the cognitive processes in classroom contexts.
5. To design questions to give systematic exercise to the complex skills of the cognitive taxonomy.
6. To develop a specialised vocabulary to facilitate communication on the products of cognitive activity.
7. To give a balanced apportionment of time to various aspects of cognitive development and with due regard for the development of other aspects of human development.

---

## AFFECTIVE AND SOCIAL SKILLS

The development of what can be called socialised behaviour is increasingly recognised as a high priority educational goal (1) on the grounds of mental health, and (2) as a necessary condition for the development of intellectual ability. Because of the limitations of an introductory text, in this discussion we are concerned primarily with the second reason because efforts in this direction contribute not only to intellectual development but also, it seems, though less directly, to mental health. The underlying assumption is that any degree of failure in the socialising process (as manifested in inadequate affective and social skills) places limits on the effectiveness of interaction with people and on the exercise of autonomy, thus restricting the range and degree of experience, and hence intellectual growth.

However, failure of the socialising process also leads to major problems of class management—for the provocative and disruptive pupil is often its typical product.

Socialised behaviour may be considered as the outcome of two inter-dependent streams of development as illustrated in Figure 3.4.

## THE DEVELOPMENT OF THE TAXONOMICALLY RELATED AFFECTIVE SKILLS

Examinations of this taxonomy which was described by Krathwohl et al.[23] (see Figure 3.4) soon make it apparent that affective skills development will be governed by the quality of self–other relationships as these must be central to the lower level skills of the taxonomy—i.e., receiving, responding and valuing. The significance of this for intellectual development lies in the importance of listening, responding and valuing in communication as central to teaching and learning processes.

Conditions, then, which promote the development of the pupil's self-confidence in self–other relationships will favour development of affective skills and, concomitantly, of intellectual ability.

But there is the possibility that some of these affective skills may be amenable to direct instruction as, for example, Canfield[25] has shown that listening skills are amenable to such instruction.

## THE DEVELOPMENT OF CONSCIENCE AS THE "CORE" OF CHARACTER

Ausubel has described the psychological abilities underlying conscience as "that aspect of ego structure concerned with the cognitive-emotional organisation of moral values".[26]

These psychological abilities also are considered related as in a taxonomy. When they are placed alongside the taxonomy of affective skills, further possibilities of teacher action to promote socialisation become apparent. It is evident, for instance, that the higher-level skills and abilities are necessarily complementary and the possibility therefore exists of an interdependence between the lower levels of the two taxonomies.

Referring to Figure 3.4, this interdependence points further to the fact that the process of socialisation is dependent upon adequate development at each successive level.

The following illustrations of the course of development of the basic psychological abilities underlying conscience emphasise the importance of understanding affective and social skills in teaching.

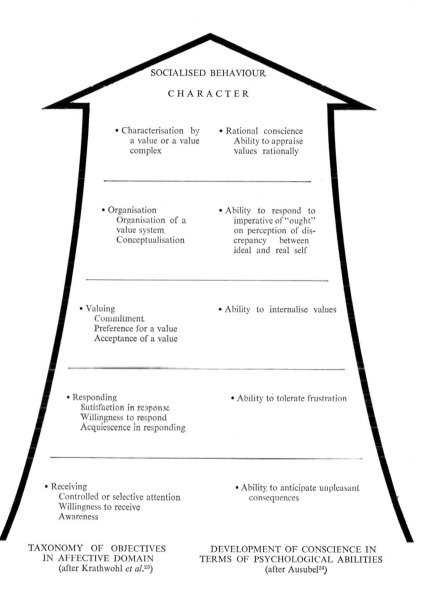

SOCIALISED BEHAVIOUR

CHARACTER

• Characterisation by
  a value or a value
  complex

• Rational conscience
  Ability to appraise
  values rationally

• Organisation
  Organisation of a
  value system
  Conceptualisation

• Ability to respond to
  imperative of "ought"
  on perception of dis-
  crepancy between
  ideal and real self

• Valuing
  Commitment
  Preference for a value
  Acceptance of a value

• Ability to internalise values

• Responding
  Satisfaction in response
  Willingness to respond
  Acquiescence in responding

• Ability to tolerate frustration

• Receiving
  Controlled or selective attention
  Willingness to receive
  Awareness

• Ability to anticipate unpleasant
  consequences

TAXONOMY OF OBJECTIVES
IN AFFECTIVE DOMAIN
(after Krathwohl et al.[23])

DEVELOPMENT OF CONSCIENCE IN
TERMS OF PSYCHOLOGICAL ABILITIES
(after Ausubel[24])

Figure 3.4: Aspects of the process of socialisation

1. *Ability to anticipate consequences.* Ausubel suggests that

> the operation of conscience presupposes a capacity to anticipate unpleasant consequences. Regardless of whether the deterrent is punishment, insecurity, anxiety or guilt it could not lead to inhibitory control of behaviour if the child were not able to project the consequences of his actions into imagination in advance of their execution.[27]

While this ability is basic to the development of conscience, its significance, for many, is not outgrown: it remains one of the most critical factors in their relationships with others. For example, those pupils who have limited intelligence or have a limited value system may be placed in a social situation which is too complex for them to appreciate the consequences of their actions. All too frequently they are then punished for what is simply ignorance. In such cases the legal maxim *ignorance of the law is no excuse* is a denial of professional accountability.

It seems a reasonable supposition that the skills of receiving and responding will be dependent upon the expectation of some degree of stability in the experience of anticipating consequences.

2. *Ability to tolerate frustration.* The development of self-control implies the existence of some compensatory force. On the one hand is a pull for immediate satisfaction, on the other is a pull which justifies postponement. A child who wishes to retain the approval of his parents learns to postpone gratification of those impulses which give him pleasure but which run counter to parental wishes.

Ability to tolerate frustration is a condition for the kind of mutuality underlying effective *receiving* and *responding*, i.e., the self–other relationships implicit to these affective skills require this kind of *self-discipline*.

When parents over-value or are too permissive with their children, the children's toleration of frustration remains low and becomes a strong limiting factor in the development of conscience and the affective skills, and hence of overall socialisation.

3. *Ability to internalise values.* This psychological ability refers to

> the capacity to assimilate external standards, or to evolve new standards which in either case exert a relatively stable *internal* directional influence on behaviour. . . .
> The process of internalisation in relation to conscience development differs from the internalisation of any other value only in the fact that a moral issue is involved.[28]

Internalisation of values may occur in several ways: through emotional identification with another person (e.g., child with mother who is seen to be loving); adoption because of utility or expediency; or as the result of rational appraisal and adoption because of worth. The most significant variables in this situation are the quality of self–other relationships and the values manifested in the behaviour of the people with whom the individual is interacting. Thus the pupil who defines adults generally as hostile has a limited source of values, as has the pupil who comes from a home where both parents lack an integrated value system.

## SIGNIFICANCE OF A FAILURE OF SOCIALISATION FOR TEACHERS

The proposition is that teachers need to be able to discriminate between the pupils whose behaviour is maladaptive primarily because they regard themselves as intolerable or inadequate in relation to others, and those suffering from immaturity of character, or even character disorder, as a result of a failure of socialisation. Further, that teachers must also be able to respond appropriately—if only because it is in the interests of their *own* mental health.

The distinction is important. The individual who, though socialised, acts as though his arms were in chains may only need *insight* to improve his capacity to cope with life. On the other hand, those whose socialisation is inadequate behave as if they had wizened arms, for their greatest need is *nurture*.[29]

Thus the individual whose socialisation began to fail when he failed to achieve a minimal frustration tolerance needs to have his environment organised so that it shapes his behaviour in the direction of exercising self-control under conditions which promote the development of this ability. Such experiences appear to be most profitable in this context when they provide for the exercise of autonomy and the facing of consequences.

---

*Areas of specialised skill highlighted by the above discussion are implicit to the following abilities:*

1. To discriminate between those whose primary need is for insight and those in need of nurture in the area of socialisation.
2. To counsel individuals and groups whose primary need is insight.
3. To plan and carry out behavioural programmes designed to promote socialisation under school conditions.
4. To recognise the approximate level of socialisation in pupils and to respond appropriately.

---

## THE DEVELOPMENT OF PSYCHO-MOTOR SKILLS

It seems obvious that this category of skills should be considered, along with cognitive and affective skills, as a necessary part of the domain of pedagogy, but the literature provides little material which is comparable in significance with that of the taxonomies of the cognitive and affective domains.[30]

At this stage it does not appear possible to integrate psycho-motor skills into the domain of pedagogy because the taxonomies that have been produced lack the credibility of those available in cognitive and affective areas; regretfully we must note its potential significance for *general* pedagogy and pass on.

## THE CONCEPT OF READINESS

As the concept of readiness is thoroughly covered in educational psychology texts, for example, in Ausubel and Robinson,[31] only the main features of its applications in the present context need to be stated.

Educational psychology texts usually give priority in *their* discussion of the concept to the notion that the teacher must gear instruction to the pupil's level of intellectual development—to his state of knowledge and to the level of development of his cognitive skills.

The viewpoint adopted here, however, gives priority to the readiness of the teacher to be genuinely more concerned for his pupil than for himself, and to show this readiness in reality by communicating effectively with his pupils, both verbally and non-verbally.

But to be consistent with the theme of the above discussion on socialisation, the teacher needs to consider at times (particularly in English and Social Studies) the relevance of the content of his lesson to the general level of *socialisation* achieved by his pupils.[32]

---

*Areas of specialised skill highlighted by the above discussion are implicit to the following abilities:*
1. To assess the self in relation to a particular class and its individuals and to organise relationships so that a greater concern for the class is manifest than concern for self.
2. To assess the stage of cognitive and affective development of pupils as previously listed under other sections of this discussion.

---

## THE SIGNIFICANCE OF GOALS

Presumably no teacher reads the minds of his pupils; yet the "man from Mars" might justifiably conclude that most teachers do. "I want my pupils *to develop intellectual power*, to understand, to appreciate . . ," says the teacher, and who would deny these are worthy educational objectives? However, as Skinner points out:

> The role of the teacher in fostering mental prowess has a certain prestige. It has always been held superior to the role of the trainer of motor skills. *And it has the great advantage of being almost invulnerable to criticism.* In reply to the complaint that he has not produced observable results, the teacher of the mind can lay claim to invisible achievements. His students may not be able to read, but he has only been trying to make sure they wanted to learn. They may not be able to solve problems, but he has been teaching them simply to think creatively. They may be ignorant of specific facts, but he has been primarily concerned with their general interest in a field.[33]

If the teacher cannot read minds, how can he know that he has achieved these goals, unless he can infer it from some pupil performance or behaviour which is a *valid* demonstration of understanding, appreciation and the like? The question is, of course, how does one determine what would be valid for such general goals?

Skinner suggests:

> Perhaps this can be answered by redefining traditional goals: instead of imparting knowledge, one could undertake to bring about those changes in behavior which are said to be the conspicuous manifestations of knowledge, or one could set up the behavior which is the mark of a man possessing well-developed rational power. But mentalistic formulations are warped by irrelevant historical accidents.

The behavior of the educated student is much more effectively analysed directly as such.[33]

The ambiguity of the terms used in the traditional expression of goals implied by Skinner has been shown by Mager.[34]

The need to specify objectives in the form of a *terminal behaviour*, i.e., what the pupil will be able to do at the end of the lesson, which can be accepted as characteristic of competence at a designated level of development seems inescapable. The *raison d'être* may well be, simply, that unless such a terminal behaviour is known, the teacher planning a lesson has little prospect of establishing the conditions necessary for *learning* to take place.

---

*Areas of specialised skill highlighted by the above discussion are implicit to the ability:*

To specify worthwhile instructional goals in terms of terminal behaviour in a form which ensures that the course of instruction required to achieve them can be both explicit and manageable.

---

## CONDITIONS OF LEARNING

After a teacher has determined the behaviour which is to be his goal, he needs to plan, i.e., to prepare to establish the conditions necessary to achieve the goal he has set himself.

### CONDITIONS OF LEARNING IN THE AREA OF COGNITION

Choice of conditions in the area of cognition will be limited by the kinds of learning implicit to the achievement of the teacher's goal. As Gagné puts it:

. . . there are as many varieties of learning as there are distinguishable conditions for learning. These varieties may be differentiated by means of descriptions of the factors that comprise the learning conditions of each case. In searching for and identifying these, one must look, first, at the capabilities internal to the learner, and second, at the stimulus situation outside the learner. Each type of learning starts from a different "point" of internal capability, and is likely also to demand a different external situation in order to take place effectively.[35]

Thus Gagné identifies eight varieties of learning and specifies for each the internal capabilities and external conditions of management. The eight types are:

*Type 1: Signal Learning.* The individual learns to make a general, diffuse response to a signal. This is the classical conditioned response of Pavlov (1927).

*Type 2: Stimulus-Response Learning.* The learner acquires a precise response to a discriminated stimulus. What is learned is a connection (Thorndike, 1898) or a discriminated operant (Skinner, 1938), sometimes called an instrumental response (Kimble, 1961).

*Type 3: Chaining.* What is acquired is a chain of two or more stimulus-response connections. The conditions for such learning have been described by Skinner (1938) and others, notably Gilbert (1962).

*Type 4: Verbal Association.* Verbal association is the learning of chains that are verbal. Basically, the conditions resemble those for other (motor) chains. However, the presence of language in the human being makes this a special type because internal links may be selected from the individual's previously learned repertoire of language (see Underwood, 1964).

*Type 5: Discrimination Learning.* The individual learns to make *n* different identifying responses to as many different stimuli, which may resemble each other in physical appearance to a greater or lesser degree. Although the learning of each stimulus-response connection is a simple type 2 occurrence, the connections tend to interfere with each other's retention (Postman, 1961).

*Type 6: Concept Learning.* The learner acquires a capability of making a common response to a class of stimuli that may differ from each other widely in physical appearance. He is able to make a response that identifies an entire class of objects or events (see Kendler, 1964). Other concepts are acquired *by definition*, and consequently have the formal characteristics of rules.

*Type 7: Rule Learning.* In simplest terms, a rule is a chain of two or more concepts. It functions to control behaviour in the manner suggested by a verbalised rule of the form, "If *A*, then *B*", where *A* and *B* are previously learned concepts. However, it must be carefully distinguished from the mere verbal sequence, "If *A*, then *B*", which, of course, may also be learned as type 4.

*Type 8: Problem Solving.* Problem solving is a kind of learning that requires the internal events usually called thinking. Two or more previously acquired rules are somehow combined to produce a new capability that can be shown to depend on a "higher-order" rule.[36]

However, school instruction is concerned mainly with concept and rule learning and problem solving. From the teacher's viewpoint, the most significant differentiating condition is that of prerequisites which Gagné sees as follows:

Problem solving (type 8) *requires as prerequisites:* rules (type 7) *which require as prerequisites:* concepts (type 6) *which require as prerequisites:* discrimination (type 5).

## CONDITIONS OF LEARNING IN THE AREA OF SOCIALISATION

As far as is known, no one has explicated the conditions of learning for affective and social skills in the way Gagné has for the area of cognition. In view of the taxonomical structure and interrelationship of affective and social skills as described above, a useful rule of thumb for management might well be to adopt Gagné's principle of *prerequisite learnings*. Thus, as has been described, the development of the ability to internalise values will depend upon the ability to *tolerate frustration*, to *anticipate unpleasant consequences* and to *receive* and *respond*.

## CLASS CLIMATE AND CONDITION OF LEARNING

The class is a community whose morale has a considerable influence upon the course and outcome of instruction. Consistent with the views expressed above, it is suggested that if a teacher can successfully demonstrate a concern for his pupils greater than for himself he will have laid the foundations of good morale.

Further, if in addition he provides for pupil *involvement* in the lesson to exploit the intrinsic motivation of conceptual conflict,[37] together with the opportunity to exercise autonomy (making choices and facing consequences), he will be raising morale to the extent that the general class climate should promote learning.

---

*Areas of specialised skills highlighted by the above discussion are implicit to the abilities:*

1. To discriminate between varieties of learning, in both the cognitive and affective domains.
2. To establish and manage conditions of learning in the areas of the cognitive and affective domains.
3. To establish and manage a general class climate which favours learning.

---

## STRATEGIES

The many verbal contingencies involved in the teaching and learning processes are so complex that it seems only common sense to prepare for the more important. It is suggested, for instance, that enough is known of conceptual development and of the logical processes involved in basic intellectual skills, for a necessary part of a teacher's planning to be a *prestructuring of the framework of classroom verbal interaction* to increase the likelihood that goals will be achieved.

The framework of verbal interaction is seen in terms of statements and questions which are designed to perform quite specific but interacting roles in an organisational unit or episode.

However, the implied constraints of even a *framework* for verbal interaction is usually found outrageous by those dedicated to a conception which stresses the unhindered expression of "soul", on the assumption that this promotes autonomy of the individual. The viewpoint adopted here is that the two positions are complementary. Whitehead makes the point:

> My main position is that the dominant note of education at its beginning and at its end is freedom, but that *there is an intermediate stage of discipline with freedom in subordination*. Furthermore, that there is not one unique threefold cycle of freedom, discipline, and freedom; but that all mental development is composed of such cycles, and of cycles of such cycles. Such a cycle is a unit cell, or brick; and the complete stage of growth is an organic structure of such cells. In analysing any one such cell, I call the first period of freedom "stage of Romance", the intermediate period of discipline I call the "stage of Precision", and the final period of freedom is the "stage of Generalisation".[38] (My italics)

In terms of the theme *putting minds to work*, the teacher who is planning must prepare the framework of verbal interaction in order to be able to

E

establish the conditions of learning consistent with the needs of the particular stage of development.

## CHOICE OF STRATEGY

There are, however, many forms which the prestructuring can take, as it necessarily reflects the particular strategy the teacher chooses to adopt after consideration of the readiness of his pupils and his own particular preferences of style. Thus, given a particular goal and a class of a particular state of readiness, one teacher may choose to plan according to a strategy which could be described as beginning with intuitive thinking but concluding with inductive thinking—an intuitive-inductive strategy, in short. On the other hand, another teacher in this case might adopt a deductive-inductive strategy. Again the choice may be between an emphasis on the intellectual rather than the aesthetic, or the converse; or on reception learning rather than discovery.[39]

## PLANNING AND MANAGEMENT

The skills of planning and management comprise all those skills associated with each aspect of the domain of pedagogy—they can be considered as organised in many ways depending upon the particular strategy chosen after consideration of pupil readiness and teacher preference.

But it should be noted that the planning implicit to the above would be useless in practice if teachers implemented a plan irrespective of the actual responses of pupils, i.e., if they ignored the priority that must be given to communication in teaching. Planning is certainly seen as tending to be *subject-centred*—but the teaching must fail if it is not *pupil-centred* and *flexible* at the stage of management.

## WHO IS PROFESSIONAL?

When one now considers the areas on which pedagogy is based, one can see the significance of the ILO-UNESCO definition of teaching as a profession. The professional teacher is surely distinguished by his ability to cope with the various elements of the domain of pedagogy, described above, as exemplified in the skills of his planning and management.

## REFERENCES

[1] NEW ZEALAND EDUCATIONAL INSTITUTE, "Progress in Professional Promotion and Protection—A Summary", *National Education*, Journal of the N.Z.E.I., Wellington, 1970, p. 256.

[2] G. ALLPORT, "Crisis in Personality Development", in R. D. STROM (Ed.), *Teaching and the Learning Process*, Prentice-Hall, Englewood Cliffs, 1971, p. 497.

[3] D. P. AUSUBEL, *Ego Development and the Personality Disorders*, Grune and Stratton, New York, 1952, p. 151.

[4] O. POLLACK, "Treatment of Character Disorders: a Dilemma in Casework

Culture", in E. Younghusband (Ed.), *Social Work and Social Values: Readings in Social Work*, Allen and Unwin, London, 1967, III, pp. 121-41.

[5] See K. Y. Smith and M. F. Smith, *Cybernetic Principles of Learning and Educational Design*, Holt, Rinehart and Winston, New York, 1966, pp. 455-80.

[6] See B. S. Bloom (Ed.) *et al.*, *Taxonomy of Educational Objectives—The Classification of Educational Goals, Handbook I: Cognitive Domain*, David McKay, New York, 1956.

[7] Bloom (Ed.) *et al.*, op. cit.

[8] J. S. Bruner, *The Process of Education*, Harvard University Press, Cambridge, 1961.

[9] R. M. Gagné, *The Conditions of Learning*, Holt, Rinehart and Winston, New York, 1965 and 1970.

[10] J. Piaget, *The Psychology of Intelligence*, Routledge and Kegan Paul, London, 1950.

[11] Gagné, op. cit., 2nd edition, 1970, p. 263.

[12] Gagné, op. cit., 1st edition, 1965, p. 245.

[13] J. S. Bruner, *The Process of Education*, op. cit., p. 17.

[14] J. Piaget, *The Origin of Intelligence in the Child*, Routledge and Kegan Paul, London, 1953.

[15] D. E. Berlyne, "Recent Developments in Piaget's Work", in R. J. C. Harper (Ed.), *Readings—The Cognitive Processes*, Prentice-Hall, Englewood Cliffs, 1964, pp. 312-19.

[16] Berlyne, op. cit., p. 319.

[17] D. P. Ausubel and F. G. Robinson, *School Learning*, Holt, Rinehart and Winston, New York, 1969, pp. 191-92.

[18] N. M. Sanders, *Classroom Questions: What Kinds?*, Harper and Row, New York, 1966.

[19] Ausubel and Robinson, op. cit., p. 191.

[20] Ibid., pp. 183-90.

[21] Ibid., p. 190.

[22] Smith and Smith, op. cit., p. 475.

[23] D. R. Krathwohl *et al.*, *Taxonomy of Educational Objectives—The Classification of Educational Goals, Handbook II: Affective Domain*, David McKay, New York, 1964.

[24] Ausubel, op. cit.

[25] R. G. Canfield, "How Useful Are Lessons on Listening?", *Elementary School Journal*, 1961, **62**, No. 3, pp. 147-51.

[26] Ausubel, op. cit., p. 446.

[27] Ibid., p. 447.

[28] Ibid.

[29] See Pollack, op. cit.

[30] See: J. F. Travers, *Learning: Analysis and Application*, David McKay, New York, 1965.
  H. L. Kingsley and R. Garry, *The Nature and Conditions of Learning*, Prentice-Hall, Englewood Cliffs, 1957, pp. 297-98.
  R. J. Kibler *et al.*, *Behavioural Objectives and Instruction*, Allyn and Bacon, Boston, 1970.
  J. P. Guilford, "A System of the Psychomotor Abilities", *American Journal of Psychology*, 1958, **71**, pp. 164-74.

[31] Ausubel and Robinson, op. cit., pp. 201-10.

[32] For discussion of significance in the teaching of English, see B. Bernstein, "Social Structure, Language and Learning", *Educational Research*, June 1961, III, No. 3.

[33] B. F. SKINNER, "Reflections on a Decade of Teaching Machines", in R. GLASER (Ed.), *Teaching Machines and Programmed Learning II*, Department of Audio Visual Instruction, National Education Association, Washington, 1965, p. 12.

[34] R. F. MAGER, *Preparing Instructional Objectives*, Fearon Publishers, Palo Alto, 1962.

[35] GAGNÉ, op. cit., 2nd edition, 1970, p. 24.

[36] Ibid., pp. 63-64.

[37] D. E. BERLYNE, *Conflict, Arousal and Curiosity*, McGraw-Hill, New York, 1960.

[38] A. N. WHITEHEAD, *The Aims of Education and Other Essays*, Williams and Norgate Ltd., Cambridge, 1932.

[39] See D. P. AUSUBEL, *The Psychology of Meaningful Verbal Learning*, Grune and Stratton, New York, 1963.

### PART II

# Conditions of Learning and Method

*Planning* can be considered as the anticipation of contingencies in setting up and maintaining conditions of learning; and *management* as the actual control of the course of events during the lesson.

These chapters seek to establish the conditions of learning in order to derive criteria for the selection of teaching methods for planning and management under classroom conditions.

# CHAPTER 4

# Gagné's Conditions of Learning and the Classroom Reality

## THE PRODUCT OF LEARNING AS INDICATIVE OF CONDITIONS

Gagné has suggested eight varieties of learning or capabilities within the learner which build on each other, and for each of these varieties there are conditions which must be established if learning is to take place.[1] While Gagné differentiates between the three "highest" types, (concept, rule learning and problem solving) in terms of the conditions needed to bring them about, they do have major features in common. As these three are the most significant for the classroom, their common conditions are worth noting:

1. *Constituent (lower level) capabilities must already have been established.* Thus all concepts required for the statement of a rule must have been mastered before rule learning. Simply, if the product is to be a cake, it will not be a success without the baking powder

2. *Verbal instructions must be given* for the purpose of informing the student "of what he is going to achieve, reminding him of what he already knows, directing his attention and action and guiding his thinking along certain lines".[2] Simply, there must be efficient supervision of the novice cook.

3. *The learner must experience reinforcement.* Simply, the cook needs immediate confirmation of successful moves.

4. *The learner must demonstrate his understanding.* Simply, there is no other way in which the success of teaching can be established.

Gagné points out that if one is to take into account differences in conditions applicable to each kind of learning, the feature of *differential starting points* is the most crucial. This follows, of course, from the way in which the different kinds of learning build on each other. It also follows that planning of sequences of instruction is essential not only to ensure that prerequisite capabilities are established, but also to facilitate the shaping of a particular kind of learning. Sequencing is thus a major feature of planning which observes these conditions, and which is of such a nature that the end products of a learning sequence can be considered as proceeding systematically upwards in an organised hierarchy of more and more inclusive ideas. The preparation of a sequence in practice is thus a logical exercise which requires:

1. Identification of the intended products of learning according to the relationships they have with other products.
2. Organisation of learning into a hierarchy of greater and greater inclusiveness.[3]

The logical interrelationships existing between the learning products sought also largely determine the kinds of shaping of learning behaviour through verbal instructions.

## RESTRICTED APPLICATIONS OF GAGNÉ'S CONDITIONS IN THE CLASSROOM

A teacher does not need much classroom experience to accept the relevance of the above conditions. But then neither does he need much experience of trying to apply them to perceive there is something in the classroom situation that restricts their application. Attempts to plan topic sequences and to teach them under Gagné's conditions bring the realisation that many of the concepts with which a teacher is necessarily concerned are not rigorously definable and so are not amenable to teaching under the suggested conditions. Further, as much teaching has to deal with such concepts, especially in the humanities, there seems reason to doubt the value of Gagné's identification of eight types of learning and their pre-requisite conditions.

Communication provides a bridge between any planned sequence and the learner; not only the sequence of ideas, but also the verbal instructions to shape the learning have to be communicated. But many concepts have in some measure a special meaning for each individual by virtue of his autonomous interaction with his world. If, then, such concepts are a part of the product sought or of the verbal instructions, the predictability of the outcome, as sought by Gagné, must be considerably diminished. The implication is, of course, that if the variation in meaning could be "controlled" in some way, there would be greater likelihood of a successful outcome.

It is not surprising, in view of the above, that the most successful programmed books (which best meet Gagné's conditions) appear to be those on topics whose constituent concepts are rigorously definable.

## CONDITIONS OF LEARNING ARE GOVERNED BY FACTORS OF PROCESS

Conditions of learning need to be governed by factors of process inherent in the acquisition of *all* concepts. In his studies of perceptual and conceptual processes, Bruner recognised learned probability judgments as a necessary condition for effective generalisation in the acquisition of knowledge.[4] By this he meant that we have to learn the inferential weight to be given to events when they occur in association with other events. Thus, smoke on the horizon at sea is probably a ship, while on the land, depending on locality, it reveals the presence of a train or a forest fire. Bruner argues that the learning of such probability judgments is a condition for successful generalisation—*and generalisation is central to the process of acquiring concepts*. Probability judgments, by their nature, deal with uncertainty. Is this not a possible source of insight into the conditions needed to cope with the variation in meaning of certain categories of concepts?

Gagné, however, has been able to ignore the implications of learned probability judgments and associated processes because he has created his learning model around subjects and topics that can be rigorously structured. In these, the requisite conditions for the learning of, for instance, probability judgments are likely to be inherent in the verbal instructions when they are designed to shape behaviour closely to a structured sequence. But the inclusion is fortuitous—a by-product of the nature of rigorously structured sequences of instruction.

Given the additional variables of the class teaching, the inadequacies of Gagné's explication of the nature of the verbal instructions to shape learning behaviour as a condition of learning is all too apparent: learning is in jeopardy; problems of management become acute.

It appears that if we are to establish conditions of learning that are practicable under classroom conditions it will be necessary to be *explicit* concerning the conditions necessary for the acquisition of *all* types of concepts.

Gagné's model of learning focuses upon a stimulus situation bringing about a change in response:

> . . . the *stimulus situation* affects the learner in such a way that his *performance* changes from a time *before* being in that situation to a time *after* being in it. The *change in performance* is what leads to the conclusion that learning has occurred.[5]

As has been argued, this model presents difficulties. However, when concept formation is considered as essentially the grouping process in the information-processing activities of mind, some of its characteristics seem to have considerable relevance for the communication problem inherent in Gagné's model.

## THE PROCESS OF ACQUIRING KNOWLEDGE AS INDICATIVE OF CONDITIONS

The mind has to cope with an enormous flood of information poured into it from two sources: (1) the problem situation of the moment, from which information is obtained through the senses, and (2) the knowledge store, through a process of retrieval or remembering. If this information is thought of in terms of the smallest item the mind could distinguish through any one sense, it will be apparent that the total number of such items of information coming into the mind from a problem situation is astronomical. For instance, the total possible information on colour from a picture would involve many millions of discriminable elements.[6] The volume of each and every item is such that the "switchboard" would be jammed. And the mind not only has to process the *input* but also the *output* in the skill we call *communication*.

## WAYS OF COPING WITH INFORMATION

The mind develops very effective ways of coping with, or processing, this flood of information. For classroom purposes it is useful to consider these as *discriminating* or selecting; *classifying* or grouping; and *generalising* or going beyond the immediately present information.

However, while it is convenient to talk of discriminating, classifying and generalising of both input and output information, these are essentially only three aspects (though basic ones) of the complex skill of information processing. This skill encompasses not only these three aspects but *all* the cognitive skills which feature in the development of intellectual ability—a major concern of pedagogy.

## COMPONENTS OF INTELLECTUAL ABILITY

For the purposes of this discussion intellectual ability will be considered as comprising:

1. *Knowledge*—the store of information on past experience which can be available as a resource when an individual is attempting to solve a problem. We can think of knowledge in terms of:
   (a) *quantity*: the number of items of information relevant to a problem, and
   (b) *quality*: the utility of the knowledge in problem solving to the extent to which it enables new problems to be seen as special instances of what is already known.
2. *Cognitive skills*—kinds of operation upon this information about past experience. This may be grouped for pedagogical purposes into:
   (a) *thinking skills*: a number of skill complexes used singly or in association, and
   (b) *communication skills*: concerned with the organisation and presentation of information in ways designed to give information and/or understanding to another individual or, simply, to systematise it for oneself.

While it is convenient at times to talk of knowledge and the cognitive skills in this way, i.e., as if they were separate entities, the findings of research indicate they are, in fact, interdependent.

It is proposed in the next three chapters to explore the process of concept formation from the above point of view in search of the missing conditions of learning.

# REFERENCES

[1] R. M. GAGNÉ, *The Conditions of Learning*, Holt, Rinehart and Winston, New York, 2nd edition, 1965, pp. 172-73.

[2] Ibid., p. 27.

[3] Ibid., p. 188.

[4] J. S. BRUNER, "On Going Beyond the Information Given", in R. J. C. HARPER (Ed.), *Readings—The Cognitive Processes*, Prentice-Hall, Englewood Cliffs, 1964, p. 298.

[5] GAGNÉ, op. cit., 2nd edition, 1970, p. 5.

[6] BRUNER, op. cit., p. 294.

# CHAPTER 5

# Implications of Discrimination as Involved in Concept Formation

## NATURE OF THE PROCESS

### INFORMATION IS PROCESSED AT DIFFERENT LEVELS OF THE MIND

Information is processed at different levels of the mind. Some is processed right at the foreground and some in the background of consciousness, and a considerable quantity is processed *below* consciousness, in the sense of being beyond any degree of awareness. It is not, however, a case of a simple dichotomy—the forefront of mind, the conscious and the unconscious—they are dynamically related. For instance, the focus of attention adjusts to changes of attitude. What is in the foreground of the mind at any time is played out against a passing parade of events in the background of the mind, some of which can become impressed on the foreground of mind and even supplant what is there.

Consider the case of Murray, who is hurrying through a crowd to meet the young lady he is courting. Undoubtedly he will fail to register most of the information his mind must process to steer him through the crowd, but in spite of his preoccupation with (say) a matter of strategy, popping the question that night, he will nevertheless note some features of the crowd through which he is passing: the young woman with twins in an outsize pram; the man with an old-fashioned coat and military bearing— "seen him before"; the kid from round the corner . . . . In this case, where one thing dominates the mind, the people he notices are only the outstanding features of the background of mind. They receive only peripheral attention and make a brief impression on consciousness and, if nothing happens to make them otherwise remarkable, they are soon forgotten.

In ordinary situations there may be quite rapid changes in the priorities to which consciousness is responsive as we focus upon different parts of our environment in successive acts of adjustment to it. For example, I must concentrate on doing the dishes because I am running late, plan what I am going to say to Charles at the meeting (a matter of considerable uneasiness), and make some effort to appear interested in what Katherine is saying (it is the first time that we have had a chance to talk today). At the moment Katherine is just talking for the sake of talking, so I think about the dishes and Charles alternately. Katherine, however, is now telling me something which is important for her, so as a responsible parent I must pay attention in order to make intelligent comment. The problem of Charles is dismissed to the background of mind for a while, and so on, with alterations of the focus of attention in response to re-appraisals of the priorities of the changing situation. Again, for Murray, even such an absorbing topic as his impending proposal of marriage can be pushed to the background of mind by some more urgent matter such as a threat to safety—"the bus is careering downhill"; or to dignity— he is developing a cold and discovers he has left his handkerchief at home.

Such reversals of the focus of attention occur in response to an individual's changing appreciation of what is most significant in his world in successive acts of awareness. This appreciation is very much influenced by more or less stable attitudes he has developed to classes of experience, such as the matters of a particular church, authority, tennis, solving problems, gardening, the opposite sex, success in school.

Somewhat similar reversals occur between the conscious and un-conscious. But here the appraisal of events may be only nominally con-scious—it may depend, in reality, upon "judgments" of the situation conducted below the level of consciousness. Thus emotionally charged attitudes (of which we may be quite unaware) may influence substantially a particular situation. For example, we may assume that we are opposing a motion at a meeting on impeccable grounds of logic, but, in fact, the opposition may be induced by a dislike of the proposer

## Attitudes can Limit the Input of Information

One of the most significant features of these changes in the focus of mind is that the entry of information is facilitated or impeded to effect the changes. As Bruner suggests, ". . . perception acts sometimes as a welcoming committee and sometimes as a screening committee".

Bevan is infatuated with Margaret: he fairly soaks up anything even remotely connected with her, even descending to engineering changes in conversation so that she can be discussed. His mind is wide open on this topic. On the other hand, his mind also screens out information. Bevan is quite unresponsive to signs that Margaret is going to be a nagger—just like her mother.

It is as if each individual has a limited set of lenses through which he views his world: his selection of focus is of varying degrees of appropriate-ness for any one situation. In fact discrimination processes display such uniformities in each individual that we expect to be able to predict in various degrees the behaviour of those we meet. We tend to know, for instance, who will be interested in the theme of a recent controversial play and who will not. What we attend to and what we disregard is to a large extent predictable.

## SELECTION AND LEARNED PROBABILITIES

### Selection is on the Basis of Stable Expectations set up from Learned Probabilities

The mind operates to minimise the amount of adjustment it must make because of the operation of chance; it shows a marked preference for stability of expectation. If you go to the station expecting to meet Uncle Mac, you do so on the basis that it is highly probable that he will be there. You cannot, however, justifiably be absolutely certain. He may have died, had a fit of the sulks and decided not to come, or even eloped with his secretary.

In one sense we obtain stability of expectation by *ignoring* possibilities, as for instance, the many possible reasons why Uncle Mac may not be there. However, we learn to do this ignoring by *learning the probabilities* to associate with particular events in particular kinds of settings. It is most probable that Uncle Mac will be there, though he might not; or again, smoke on the horizon—it is a ship; whereas out on the plains it is a railway train.

Consider too, the following:

> Gary did not have his usual game of marbles with his friends behind the bicycle shed. He was waiting for Elizabeth. He was very disappointed and rather upset when she did not come out at the usual time; he thought he had missed her. At last she arrived and they went home together.

At first sight this is obviously a budding romance, but many young children when given this paragraph will equally confidently assert that Gary and Elizabeth are brother and sister. They have not had sufficient experience to enable them to learn the inferential weight to give to the different events in the paragraph—especially "He was very disappointed and rather upset when she did not come out at the usual time". As children just a little older remark: "A *brother* would not behave like that!" The second interpretation is *possible* (brother and sister have recently lost their parents and have drawn close together) but we learn to assess it as *less likely*.

A very large number of the judgments we make about our environment are made on the basis of such learned probabilities. The mind selects from the range of *possible* events the one it has found most *probable*— in this way it achieves a basis for stable expectation. As Bruner says, we must learn the *probability texture* of our environment.[1]

### Selection of Information is on the Basis of Relevance

As we have seen, an individual selects what he will attend to by changing his general focus of attention: thus one person may select chess in preference to football, and this would be a reflection of a fairly stable set of priorities built up over the years. But the selection process also operates *within* the field of focus, for what is perceived within that field will in large measure be determined by judgments of *relevance*, i.e., whether it is related to the matter in the focus of mind.

This is brought out in the following exercise taken from a set designed to develop skill in judgments of *relevance:*

*Instructions:* The following are some jottings on "My Family". Select those which you consider suitable for use in a "story" you might have to write on "A Wet Sunday", the theme being *irritability.*

1. Rain all the week.
2. We have had a glorious Christmas.
3. The pre-school members of the family have not been outside all the week.
4. Dad usually plays golf on Sundays.
5. Mum has a heavy cold and is feeling really miserable.
6. The cat caught three mice last week.
7. We have seven in the family.
8. I wish Dad were not so cracked about vintage cars.
9. The dog's kennel is leaking.
10. Mum does not like "that dog" in the house.

If a number of pupils are given this exercise they will select different sets of notes. Asked to justify their particular choice, in the end they will have to refer to co-ordinating themes or subsuming ideas—and the relatedness of items to them. For instance, they frequently justify the inclusion of numbers 9 and 10 above by referring to the idea of a conflict of wills being *likely* to add to tension and hence irritability (the overall theme). They argue that if the children are upset at the dog's discomfort then they will be in conflict with the mother who does not want it in. However, other pupils will make other groupings and justify them in terms of different ideas. Thus the perception of relevance depends upon judgments which must take account of learned probabilities.

### Selection of Information is also on the Basis of its Significance

Information is not sampled for relevance alone but also for the degree of its relationship to a particular idea. Information can, for instance, be relevant but so remote from the central idea as to have little weight or significance for the subsuming idea in mind. A feature of the discrimination processes, then, is a weighting or ranking of what is relevant and a disregard of the relevance of that which lacks a certain minimum of weight, or significance. This is variously expressed: "That has little relevance"; "little significance"; etc. Relevance and significance must be considered as the two sides of the same penny. Such judgments again depend upon learned probabilities and on the degree of association between ideas.

This is brought out in the following exercise taken from a set designed to develop skill in making judgments of *significance.*

*Instructions:* The following notes are of an accident to a pupil. A teacher has to telephone the mother to tell her of the accident.

—Which information is the most significant?
—Rank the remainder in order of significance (group items if necessary).
—Which has so little significance as to be irrelevant?

1. Fell in front of car.
2. On the way to church.
3. Riding a bicycle.
4. Accompanied by Julie.
5. Too fast at the corner.
6. Loose gravel.
7. Tore her stocking.
8. Dented grandmother's cake-tin.
9. Broke leg.
10. In hospital.
11. Not serious.
12. Car driven by a *man*.
13. Car went over the back wheel of bicycle.

All of these items are relevant to a general account of the accident, but not all of them are of sufficient importance under the designated theme (a teacher telling the mother of the accident) as to have significance. In this exercise items 9-11 inclusive would be most likely to be accorded rank one—as the most significant items. On the other hand, No. 8—"Dented grandmother's cake-tin"—would be considered to be likely to have so little significance as to be ruled irrelevant. Notice here, that judgments of relevance cannot really be made without consideration of significance and that if an item is not significant *enough* it must be also judged irrelevant.

It will also be apparent that judgments of significance must rely on evaluative criteria set up for each situation. For instance, "Dented grandmother's cake-tin" would be relevant for the situation of a *complete* description of the accident, though of little relevance and no significance (therefore ruled irrelevant) in the situation that the accident was being communicated to the mother by the teacher. On the other hand, the communication of the accident by the mother at a tea-party of relatives, but excluding Grandma, might well accord the item sufficient significance for inclusion, and even give it second ranking, Grandma being the dragon she is.

## IMPLICATIONS FOR PEDAGOGY

In the information processing needed to achieve a new concept, processes of discrimination play an important part.

### ATTITUDES AND SELECTIVE SCREENING

The most significant effects of negative attitudes on selective screening in classroom situations would appear to fall into two categories:

1. Tensions between individuals which, in communication contexts, lower efficiency and can be disruptive.
2. A restricted interaction with available information results in a lower level of performance.

Efforts by the class teacher to improve the class climate would appear to have a special "payoff" for processes of discrimination which should operate more efficiently. Dramatic improvements to the volume of pupil-originated ideas in discussion can be achieved, for instance, simply by ensuring that the teacher and the pupils accept the obligation never to reject a new idea without reason—no matter how strange or poorly expressed it may be. In this case the *snigger* or remark of *dismissal* is replaced by the question asking for more information: "What do you mean by . . .?", "Could you tell us more about that?" Again, when the teacher provides for pupils to have choice of courses of action and some freedom to go about things their own way, there can be an equally dramatic lowering of class tensions and improvement in individual and group productivity.

---

In the two representative courses of action above, the teacher is aiming to counteract the effects of negative attitudes on selective screening by:

1. Improving security for individuals and so lowering the defensive threshold, which permits screening to be less restrictive.
2. Permitting the exercise of autonomy which research has indicated as a powerfully motivating interaction with the environment, thus increasing the input of information.[2]

---

## LEARNED PROBABILITY JUDGMENTS

The young children who inferred that Gary was *waiting for his sister* in the example above when he "did not have his usual game of marbles" and "was disappointed she did not come" had yet to have a number of experiences with family relationships before they would be able to infer that Gary was in fact "very friendly" with Elizabeth rather than "waiting for his sister". They lacked the requisite fund of probability information.
Such learning is complex and typical of much school learning. The conditions needed for this kind of learning are suggested by Smith and Smith:

> When it comes to general education — to the teaching of basic knowledge and skills that are to be used adaptively by the individual in countless different situations throughout life — there can be no simulation training as such. The best we can do for the learner is to provide him with a diversity of sensory experience and encourage him to react in diverse ways.

> An individual extends his knowledge, understanding and control of the environment by responding to it under many varieties of perturbed feedback. In this way he establishes an ever-expanding accumulation of adaptive response patterns and stable symbolic meanings.

> A basic principle of training is to perturb the feedback properties of response systematically in order to provide the learner with opportunities to extend his understanding and control of his own action in relation to the environment.[3]

The stability of expectation which underlies discrimination processes appears to depend upon experiences of the new concept in a variety of contexts under conditions requiring the learner to accommodate the new concept to the successive contexts in systematically varied ways.

F

If, then, pupils are going to achieve the fund of probability information necessary for effective discrimination, it would seem that new ideas must be presented in a variety of contexts, under conditions of perturbed feedback and with some degree of autonomy.

## RELEVANCE AND SIGNIFICANCE

The exercises used to illustrate relevance and significance above were used initially under experimental conditions in an exploration of processes of concept formation under classroom conditions. However, it was noted that when teachers required pupils to continue using the new terms and to apply them in the context of class discussion, the terms were used correctly and as well they added considerably to the quality of discussion when they were used to perform an evaluative function. A pupil would say to another: "That is not relevant—it has nothing to do with the . . ." and the like. If appeal to the teacher or the class was necessary, the matter could be settled with greater despatch and objectivity than before.

It was inferred from the above experience and others that:
1. Pupils should be trained in these skills. Specifically they should:
    (a) have practice verbalising the idea determining relevance,
    (b) have practice ranking ideas for significance relative to a given idea and verbalising their reasons for the ranking, and
    (c) have practice in making judgments of relevance and significance in relation to a given idea.
2. Pupils gain from a self-conscious awareness of the use of these skills.

As discrimination, classification and generalisation skills are here conceived as interdependent in concept formation, further implications for pedagogy will emerge from discussion of the following five chapters.

## REFERENCES

[1] J. S. BRUNER, "On Going Beyond the Information Given", in R. J. C. HARPER (Ed.), *Readings—The Cognitive Processes*, Prentice-Hall, Englewood Cliffs, 1964, p. 295.
[2] See K. Y. SMITH and M. F. SMITH, *Cybernetic Principles of Learning and Educational Design*, Holt, Rinehart and Winston, New York, 1966, pp. 474-75.
[3] Ibid., pp. 469-70.

# CHAPTER 6

# Implications of Classification as Involved in Concept Formation

The mind creates order out of an enormous flood of information by a classifying process in which grouping, and the ranking and organising of groups are salient characteristics.

## THE NATURE OF THE PROCESS

### GROUPING

#### Grouping is Discriminatory: The Concept

When asked to apply immediately one word which describes the group in Figure 6.1(a), adults answer *furniture*. But when asked to do the same for Figure 6.1(b) there is usually considerable hesitation, with many declining to make the attempt.

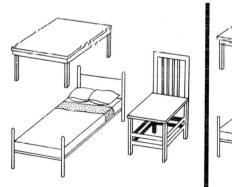

Figure 6.1 (a). The word which describes the group is......................

Figure 6.1 (b). The word which describes the group is......................

If *chattels* is suggested as the answer for Figure 6.1(b) it is usually received with delight or protest, depending on sex. The problem, of course, is that one must perceive the woman as "movable property" to be able to accept her as a member of the group *chattels*. If she can be so regarded, then in spite of the differences between her and the furniture, *chattels* becomes the answer. The exercise illustrates the dependence of the grouping process upon the development of two complementary abilities:

1. To accept things as equivalent because they possess certain qualities or attributes in common.
2. To ignore the ways in which the members of this group are different.

Thus, though *mouse* and *elephant* have very substantial differences, they do have certain attributes in common which enable us to accept them as members of the group named *mammals*.

| Some attributes of mouse and elephant | | A group in which recognised as equivalent |
|---|---|---|
| Common features noted | Some differences ignored | |
| vertebrate<br>suckle young | food<br>shape<br>habits<br>height<br>weight | mammal |

Figure 6.2 Example of grouping

By changing the attributes specified to be held in common it is possible for mouse and elephant to belong to other groups, e.g., *animals* and *living things*. All of these names of groups can themselves be grouped and are given the group name of *concept*. In terms of the above discussion, a concept can be defined as *a set of specifications whereby membership of groups can be determined*.

### Learned Probabilities and the Discriminatory Processes of Grouping

The ease with which a new concept is achieved appears to be critically influenced by learned probabilities. As has been implied, the acceptance of things and events as equivalent depends upon accepting some attributes and ignoring others. If then we enter the learning situation with a tendency to accept attributes which should be ignored and vice versa, learning will be difficult. Mednick, in a discussion of the work of Underwood and Richardson, states:

> As might be predicted it has been found that the greater the average probability of the stimulus-concept association in a group of stimuli, the faster the concept is attained.

Take the four words:

Baseball          Head          Button          Knob

What sensory-impression do they represent? No doubt you very quickly come up with "round". You might have also noticed "hard". But you were most likely to come up with round first because as a sensory association it has an average probability of $66 \cdot 25\%$. Hard has an associative probability of only $8 \cdot 25\%$.

If we take another group of four words, however, we can reverse the situation; take

Knuckle          Hailstone          Skull          Stone

What sensory-impression concept do these four suggest? In this case "hard" is your most likely response (average associate probability of 52·5%); "round" is considerably less likely with an average association probability of 11·25%.

Underwood and Richardson have shown that the *probability of the concept association is an extremely powerful variable determining ease of concept attainment*.[1] (My italics).

## NOT ALL NAMES ARE THOSE OF CONCEPTS

Some names are of particular things or events; that is, they do not name groups. *Katherine* and *World War I* are therefore not concepts; though it should be noted that *World*, *War*, and *I* taken separately are all concepts.

---

*Exercise:* Which of the following are concepts?

1. Fielding Tennis Club
2. Justice
3. Cosmos
4. Hitler
5. News Media

Correct answers are indicated by the digits 2, 3 and 5.

---

## CONCEPTS CAN EXIST WITHOUT KNOWLEDGE OF SPECIFICATIONS

The process of concept formation occurs at both the conscious and unconscious levels of the mind—so it is possible to learn a concept without being aware of the common features of the instances of the concept one can recognise.[2] In fact, as Osgood observes: "adults use many concepts more or less accurately that they find hard to define".[3] Concepts, then, can exist and be used more or less successfully without the common features being made explicit. How many adults, for instance, who use the concepts *freedom*, *democracy*, *justice*, and *romance*, are able to give their specifications?

Carroll observes that

> Because such "unconscious" concept formation is possible in some contexts, it is useful to define concept learning in terms of ability to recognise instances and the ability to formulate descriptions, or to construct instances of the concept.[2]

## KINDS OF CONCEPTS

The specifications of concepts vary with the nature of the group. Bruner, Goodnow and Austin suggest the following three types; their second type is considered here a sub-category of the first.[4]

1. *Conjunctive:* the specifications list attributes which all members have *in common*, i.e., *all* the attributes must be present.

*Example: Chair:* (furniture); *seats one person, has a back, and is usually movable.*

---

(a) *Disjunctive:* the specifications list *alternative* sets of specifications such that anything possessing any *one* set is thereby a *disjunctive* concept.

---

*Example:*

| Concept | Alternative Specifications |
|---|---|
| *foul* (in boxing) | To use the knee to strike an opponent. |
| | *OR* |
| | To punch below the belt. |
| | *OR* |
| | To use the head in a butt. |

---

Note that the disjunctive concept necessarily includes specifications which all *fouls* have in common (and is to that extent conjunctive, but differs from conjunctive concepts in going on to give alternative specifications for particular cases of the concept—a foul in boxing is not the same as in water-polo.)

2. *Relational:* these specify the relationship which must exist between the attributes of an instance of the concept.

---

*Example:*

| Concept | Specification |
|---|---|
| Direction | Implies a specific movement between one point and another relative to a base line. |

---

| Conjunctive | | Relational |
|---|---|---|
| Conjunctive | Disjunctive | |
| reptile (biology)<br>sphere  (maths) | strike (baseball)<br>form  (furniture) | distance<br>velocity |

Figure 6.3 Examples of the types of concepts

---

*Exercise:* Which of the following are *relational* concepts?

| | |
|---|---|
| 1. furniture | 4. mass |
| 2. time | 5. geography |
| 3. ratio | 6. average |

The answers are indicated by the digits 2, 3, 4 and 6.

## THE RANKING OF GROUPS

### Concepts can be Ranked in Terms of Degree of Abstraction

A concept is said to be *concrete* when the members of the group it identifies can be directly perceived by the senses. Examples of *concrete* concepts are: *pin, cover, range, floor, stone,* and *water.* The term is, unfortunately, rather misleading because any concept, by virtue of being a group name, is an abstraction; for example, one can touch *five blocks* but not *five.* A more helpful notion from a teacher's viewpoint is to rank concepts in terms of *degree of abstractness,* or the extent to which they name groupings of other concepts. In the example below, Figure 6.4, *wealth* is the most abstract concept because it includes the concepts of *property* and *money* and all the concepts which they in turn include in their respective groups, and so on.

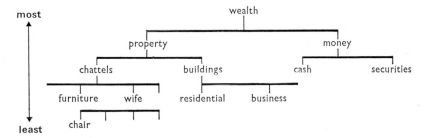

Figure 6.4 Degrees of abstractness of concepts related to the concept of wealth

The concept *chair* would be the *least abstract* of those listed.

Thus concepts can be ranked in terms of the remoteness of the group from the perceptual world.

---

*Exercise:* Rank the following set of concepts in order of increasing abstraction:

1. mathematics
2. blocks
3. number
4. arithmetic
5. three

(The correct order is indicated by the following initial letters: b, t, n, a and m.)

---

### Specification Requires Various Degrees of Abstraction

When *chair* is defined as an item of furniture—seats one person; has a back; is movable—the specifications express the attributes through the interrelationships of a number of concepts. However it is necessary to realise also that this specification is a mixture of concepts of various degrees of *abstraction;* each particular concept is chosen at the level which will permit the best differentiation of instances of chair from other furniture which closely resembles a chair, e.g., *stool and form* (*with a back*).

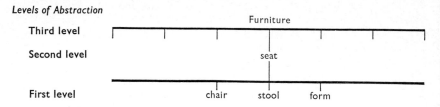

Figure 6.5(a) Levels of abstraction of selected items of furniture

| CONCEPT | | SPECIFICATIONS | | |
|---|---|---|---|---|
| Second level of abstraction | SEAT | a number; from one to — | shape to permit sitting | various degrees of movement |
| First level of abstraction | CHAIR | seats one | has a back | movable |
| | STOOL | seats one | has no back | movable |
| | FORM | seats several— usually 4-6-8 | backed *or* backless | movable |

Figure 6.5(b) Specifications of items of furniture of Fig. 6.5(a)

Thus, as illustrated in Figure 6.5(b), the specification of chair begins by citing furniture and seat (from the two levels of abstraction above it) and then, to detail the specification, must go to a lower level of abstraction than is necessary for the specification of *seat*, e.g., *back* is less abstract than *shape*.

## THE ORGANISING OF GROUPS: KNOWLEDGE

As will be apparent from the discussion on their specification, concepts do not exist in isolation but are linked in networks. The totality of this network we know as *knowledge*. Considered as an organised system to store information when value depends critically upon retrieval, knowledge is in some ways analogous to a fishing net. The whole or part may be tangled (confused knowledge); may have unconnected or loose ends or inappropriately sized mesh (gaps in knowledge); or may be of appropriately sized mesh and folded in a systematic way for use (mastery).

The network in knowledge may also be considered as analogous to an electrical reticulation system, where there are sub-stations which can be ranked in order of importance in terms of the number of outlets and the amount of energy distributed. Concepts can be ranked in a similar way, that is, according to the number of relationships existing with other concepts and to their usefulness in organising other concepts.

The source of the network of relationships, however, is wider than that implicit to degrees of abstraction or power to subsume other concepts. This will now be explored.

## Concepts can be Linked by Propositions

Propositions are statements which express a pattern of relationships between two or more concepts.

---

*Examples:*
1. Two plus two equals four.
2. Force is proportional to the product of mass and acceleration.
3. Round things roll.
4. Ignorance is bliss.

---

Propositions have a stabilising effect on linkages between concepts in that they are explicit formulations of a pattern of concepts and they are intended to be remembered in that pattern. This explicit statement of relationships is a major source of stability in knowledge as a whole— especially when associated with the intention to remember. This is because the stability of each proposition also tends to stabilise the linkages between other concepts which are included in the specifications of the concepts it names.

### PROPOSITIONS MAY BE SINGULAR OR GENERAL

Propositions may be singular statements (such as *John loves art*) about a particular thing (or person, in this case), or be general statements (such as *two plus two equals four*); that is, propositions may be *singular* or *general* depending upon whether they are about a *particular* thing or about a *group* or *class* of things.

---

*Examples:*
> John loves art. (singular)
> Two plus two equals four. (general)

*Exercise:* Which of the following are general propositions?
  *Note:* Imagine the phrase "In all cases" as understood in front of the above example of a general proposition.
1. Mixed farming on the Canterbury Plains exploits the need to renew pastures frequently.
2. Jackson's barn was razed last night.
3. The *Titanic* disaster was the sinking of a new passenger liner with large loss of life.
4. Appreciation involves (a) comprehension, and (b) evaluation against both public and private criteria.
5. To change the order of an addition does not affect the total.

The digits of one hundred and forty-five indicate correct answers. Remember: a general proposition is about a *group* or total class of events.

---

General propositions are called by several names: concepts, generalisations, principles, laws, rules, hypotheses or definitions, depending sometimes upon the actual context of use, sometimes upon conventional usage, and sometimes upon the whim of the user! Thus, for example, the general proposition "Four-year-old boys are incorrigibly naughty" would be considered a *generalisation* because it certainly would not have universal acceptance; whereas $2 \times 2 = 4$, and "round things roll" would be considered *principles* because there would be the necessary degree of acceptance. Then again, we refer to the *Principle* of Archimedes but to Boyle's *Law* of Gases, the difference being one of convention. It will be apparent that the formal specification of a concept must be a general proposition, which perhaps accounts for part of the confusion of names.

### THE STRUCTURE OF KNOWLEDGE

The concept of structure is used to refer to the systematised pattern of relationships which is characteristic of organised or formal knowledge at the level of mastery of a topic or subject. Formal knowledge is characterised by the disciplined attempt to use concepts whose specifications are defined as rigorously as is possible for the particular topic and/or subject. In fact, agreement on specifications of concepts is a major preoccupation of those studying the subject. Informal knowledge, on the other hand, has concepts whose specifications owe much to fortuitous association. For example, the concept of mother for two illiterates (who thus would not have the compensating vicarious experience of reading) would vary: one whose mother was loving, the other rejecting.

To structure a topic, then, is to organise its concepts in such a way that the implied interrelationships between them are consistent with those that follow of logical necessity from their specifications.

## IMPLICATIONS FOR PEDAGOGY

### IMPROVING THE DISCRIMINATORY ASPECT OF GROUPING IN CONCEPT LEARNING

Learners come to each task with different capabilities to manage grouping processes. The teacher, it seems, must give high priority to the creation of conditions which help the learner to perceive and to note the significance of what is common and to ignore what is different.

### Experiences with Non-instances

A frequently used exercise to test intellectual ability is to require the testee to identify the "odd man out" or one which "does not belong" as in the example below:

tiger, lion, elephant, leopard.

If one thinks about the process whereby *elephant* is identified as the one which does not belong, it is readily apparent that there is increased awareness of what the other three have in common. This can be exploited to advantage in the teaching of concepts.

A well chosen non-instance of a concept can serve to highlight the significance of a concept attribute. Therefore, in the teaching of a concept, the non-instance can be used to *compensate for the low probability of a particular attribute being perceived.* Such non-instances ideally should possess all attributes except one whose absence in the presence of instances is very likely to be perceived. In the case of the concept *chair* (see Figure 6.6), a stool is chosen as a non-instance in association with a group of instances of the concept *chair*, so it will highlight the attribute *no back*; whereas if form (with a back) is used, it will highlight *seats one person.* On the other hand the use of a *backless form* would have little value as it lacks *two* attributes, i.e., it seats more than one and lacks a back.

Good non-instances

Instances of chair          Poor non-instance

Figure 6.6: Some instances and non-instances of teaching the concept of the chair

But in teaching a concept using non-instances, Braley states that it is difficult to learn from non-instances unless good examples of the concept accompany them.[5]

### Verbal Instructions

As de Cecco advises:

> Teachers must give aural or visual emphasis to attributes which are obscure and yet important in identifying the concept. In defining concepts teachers traditionally resort to vocal inflection, hand and arm gesticulation, underscoring, diagramming, drawing and so on, to make obscure attributes obvious. Unless this emphasis is provided the student will learn some attributes and not others and, thereby, fail to learn the complete concept.[6]

### The Need for Variety: a Multi-media Approach is Essential

The dietitian insists that there be variety in the diet to ensure adequate coverage of the body's nutritional needs, both because of the range of individual differences in needs and the unpredictability of the nutritional value of particular foods eaten. For a similar reason it is necessary to ensure a sufficient variety of contexts in which instances of a concept are experienced, for individuals vary in their facility of perception through the different senses and therefore in the likelihood of their perception of particular attributes.

## CONCEPTUAL RESOURCES WHICH FAVOUR LEARNING NEW CONCEPTS

### Relation to More Abstract Concepts

In the discussion above it was found that to give the specifications of the concept *chair* it was necessary to call on concepts of a various degree of abstractness, *two of which were of a higher level than chair*. The implication seems clear: the teacher must ensure a sufficient familiarity with the context of the new concept so that its more abstract concepts can provide a framework for the perception and organisation of attributes.

Figures 6.7(a) and (b) illustrate this. When groups as large as 250 graduate students were asked to identify Figure 6.7(a) they have invariably failed, their best suggestions being "something to do with TV" and "frames of a film strip". When, however, they have been shown Figure 6.7(b) there is immediately a chorus of "the first is a view of the nut"—and this answer comes from many who are quite unfamiliar with technical drawings. The point is that awareness of the significance of the "nut" serves to change the probability values of the elements perceived in Figure 6.7(a), just as knowledge that a chair belongs to the groups *furniture* and *seat* would considerably improve the likelihood that essential attributes would be identified.

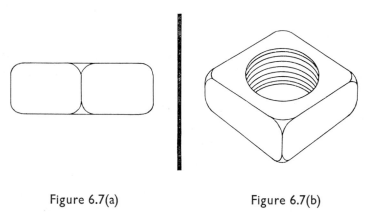

Figure 6.7(a)                    Figure 6.7(b)

What is it?

As a further example, if the concept *chattels* (see Figure 6.4), had to be taught, it would seem necessary to ensure that the concept of *wealth* was known to the extent of the attributes of *property* and *money*, as this knowledge would increase the likelihood that the significant attributes of *chattels* would be perceived.

## Rules before Examples

Carroll comments:

> A number of relevant experiments in the context of programmed instruction indicate that the teaching of concepts can be accomplished by the presentation of "rules" and "examples", in that order, more effectively than by the presentation of examples *followed* by rules.[7]

In the context of this discussion, giving the rule first would increase the likelihood that significant attributes would be perceived in the examples. However, it would be necessary for the teacher to ensure that the learner verbalised the attributes of instances as a safeguard against rote learning. Again, it would be essential that the rule given was not implicitly the imposition of a *structure* beyond the capacity of the pupils.

## Advance Organisers

Ausubel suggests the use of "organisers" in advance of certain types of complex learning, to

> provide relevant ideational scaffolding, *enhance the discriminability of the new learning material* from previously learned related ideas, and otherwise effect integrative reconciliation at a level of abstraction, generality and inclusiveness which is much higher than that of the learning material itself.[8] (My italics.)

Ausubel and Robinson[9] suggest that advance organisers should be used, generally speaking in either of two conditions:

1. *If specifically relevant ideas are not available* in the mind of the learner when potentially meaningful material is presented.
2. When relevant ideas are available *but their relevance is not recognised by the learner.*

In either case the use of an advance organiser would appear to increase the quality of discrimination exercised to achieve new concepts: the relevance and significance of ideas is then more apparent and so increases the probability that attributes and new concepts will be perceived.

# INSTRUCTION AND THE RANKING AND ORGANISATION OF CONCEPTS

## Less Abstract before More Abstract

Because of the limitations imposed by stages in the development of intellectual ability, the rule that "concrete should be taught before abstract" seems well founded, particularly in terms of a particular sequence of instruction. This is, of course, consonant with Gagné's insistence upon the sequence of instruction being ordered by a notion of prerequisite capabilities.

However it must not be assumed that the abstract concept is necessarily more difficult than the less abstract—the so-called "concrete" concept. Bruner, Goodnow and Austin concluded that the difficulty of learning a concept was influenced by its complexity and logical structure. So they found, for instance, that conjunctive concepts were easier than relational, and disjunctive were the most difficult under their experimental conditions.[10] While there is no formal evidence to support the view other than an impression from teaching, it seems that when disjunctive concepts are regarded as a sub-category of conjunctive and taught accordingly, they too are simpler than relational concepts. De Cecco states the problem with relational concepts:

> Since the concept does not adhere in the attributes themselves but in the particular relationships of the attributes, it is easy for the child (and even the adult) to become confused. For example, both the concept *distance* and the concept *direction* have as their attributes points in time and space. What distinguishes them is the difference in the relationship of the same attributes.[11]

### Structure Indicates Priorities

As Bruner observes:

> Since the goodness of a structure depends upon its power for simplifying information, for generating new propositions, and for increasing the manipulability of a body of knowledge, *structure must always be related to the status and gifts of the learner. Viewed in this way the optimal structure of a body of knowledge is not absolute but relative.* The major requirement is that no two sets of generating structures for the same field be in contradiction.[12] (My italics.)

In other words the *readiness* of the learner for a particular structuring of a topic must remain a first consideration in planning. The decision would depend upon the range of concepts and principles of the structure known, and the degree of mastery in terms of Carroll's definition of concept learning, i.e., in terms of ability to recognise instances, formulate descriptions and construct instances.

## REFERENCES

[1] S. A. MEDNICK, *Learning*, Prentice-Hall, Englewood Cliffs, 1964, p. 65.

[2] J. B. CARROLL, *Language and Thought*, Prentice-Hall, Englewood Cliffs, 1964, p. 82.

[3] C. E. Osgood, *Method and Theory in Experimental Psychology*, Oxford University Press, New York, 1953.

[4] J. S. BRUNER, J. J. GOODNOW and G. A. AUSTIN, *A Study of Thinking*, John Wiley & Sons, New York, 1956.

[5] L. BRALEY, "Strategy Selection and Negative Instances in Concept Learning", *Journal of Educational Psychology*, 1963, **54**, pp. 154-59.

[6] J. P. DE CECCO, *The Psychology of Learning and Instruction: Educational Psychology*, Prentice-Hall, Englewood Cliffs, 1968, p. 390.

[7] CARROLL, op. cit., p. 83.

[8] D. P. AUSUBEL, *The Psychology of Meaningful Verbal Learning*, Grune and Stratton, New York, 1963, p. 214.

[9] D. P. AUSUBEL and F. G. ROBINSON, *School Learning*, Holt, Rinehart and Winston, New York, 1969, p. 145.

[10] BRUNER, GOODNOW and AUSTIN, op. cit.

[11] DE CECCO, op. cit., p. 393.

[12] J. S. BRUNER, "Some Theorems on Instruction illustrated with reference to Mathematics", in *Theories of Learning and Instruction: 63rd Yearbook, Nat. Soc. Stud. Educ.*, Part I, Chicago Press, 1964, pp. 308-09.

# CHAPTER 7

# Implications of Generalisation as Involved in Concept Formation

## THE NATURE OF THE PROCESS

### INTRODUCTION

The process of generalisation, the product of which is expressed as a general proposition, is essentially a process whereby the mind goes beyond the information immediately available.[1] Thus, from consideration of the limited number of women drivers we have known (or choose to remember) we can assert: Women drivers, implying *all* women drivers, . . . Essentially then, when generalising, we infer the nature of some group or population of events which is wider than our present experience from the nature of a representative group or sample we have actually encountered. But the process is not unidirectional in the sense that it involves only a movement from sample to total population. In fact it is characterised by a *feedback* of information between sample and population as the adequacy of a succession of trial inferences about each is tested for "goodness of fit": the more complex and difficult the generalisation the more this will be so.

### PROBABILITY JUDGMENTS NECESSARY TO GENERALISATION

Going beyond the immediate information is the most distinctive feature of the generalisation process; it is made possible by the learned probability judgments or inferential weightings to be given to different parts of the available evidence. *If such probability judgments are not a distinctive feature of the recognition of something, the process is not generalisation, but simply that of remembering.*

By its nature, generalisation is an integral part both of concept use and concept formation. This is because the mind seldom waits for all the evidence before it (1) infers identity or (2) forms a set of specifications. Of course there are risks: only too frequently we infer the wrong identity or formulate faulty specifications for new concepts.

The following discussion will be concerned mainly with generalisation:

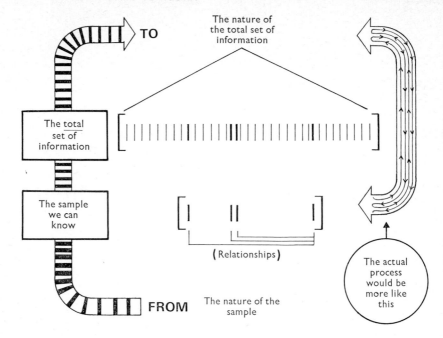

Figure 7.1: Schematic representation of the nature of generalisation

1. As a process which makes possible the *recognition* of a *new* instance of a known concept.
2. Its function in
   (a) establishing *sets of specifications* of *new* concepts, and
   (b) progressive modification of existing specifications.
3. As locatable on an intuitive-inductive continuum.

## GENERALISATION IN INFERRING IDENTITY

A decision as to the identity of something, that is, to recognise it as a new instance of a known concept, is often made on the basis of limited evidence.

We recognise an object or event when there is sufficient evidence to infer identity. But what does *sufficient* mean? In the case where I have my golf-ball in my *hand* there can be more than sufficient evidence. It is a golf-ball: size, shape, colour, texture, weight, elasticity, all within the limits of variation I have learned to associate with the characteristics of golf-balls; and it is mine because I see it has the texture of an almost new golf-ball, it is marked with Dunlop 4 and there is a slice mark through the number—but most of our thinking does not wait until this amount of evidence becomes available.

As we become familiar with the attributes of a thing, we obtain the means to infer its identity from the presence of only a few cues: a few attributes of the total set of specifications of the concept. The speck of white in the distance on a golf course is *most probably* a golf-ball, whereas an identical speck of white on the footpath at the same distance is *quite probably* a piece of paper or a cigarette packet. But on the other hand, I realise that an identical speck of white at the same distance in a fairground could be any of a large number of articles. In the first two cases I would expect to be right, though with a feeling of greater certainty in the case of the golf-ball; but I have no degree of certainty in the third case. Thus we only have *sufficient* evidence when there is some *acceptable degree of certainty*. As it is, we are very frequently in the position of having reasonable certainty of the nature of something for which there is only limited evidence present.

### The Ranking of Evidence to Infer Identity

In the case of my first experience with a golf-ball at a distance on a fairway, my experiences of small, round, white objects at a distance on backgrounds of a similar range of colour lead me to assign priorities in these circumstances to the characteristic *whitish speck*. Someone who has never had the experience of looking for such an object under these or analogous conditions would initially find the ball very difficult, or, more likely, impossible to locate from a distance, for when there is not sufficient familiarity with the object in its different kinds of settings, the ability to rank the evidence of its specifications will not have been developed. It is for this reason that a novice hunter frequently cannot see the deer he seeks even though he is looking directly at it. As we become familiar with the characteristics of objects or events under different conditions, we learn to rank their characteristics as clues of their presence. For example, we learn to expect to *hear* the high-flying aeroplane before we see it; to expect to see the colour of a small object at a distance (such as a golf-ball) before (say) the *shape and texture*.

When the setting changes, the rankings also change, for the setting is a part of the available relevant evidence from which to infer identity. If we have to find a pin among needles of much the same size, assuming the task to be novel and also assuming familiarity with the characteristics of pins and needles, we would probably approach the task expecting to find the pin on the basis of its *round knob*, or, a little less likely, its size relative to needles. On the other hand, in a new setting, such as the pin in the green grass of the lawn, we would approach the task expecting to find it quickest if we looked for it on the basis of *shininess* or brightness.

### The Ranking Process and Probability

If, given the novel task of finding a pin in the green grass of the lawn, the decision to look for *something shiny* rather than (say) the *round knob* will be on the basis of an on-the-spot assessment of the probabilities of finding the object if the search is made for different kinds of evidence. Such judgment will call on earlier probability judgments and their consequences. In the present case the process leading to the decision to look for something shiny might go rather like this:

G

Pin in the grass; previous searches like this have been most successful when conducted on the basis of *contrast*, so what provides the greatest contrast in this case? Length and shape of the pin against green grass—colour—pin is silver; sun-shininess; would catch eye—*shininess*.

From previous experience it has been learned that shininess in such a context provides the greatest probability of success; that to look, for instance, for the length and shape of the pin has less probability of success because previous experience has indicated that there is insufficient contrast in such a context.

## The Learning of Probabilities

Variety of experience of instances of a concept in different contexts allows attributes to vary in significance relative to the known specifications. Less dominant attributes of one situation may be highlighted in a new situation so that its real significance can be noted. Thus it is a sound pedagogical principle in the teaching of a concept to provide opportunity to discriminate between instances of a concept and a non-instance which lacks only one particular attribute.

## Recognition of Identity does not always Involve Generalisation

The recognition of objects or events does not necessarily involve the process of generalisation.

First, there are occasions when the full set of specifications of the concept can be seen to be present. Consider the example: this object in front of us can seat one person, has a back and is movable. Because it has all the attributes of the concept chair, it *is* a chair. In such cases the essential features of generalisation, that is, going beyond the immediate information and the use of probability judgments in so doing, are not present.

Second, in the case of repeated recognitions of the concept from limited evidence, what initially required generalisation becomes simply recall. For example, I have previously recognised a golf-ball at a distance on the fairway. On the first occasion generalisation was involved because the inference of identity was from both limited evidence and judgments on the probability of a correct inference from features of the limited evidence. But on the subsequent occasions I come to rely on the clue—*whitish speck in the distance*—through learning the clue, and I respond from habit. In this case there is an assigned probability judgment—but no weighing of probabilities which would involve a ranking of evidence. Generalisation in fact may be unnecessary in such simple cases after the first occasion of its use.

Figure 7.2 illustrates this identity-type generalisation in the example of *Gary loves Elizabeth*. From the discussion in this chapter on the processes of discrimination it will be realised that the focus of probability judgments is on the significance of the fact that *he was disappointed when she did not come out*—in the context of the other events, and relative to knowledge of the behaviour of those "in love".

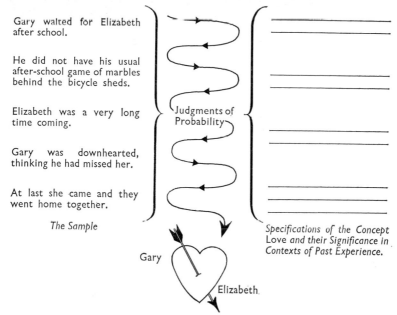

Gary waited for Elizabeth after school.

He did not have his usual after-school game of marbles behind the bicycle sheds.

Elizabeth was a very long time coming.

Gary was downhearted, thinking he had missed her.

At last she came and they went home together.

*The Sample*

Judgments of Probability

Gary

Elizabeth

*Specifications of the Concept Love and their Significance in Contexts of Past Experience.*

Figure 7.2: Schematic representation of identity type generalisation *Love* in the context of the relationships of Gary and Elizabeth

## Examples of Generalisation to Infer Identity

It is assumed in both examples that the problem involves an application of a concept not previously met.

- This is an example of *colonial exploitation*.
  (From evidence on the politico-socio-economic history of the country.)
- The solution of this problem depends upon a calculation of *inverse proportion*.
  (The problem: If four men dig a hole in six days, how long will six men take?)

---

*Exercises in Identity-type Generalisation*
1. What can we say of Joy from the following sample of behaviour?
   (a) People like having Joy around.
   (b) She has many friends.
   (c) She always has a smile.
2. What can be said of John from the following sample of behaviour?
   (a) John is hard to get out of bed in the mornings.
   (b) He always dodges doing the dishes if he can.
   (c) He never offers to help in the garden.
   (d) His only friends are very much younger.

---

Most readers should immediately identify the concept *popularity* in the first case but have to give the second some thought. Many on a first reading hit on *laziness*, but then on reading item (d) discover that (d) does not fit. A new inferential weight has then to be given (a), (b) and (c). The concept identity *inferiority complex* or equivalent would be an acceptable solution.

## GENERALISATION IN THE FORMATION OF NEW CONCEPTS

### Establishing Specifications of a New Concept

As we have seen, concept formation is essentially the abstraction of the common features of a class of objects or events which become the set of specifications whereby objects or events shall be considered equivalent within the concept group.

Generalisation in concept formation, in contrast to the recognition of identity, is primarily from *identity* to *specifications*. When the identity of a golf-ball is inferred from the speck of white in the distance on the fairway, on the first experience of having to make such identification, the generalisation is from the limited evidence of the specifications to the identity. However, when we state the specifications of a concept the process is much more complex. In the first place, the generalisation of the specifications is in the *reverse* direction, that is, *from knowledge of identity to the statement of specifications*. In the second place, the generalisation of the specification is essentially identity-type generalisation, but with the additional complication of the need to make judgments as to the inferential weight to be given to each of the concepts identified in order to determine their value as differentiating attributes. For instance, to say of round things that they *roll* is to give one of the specifications of round things. However to achieve this specification it is necessary to identify the concept *roll* from the common features of the attributes present in round things and to determine its significance as a specification.

## PROBABILITY JUDGMENTS IN CONCEPT FORMATION

All that has been said about probability judgments being central to generalisation involved in inferring identity applies with equal force to generalisation of the specifications of new concepts. As will be remembered, concept formation is essentially a grouping process which we manage on the basis of our ability to *notice* common attributes and *ignore* all others. Learned probability judgments are, however, central to the perception of these common features in that the significance of any particular attribute has to be assessed relative to any tentatively held hypothesis as to the nature of the concept for which specifications are sought. (Remember, deciding on the nature of the total set of information from a sample is a *feedback* process.) I *could* say, for instance, that all *metals* consist of matter but this does not help me distinguish *metals* from *non-metals*. What I must decide about any common attribute of metals is how significant it is likely to be in differentiating metals from non-metals. My ability to make these probability judgments will depend upon my experience of metals and non-metals in many contexts of association. I can say from experience, for example, that metals conduct electricity, are

malleable, and are shiny when scraped—in descending order of significance as differentiating attributes. My statement of this specification
of the concept *metal* would be considerably less likely to be forthcoming
if my experience of metals was restricted to seeing it used in pots, axes
and roofing without having had the opportunity to "work with" metal.

## GENERALISATION CAN BE EITHER EXPLICIT OR IMPLICIT

In the discussion of the grouping process of concept formation, it was
pointed out that concept formation can be either a conscious process or
an unconscious process. Generalisation involving concept formation may
therefore be either explicit or implicit. Apart from certain contrived
situations, such as in the classroom, concept formation is ordinarily an
unconscious process.

Because generalisation in an unconsciously formed concept is implicit,
instances of the concept can frequently be recognised but the specifications of the concept cannot be formulated. For example: "I can give you
*examples* of forces but I cannot tell you what force *is*."

### The Progressive Modification of Existing Specifications

With concepts which have complex, sophisticated specifications or which
include concepts of a high degree of abstraction, the first specification
of the learner is frequently merely a "global" statement of attributes.
The differentiation of attributes required for the more sophisticated
specification must await further experience which consists essentially of
*practice in using the concept in varied contexts which require its identifica-
tion and further refinement of its specifications.* Thus the specifications
of the concept *revolution* which would be likely to come from the *French
Revolution* alone could be considerably refined by the required perception
of the concept *revolution* in other contexts—for example, the *Industrial
Revolution* of the nineteenth century in Great Britain and contexts which
contrast *revolution* with *evolution*—and by the verbalisation of its specifications.

Of course, in relation to the processes involved in generalising specifications, each successive modification is essentially the generalising of a
"new" concept, for new rankings of the significance of all attributes must
be determined with the perception of new attributes.

## INTUITIVE AND INDUCTIVE THINKING AS GENERALISATION

Intuitive and inductive thinking as generalisation are of the same logical
order in that they are both characterised by the inference of the nature
of a total set of ideas from the nature of a sample. However, intuitive and
inductive thinking are related in such a way that they can be thought of
as the two ends of a continuum representing all acts of generalisation.
In terms of the generalisation process described above they differ (1) in
terms of the degree of rigour *implicit* to the whole process and (2) in the
degree to which the elements involved in the process can be made explicit.
Thus any generalisation can be placed upon the continuum according to
how close its characteristics are to those of intuition or induction—with

an intermediate zone where the distinction is necessarily arbitrary (see Figure 7.3).

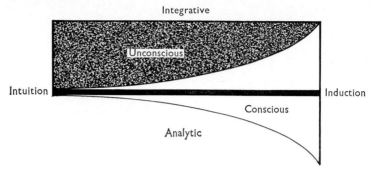

Figure 7.3: Model for range of generalisation in an intuitive-inductive continuum in terms of analytic and integrative thinking

What, then, are the differentiating characteristics? The stereotype of a woman's intuition illustrates the essential features.

Lyn and Jason are having a row. Under the stimulus of her annoyance at Jason's cutting remarks, Lyn has just "perceived" for the first time the significance of several things she has previously noticed about Jason. "You're mummy's boy!" she snaps. Jason, in high anger, finally asks that she justify this. At this point (to keep faith with the stereotype) Lyn is confused because she is unable to do so and yields the advantage to Jason on the grounds of manifest illogicality. Leaving aside all issues of the sex war and whether or not such intuitive thinking should be encouraged, it is illuminating to analyse the above in terms of processes of generalisation. First, "You're mummy's boy!" must be based on a sample of ideas which is not apprehended consciously—for the ideas cannot be recalled immediately after. To get the significance of this we must imagine that Lyn was, in fact, *better informed* than first suggested, and that before making the remark she was to some extent aware of the source of her ideas. Further, when challenged she was able to go back to these and make them to some extent explicit. There is now a very significant difference. Lyn is in some degree conscious of the sample *before* generalising and is able to go back to it *after* generalising. This is a more sophisticated form of intuition of which the differentiating characteristic is analytic thinking. Bruner says:

> Analytic thinking characteristically proceeds a step at a time. Steps are explicit and usually can be adequately reported by the thinker to another individual. Such thinking proceeds with relatively full awareness of the information and operations involved. It may involve careful and deductive reasoning, often using mathematics or logic and an explicit plan of attack.[2]

Given that analytic thinking can have varying degrees of rigour, it will be seen that it is a useful criterion for locating thinking on the intuitive-inductive continuum. So in our model the more rigorous the analytic thinking associated with a generalisation, i.e. *before* the generalisation in order to know the sample, the closer a given generalisation is to the inductive end of the continuum. (Of course, the better the sample is known *before* the generalisation the more likely its elements can be made explicit *after*.)

But there is a second factor in the stereotype of intuitive thinking, which is that the generalisation "You're mummy's boy!" must be a synthesis or integration of the ideas in Lyn's unconscious. Of course all generalisation must necessarily include this integrative process as we move from awareness of the sample to the idea which best subsumes it and the total set. But while integrative thinking must have been present in the extreme instance of the stereotype intuition, analytic thinking was not—assuming it to be necessarily a conscious process. Yet, at the other end of the continuum, inductive thinking must be characterised by a *balanced* use of the analytic and integrative thinking.

Thus we can account for the stereotype as representative of the intuitive end of the continuum of our model and as an unconscious act of integrative thinking with no analytic thinking. As generalisations are increasingly characterised by conscious attempts to know the sample, they are increasingly analytic with a corresponding decrease in the unconscious type of integrative thinking. Concomitantly there is an increase in the conscious components as generalisation becomes an increasingly disciplined process.

## DEDUCTION AND INDUCTION

These have long been considered as opposites. However, if intuition and induction are but opposite ends of a generalisation continuum, deduction should more correctly be opposed to *generalisation*. Generalisation is a reasoning from the particular to the general; deduction from the general to the particular. While this is so, there is a more significant difference for our purposes, which is that deductions follow of *logical necessity* whereas generalisations are only *probabilities*. The point is that deductive reasoning is governed by rules of inference which produce acceptance of the conclusion as a logical necessity—in marked contrast to the probability of an induction.

It needs to be noted that deductive thinking is increasingly a feature of analytic thinking as its rigour increases. But on the other hand, it is *not synonymous* with fully rigorous analytic thinking which may include procedures and methods of attack and hence has a broader connotation than deduction.

## IMPLICATIONS FOR PEDAGOGY

As a salient feature of concept formation, generalisation is a highly significant skill for those teachers who prefer to promote the development of independent minds rather than to train their pupils to be sophisticated parrots. Perhaps the most important inference to be drawn by such teachers from the above discussion is that there is considerable room for improvement in the use of generalisation in the classroom. Such improvement would appear quite practicable under classroom conditions, given the development of two complementary sets of teacher skills which are required:

1. To plan for and directly manage the process of generalisation in the achievement of ideas.
2. To contribute to the development of pupil autonomy in learning by:
   (a) quite specific development of their generalisations skills, and
   (b) planned opportunity to exercise these skills independently.

## IMPROVING DIRECTLY MANAGED GENERALISATION

### Improving the Sample

If a generalisation is essentially an inference based on the nature of a *sample*, it follows that the teacher's *selection* of that sample will be a very significant factor in determining the success of pupil generalisation. For example in Figure 7.4 below, the teacher using Sample A is very much less likely to achieve the generalisation objective than the teacher using Sample B. Why? What criteria could be used to evaluate these samples? The discussion which follows explores these questions relative to the problem of selection.

It should be noted in this and subsequent discussions that the expression to *achieve the required generalisation* refers to the *product* of the generalisation process.

*Generalisation required:* Plants need water to survive.

| Sample A | Sample B |
|---|---|
| 1. My garden has looked much better since I started using a sprinkler.<br>2. Farmers anywhere become very anxious in times of drought when everything becomes dry.<br>3. In Egypt the Nile is very important for farmers. | 1. *For observation:* A set of twelve plants of different kinds which have not been watered for four weeks. (All plants have died except the one cactus.)<br>  (a) Data on the ways cacti store water and otherwise cope with long dry spells.<br>2. Information from farms in the district on the drought the previous summer and autumn:<br>  (a) loss or drastic reduction in crops;<br>  (b) some irrigation systems broke down for various periods. For given crops note that loss or reduced cropping was related to period water not available. |

Figure 7.4: Two samples for comparison. From which sample is the class more likely to achieve the required generalisation?

### SELECTION

In preparing material for their classes, many teachers proceed as did the teacher who prepared Sample A: they rely on a selection process which requires only that the material be more or less relevant. As a consequence, their pupils have difficulty achieving the required generalisation and the teacher has to resort to strong leading questions or ends by telling them. When, however, a teacher selects material for the sample *as embodying significant concepts relative to the required generalisation*, the outcome is markedly different.

Each item of Sample A has some *relevance* to the generalisation "Plants must have water to survive", but the significance of the items is such that the class, unaided, is more likely to make the generalisation "plants *need* water for *growth*".

The point is that the selection process leading to Sample A does not *necessarily* lead to the inclusion of items of high significance relative to the required generalisation, whereas Sample B proceeds from the identi- fication of significant concepts inherent in the generalisation sought to a selection of the sample using the concepts' rankings of significance.

Thus item 1 of Sample B highlights that *most* plants die without water and 1 (a) could confirm that *all* plants need water to survive. Item 2 (a) could establish the generality of the proposition, i.e., true of all plants, not just pot plants; 2 (b) gives a suggestion that it is not just *any* amount of water during a period of time.

From the above it will be apparent that if a teacher is to select a good sample he will need to *explicate* an idea he wishes to teach—to identify what is significant and to rank it and thus establish criteria for selection.

The importance of selection is such that the explication is considered necessarily done under discipline—hence it will be discussed in the chapter on the *topic analysis discipline* (Chapter 11) which was developed to cope with this and certain other problems.

## ADEQUATE RANGE OF IDEAS IN THE SAMPLE

One sample may be better than another in terms of the *range* of ideas relative to the concepts implicit to the required generalisation. Thus, it would easily be possible in Sample B above for a class to achieve the generalisation with only items 1 and 1 (a) but the inclusion of 2 (a) and (b) adds to the range of the sample in a significant way, i.e. in establishing the universality of inferences about 1 and 1 (a). Again, if the range of Sample B included only 1, the generalisation would *still* be achieved, but it would have considerably less value for the class, being based on such a restricted sample. Given, then, the identification of significant ideas inherent in the generalisation to be achieved, there must be an estimate of how many of these should be included in the sample. Obviously the readiness of the pupils will be a major consideration; thus some teachers of Grade 3 would probably object to the inclusion of 2 (b) as a confusing complexity for their class. That is their judgment! However, as a practical point it seems good sense to have a larger sample prepared, on the assumption that the assessment of readiness may be in error. Teachers who do so prove much better able to cope with un- expected pupil contribution—a bane of the unprepared teacher. On the other hand, the range may be so inadequate that the generalisation is not likely to be achieved on the basis of valid inference, as in Sample A above.

## EXPLORATION OF THE SAMPLE

While a teacher may have a good sample, his class may need (or teacher preference of strategy may dictate) his assistance in its exploration of the sample and the inference about the nature of the "whole". The *need* that pupils have for this assistance with generalisation is never more apparent than with the so-called *slow learners*. All too frequently these pupils are dismissed as incapable of mastering certain ideas and relegated to the educational slums of "fact learning", when all that is needed is some practical assistance with the process!

The difference between the "slow learner" and the highly intelligent pupil in the matter of generalisation, from the viewpoint of the teacher who has experience with both, seems only a matter of *degree*, not *kind*. Work with the highly intelligent soon makes it apparent that they also need the same kind of assistance when the concept is very abstract and complex relative to their knowledge resources.

## THE FUNCTION OF QUESTIONS

The solution of a question which states a problem requires relationships to be perceived between the elements of the problem situation. In the exploration of the sample itself and its relationship to the "whole" of which it is representative, questions can provide guidance and support as the learner gropes his way through the intricacies of inference needed to achieve a complex generalisation.

If questions are to serve this purpose economically, they need to be devised with the following points in mind:

1. The *kind* of thinking, i.e., the particular cognitive skill needed to solve the particular problem. It may be necessary to indicate the particular cognitive skill because the problem is difficult enough without making it a guessing game as to which skill is appropriate.[3] (This topic will be discussed further in the following chapter on Communication.)

2. The order of their presentation. When questions are asked in succession they can add to or detract from overall understanding depending on the *order* in which they are presented.

## ORDER AND EXPLORATION OF THE SAMPLE

Because generalisation depends critically upon learned probability judgments, and these are more accessible and useful when the need for them arises in contexts that are well known (in the sense of familiarity and diversity of experience), pupils will need to proceed from the *known* to the *unknown*. However, the maxim must be qualified in this context, for what is known must be selected for its significance in developing a train of thought in which the significance of the most pertinent item in the sample will be given its proper inferential weight. Compare the two samples of Figure 7.5 where $A_2$ is a variation in the order of $A_1$.

| Sample A₁ | Sample A₂ |
|---|---|
| 1. My garden has looked much better since I started using a sprinkler. | 1. Farmers anywhere become very anxious in times of drought when everything becomes dry. |

*Sample A₁—cont.*

2. Farmers anywhere become very anxious in times of drought when everything becomes dry.

3. In Egypt the Nile is very important for farmers.

*Sample A₂—cont.*

2. In Egypt the Nile is very important for farmers.

3. My garden has looked much better since I started using a sprinkler.

Figure 7.5: The significance of order in a sample

If the class meets item 1 of $A_1$ first, they will in all probability infer that I am referring to the health and vigour of growth in my garden. They will therefore be predisposed to examine the items which follow as to their inferential weight for the hypothesis that *growth* is the "controlling idea" in the sample.

However, in Sample $A_2$ where the class encounters the farmers' concern about *dryness* first, there is a high probability that pupils will perceive everything being *dry* as signifying the *possible death* of the plants. Item 2 on the Nile would be assessed from this viewpoint and Item 3 may be interpreted in consonance.

The tendency of the first item encountered to generate what is in effect a mental set, determining the inferential weight of subsequent items when there is a complex sample (we almost compulsively create *any* sort of order from disorder), indicates a need for care in determining not only the first item but also the placement of other items relative to their value in facilitating perception of significance.

### INSTANCES OF GOOP

A bird on a cinema seat as people go to their seats

A *Bible* on a lectern in a large city garage workshop.

A naked man walking down the aisle of the church during a funeral service.

*Note*

1. This sample illustrates *selection* and *order* of presentation.

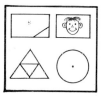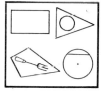

2. To present the geometrical instances first is to lower considerably the possibility of success.

### A NON-INSTANCE OF GOOP

Absentmindedly walking out of a shop without paying and being accused of shoplifting.

Figure 7.6*: Sample for teaching the concept of "Goop". What *is* a Goop?*

*Specification of "Goop".* Situations in which something appears in such an incongruous setting as to give the onlooker a substantial degree of surprise, amounting at times to shock.

### Levels of Generalisation Implicit in Knowing the Sample Need to be Sequenced

A sample may be so complex that it is necessary to group its items and to generalise in order to understand the nature of each part. When all parts are known in this way, their collective generalisations constitute a new "sample" from which the overall generalisation is derived. Figure 7.7 illustrates this.

| | | |
|---|---|---|
| Required generalisation | A The physical and social environment influences the way in which an individual will behave. | |
| New sample 1st level of generalisation | I The physical environment makes demands on the individual which directly affect his relations with others and his concern with survival. | II Through both formal and informal social controls, society imposes standards on social behaviour. |
| Items of original sample | | |

Figure 7.7: Generalisation from a sample may require several levels of generalisation which will need to be sequenced

The original sample must be organised so as to facilitate the first level generalisations I and II, yet contain a *selection* and *range* which will facilitate the generalisation of "A" from I and II as the new sample.

### A Frame of Reference for Questions is Necessary

Observation of pupils answering teachers' questions indicates all too frequently a hiatus between the manifest intention of the teacher (assuming the observer to be equally sophisticated in the subject) and the pupil response. When such a pupil is examined closely on what he thought the teacher meant by his question, the teacher and the pupil will frequently be found to have different *frames of reference*. A major feature of the teacher's guidance in the exploration of the sample must necessarily be communication of *his* frame of reference, so that pupils can know *the pattern of inferential weightings to attach to items* of experience that may be relevant to the questions asked.

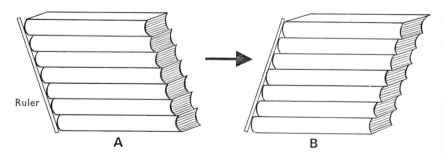

Figure 7.8: A lesson on "shearing" in transformation geometry

Compare the following questions on the movement of the books between positions A and B in Figure 7.8 for communication of the teacher's frame of reference.

1. "How would you describe the movement of the top book?"
   Correct answers: It moves furthest.
                    It moves parallel to the table top.
2. "Relative to the table top—how would you describe the movement of the top book?"
   Correct answer: It moves parallel to the table top.

It will be apparent that by communicating the frame of reference— *I am looking at this book's movement* only *in relation to the base*—pupil thinking is on the same wavelength as the teacher's. This, of course, is not meant to suggest that the following question is not desirable:

"What can you tell me about the movement of the top book?"
which has the *implicit* frame of reference—

"*I want you to tell me all you can about it.*"
Obviously the frame of reference makes explicit what is implied in the order of presentation. This is particularly necessary when there are shifts of viewpoint in the exploration of a complex sample.

While the illustration above involves what Guilford has called "convergent thinking", a very strong case can be made for the communication of a *frame of reference* for his "divergent thinking" to be optimally productive.[4] This will be discussed in the final chapter.

## Controlled Learning of "Probability"

In the learning of difficult ideas a good teacher uses gestures, underlining, tone of voice, etc. to highlight attributes of concepts whose significance might otherwise be overlooked by the learner. There are occasions when statements and questions can be used to require pupils to verbalise the *inferential weight* or significance of a particular attribute of a concept along the lines of justifying the generalisation as being a "good fit" for the sample. The value of this is that it ensures that the class as a whole has a sound "measuring stick" for subsequent probability.

Thus in the example of the sample from which we generalised *Gary loves Elizabeth* (Figure 7.2), pupils may be asked to justify this generalisation rather than *Paul feels responsible for his sister*. The process of justification will necessarily involve a verbalisation of the inferential weight to be given each of the items of the sample—and thus will lead to a more soundly based generalisation.

A simple extension of this procedure is to supply a class with a sample, (say) Sample B of Figure 7.4, *and* to provide two or three generalisations purporting to be from the sample. The class is asked to select the best one and to justify the selection or rejection of each. The end point is invariably better understanding—provided there is a good selection of sample and competing generalisations.

## Differentiation of Specifications

The further development of complex concepts depends upon their use in a range of contexts which make successive refinements of the original specifications possible. The *selection* of the range of contexts needs to be as disciplined as for the original sample. (See the set of problems on *shearing* at the end of the lesson plan in mathematics, Chapter 14.) Further, the exploration of the concept in each of the contexts will need the same kind of guidance as would be needed for any generalisation, whether it is presented as a problem requiring identity-type generalisation or reformulating of specifications, or both.

## PUPIL AUTONOMY

### Specific Development of Generalisation Skills

Generalisation and other cognitive skills are essentially *tools* we use to operate on knowledge as the material of thinking. By simple analogy from developing a tradesman's skill it can be argued that the use of such tools may well be improved by specific instruction. There is some research evidence to support this, though it has tended to be overshadowed by the wealth of findings on developmental stages. Informal classroom trials by many teachers (supervised by the writer) have shown, in fact, that pupils gain substantially in skill when they are aware of the mental processes involved in all aspects of concept formation. For that matter it was found that comprehension could be considerably improved by alerting pupils to the logical structure of the usual categories of comprehension questions.[5] As the development of such skills is largely in terms of communication skills, further discussion will be deferred to the next chapter under the heading of *specialised evaluation vocabulary*.

### Opportunities for Independent Thinking

In the discussion of Gagné's conditions of learning, it was noted that many concepts are not rigorously definable and always retain a significant idiosyncratic content. If pupils are to achieve adequate mastery of such concepts, they will inevitably be calling on resources of concepts which have similar idiosyncratic content. Presumably no teacher teaches by reading minds, so it seems imperative for pupils to have the opportunity to explore the domain of such ideas *independently*, that is, working autonomously within broadly defined bounds rather than proceeding by lock-step inference.

The reason for the above requirement is that each individual has different strengths and weaknesses relative to gaining and processing information through the different senses—autonomy permits the individual to resort to the sensory mode(s) which makes his world most intelligible to him. When a pupil is able to exercise autonomy in the exploration of new ideas, it is more likely that he will learn the inferential weightings to be given to constituent attributes and ideas in different contexts (which have greater transfer value), simply because they are developed from his own way of interpreting his world.

Teachers who respect this facet of individuality in the teaching of *all* new ideas can only gain, for in the last resort the pupil who is generalising must be in *control* of his own cognitive processes in making judgments which are based on probabilities and which enable him to give meaning to the new experience of *his* world. Provision would appear to be of two kinds: (1) discovery-type exercises, and (2) opportunities for intuitive thinking.

## DISCOVERY-TYPE EXERCISES

As applied here this kind of exercise presupposes familiarity with the concepts that must be applied to the problem area if a solution is to be achieved. The *discovery* process involves *independent* application of these concepts, as in cases where there are a number of alternative "correct" answers to a problem.

## INTUITIVE THINKING

When a teacher establishes a class climate which results in the "ill-formed" idea or the "guess" or "fumble" (for which a pupil may be entirely unable to give supporting evidence) being acceptable, he is establishing that *intuitive* thinking is permissible in his class. If he fails to do this, a very substantial resource of learned probability judgments for generalisation will remain untapped, at great cost to the class's ability to think independently. Intuitive thinking essentially implies grasping the significance or structure of a problem or situation, even though its relationship to other features of the problem area cannot be made explicit. The recognition of significance of intuition is an invaluable reference point or measure for further inference. So valuable are such reference points that many teachers start on a complex idea with a question which seeks to exploit the pupils' already-existing but ill-formed, incomplete and unorganised ideas on a topic. Their intuitive ideas on the topic provide reference points for them and for their teacher in the inferential weighting to be given ideas which must be a part of the systematic learning of the idea. For example, a teacher starting on the topic *Traditional Japanese Music* asked the class how they would describe an example of the music they had just heard. One pupil commented: "It reminds me of a circus." Exploration of this intuitive response made it apparent that there was a general responsiveness to the multiplicity of sounds, unexpectedness of development, range of "colour", etc. These become anchoring points for the subsequent lesson development, but also provided insight for the teacher into the *inferential weight* his class would give to different features of his planned lesson.

## REFERENCES

[1] J. S. BRUNER, "On Going Beyond the Information Given", in R. J. C. HARPER (Ed.), *Readings—The Cognitive Processes*, Prentice-Hall, Englewood Cliffs, 1964, pp. 293-311.

[2] J. S. BRUNER, *The Process of Education*, Harvard University Press, Cambridge, 1961, p. 57-58.

[3] See R. J. KIBLER *et al.*, *Behavioural Objectives and Instruction*, Allyn and Bacon, Boston, 1970.

[4] J. P. GUILFORD, "Three Faces of Intellect", *American Psychologist*, 1959, **14**, pp. 469-79.

[5] See B. S. BLOOM (Ed.) *et al.*, *Taxonomy of Educational Objectives—The Classification of Educational Goals, Handbook I: Cognitive Domain*, David McKay, New York, 1956.

## SELECTED READING

BRUNER, J. S., "On Perceptual Readiness", *Psychological Review*, 1964, pp. 123-52.

BRUNER, J. S., *The Process of Education*, Harvard University Press, 1961, pp. 55-68 for a rather different treatment of intuitive and analytic thinking.

BRUNER, J. S., "On Going Beyond the Information Given", in Harper, R. J. C. (Ed.), *Readings—The Cognitive Processes*, Prentice-Hall, 1964.

BRUNER, J. S., "The Course of Cognitive Growth", *American Psychologist*, 1964, **19**, pp. 1-15.

GUILFORD, J. P., "Three Faces of Intellect", *American Psychologist*, 1959, **14**, pp. 469-79.

# CHAPTER 8

# *Communication*

Communication is basically a transmission of information by verbal and non-verbal means.

This chapter, however, is restricted to a discussion of *verbal* communication in the classroom and to those situations where information is transmitted to achieve some degree of understanding. Non-verbal aspects are considered more economically developed in a practical programme designed to develop *personal* skills of class management.

While planning and management skills together subsume the significant categories of the domain of pedagogy (see Figure 3.1), the communication category is so pervasive as to be considered the principal determinant of teacher efficiency. In the view adopted here, no matter how sophisticated a teacher's knowledge of the other categories of the domain, his skill in each category depends upon his knowledge of and skills in communication as a process.

Our special concern here is with the *nature* of communication—more particularly with its logical structure relative to purpose, and with the psychological conditions necessary for communication to achieve its purpose of understanding.

## THE NATURE OF THE PROCESS

Communication in the classroom typically involves a two-way exchange or transmission in which two parties alternate roles of transmitter and receiver of information. The quality of this communication depends logically upon the quality both of the *structure* of transmissions relative to purpose, and of *feedback* throughout the communication. Psychologically, the quality of communication depends upon the *listening* and *responding* skills of both parties.

For reasons of clarity the psychological conditions for effective classroom communication will be discussed first.

### LISTENING AND RESPONDING

On a common-sense basis the ability to listen is indicated by the appropriateness of the response, assessed in terms of the degree of congruence

H

between the meaning inherent in the original transmission and the meaning inherent in the response. Such meaning may be *explicit* or *implicit*. In the example below, for instance, the attitude of the pupil to maths is explicit but his feelings about failure are implicit.

> *To a pupil who is a frequent source of disturbance.*
>
> *Teacher*   Why don't you settle down and do some work? (Rather peremptory tone.)
>
> *Pupil*   I hate maths! I'm always getting everything wrong! (Dispirited tone.)
>
> *Teacher*   You'll need it for your career you know; you'll just have to keep trying. (Mollifying tone.)

Obviously the statement of feelings, though only implicit, is the more significant part of the meaning. The teacher in this transaction would be assumed to be a poor listener—he responded only to what was explicit. But the situation is more complex than appears on the surface.

When this teacher was questioned on the transaction, he was at first unable to accept that any more than a dislike of maths had been communicated. However, in a subsequent counselling session, it became apparent that while he had the capacity to perceive implicit meaning that related to feeling, he habitually "screened it out" because of his need to protect himself from involvement in the feelings of others.

> . . . I suppose I can manage feelings like the hatred of maths because he [the pupil of our example above] is not relating to *me*. We are talking about maths but not *us*. But when he tells me (in effect) that he is disheartened, he is relating to *me*. He is asking *me* to accept his feelings—to help him. . . . When I have to face that sort of thing I cringe inside.

People who have this need to insulate themselves from involvement with feeling are usually able to communicate coherently because people do not usually make their inner feelings explicit, but rely on cues of implicit meaning which are perceived only by those with the sensitivity to enter into a real dialogue. So widespread is the need for insulation from feelings in our society that the relatively passive "selective screening" described above has an aggressive counterpart in the "bedside manner" of doctors, nurses, teachers and other professionals who structure situations likely to produce communication on feelings so that anything significant in this area is exceedingly unlikely.[1]

The operation of selective screening in cognition leads similarly to inefficient listening. Perhaps the most common cause for it is the teacher's fear that he may jeopardise his subject matter superiority. Typically he then tends to ignore or reject outright any unexpected but significant ideas. Some teachers even blatantly signal their selectivity with the response, "That's not what I have in mind"!

Again, when a teacher has a low toleration of uncertainty, he tends to structure classroom situations so as to diminish the likelihood of the unexpected. He is so uncertain of his ability to manage novel situations (particularly dealing with people) that he requires the outcome of inter-personal exchanges to be highly predictable before he will risk his reputation for competence. Such a teacher avoids, for instance, discussion where there could be an interplay of independent minds with an unpredictable outcome.

But communication is a two-way process: if the pupil also can neither listen nor respond efficiently, prospects for learning are poor. Inefficiency of pupil listening and responding would appear to have much the same psychological origins as for his teacher and are manifested in much the same ways in the contexts available to him as a pupil. The implication seems clear—teachers *and* pupils must be involved in any move to improve communications.

Given, however, a teacher and pupil who *listen* reasonably efficiently, the overall quality of communication between them from the viewpoint of achieving understanding will depend upon the adequacy of the response as *feedback*, i.e. as information returned to the original transmitter for correction and adjustment. To achieve such feedback the pupil must feel free to alternate with his teacher as transmitter of information and his teacher must be prepared to support this by soliciting feedback and also by being ready to accept unsolicited feedback.

## The Need for Trust

On the above account inefficient listening can be largely attributed to the individual's need to safeguard himself from that which he considers threatening. Characteristically teachers who are poor listeners talk "at" their pupils rather than "to" or "with" them. In conversing with his peers such a teacher is also likely to "wait for a chance to talk" rather than to listen, because he fears intimacy with its exposure of self.[2]

But there are, of course, those who have simply developed the habit of not listening because few around them have the habit of listening—such people respond quickly to training.

Traditional forms of dialogue between teachers and pupils reinforce many pupils' expectations that they can be badly hurt in the realm of communication if they are not wary. To overcome this a teacher must establish *trust*—not only between himself and a particular pupil but between all members of the class as a group. The power of trust to increase the quality of learning is easily demonstrated in a classroom where the class has habitually scorned pupils' offerings which have not been expressed as felicitously as the teacher would like. A new teacher, who has no need of such a negative form of control, can transform the learning climate merely by indicating his respect for "silly" or poorly expressed ideas—what can be called *fumbles* (to be discussed below). With a well chosen illustration of (say) scientists' "brainstorming", and an explanation of the technique reinforced by moral indignation at the first lack of respect for a "fumble", the climate of trust is usually sufficiently established to generate its own reinforcement. However, while a general class climate of trust is necessary, it is not sufficient to establish efficient listening and responding.

## The Need for Reflection

When the client communicates his innermost feelings in counselling, he is usually only able to do so because he can trust the counsellor. This trust has to be earned by the counsellor who must demonstrate his *empathetic* understanding. He must demonstrate this particularly through his *reflection* of the thoughts and feelings of his client as expressed in the totality of explicit and implicit meaning of the communication. Reflection is the deliberate repetition of the total meaning of the client's communication as a proof that it was *heard, understood* and *accepted*. Necessarily it involves the perception of the most significant elements of the meaning, often indicated by feeling—tone and by what is implicit—and the reorganisation of the original to indicate this perception of significant meaning.

Thus if the client (a fourteen-year-old boy) said:
I'm always thinking about girls (pause) I can't stop it. I'm always thinking about (pause) you know (long pause) and there's one girl in particular . . .
and the counsellor said:
You're worried, you think about girls and sex (pause) about sexual intercourse (pause) and you think of one girl in particular in this way . . .

the counsellor would be demonstrating to his client not only that he had heard but had *understood* and *accepted* the client's thoughts and feelings without expressing a judgment. Note that he has made explicit the *implicit* reference to *worry, sexual intercourse*, and thinking of one girl *in this way*. The client is much more likely to continue talking about his *real* problem because a basis for the building of trust has been established—proven ability to understand and accept.

---

*Exercise*

Which of the responses below, A, B, C or D, is the best *reflection*?*

*Principal*  Mr Franks says your work has slipped badly since the second term.

*Pupil*  I would do all right if he taught us, but he just doesn't begin as a teacher.

*Principal*  A.  That's hardly the way I expect a pupil to speak of a teacher in my school!
B.  You feel the blame lies with Mr Franks' bad teaching rather than with you.
C.  You were doing well enough the first two terms, I would point out.
D.  There's not much point in being angry. Let's talk about this calmly.

---

* *Discussion of exercise.*

A. The principal is *defensive*—unable to tolerate what he interprets as aggression—so he diverts attention to the act of aggression rather than the content of the communication.

Reflection is equally valuable in classroom communication and for essentially the same reasons. A pupil who is groping his way to a new idea, and particularly if he is exposing his *real* feelings in venturing an opinion and his own experience, has equal need of trust of his teacher.

Consider the following transcript from a lesson where the goal is to teach the concept of *colonial exploitation:*

> T1      The term *colonial exploitation* is often used these days not only in geography but also in history, current events . . . in referring to places like Vietnam, the Congo, Mexico, Malaya . . . colonial exploitation . . . any idea what it means? What do you think?

> P1      *The taking of advantages of people that live in a certain place that cannot uplift and get out of themselves.*

> T2      Yes, that's quite a good *general* idea. I think we'll just take it word by word though. The word *exploitation*. What does it mean?

This teacher has quite failed to exploit a quite reasonable "fumble". He *has* acknowledged it is quite a good *general* idea but has responded most inadequately to the pupil's idea. In cases like this where the expression of ideas is crude—*taking advantages of people; that cannot uplift; get out of themselves*—reflection increases the probability of further *pupil* clarification of thinking. If the teacher had made explicit the significant but implicit idea of *unfairness* in this example—as for instance in:

> T2      You think that it means cases where foreigners *unfairly* take advantage of the limited knowledge and skills of the people who live in a certain place?

he would have established he had heard, understood and accepted the pupil's idea. In so doing he would not only provide feedback, but also meet the condition of trust that may well have been necessary for this pupil to venture an idea of even greater insight.

A teacher's ability to earn trust in this way depends upon certain abilities inherent in good reflection:

1. The ability to treat his pupils as *individuals.*
2. The ability to recognise that the immediately apparent facts of a communication are frequently less important than the reasons people feel as they do.
3. The ability to empathise with people of different cultural backgrounds, to accept differences of vocabulary, verbal facility, attitudes and values.

---

B. Reflects pupil's feeling that Mr Franks is to blame, thereby indicating acceptance of the content and implies "tell me more". (*Acceptance* of content does not mean that it is *approved.*

C. Similar to A but diversion is by means of a denial of the rationality of the viewpoint.

D. A rejection of the pupil's feeling. Pupil will know that communication of feeling is not permissible—yet it might be the most significant factor in the situation.

Elaboration of these three points will be deferred to the next chapter on Interpersonal Relationships in the Classroom, as it involves consideration of a number of topics more properly discussed there.

### Responding to Feedback

Given a climate of trust and the teacher and pupil sharing the common goal of pupil understanding, each seeks to supply feedback to the other to help him play the role he has adopted for a particular teaching strategy. Each seeks to provide the other with the kind of information which will facilitate his making those corrections and adjustments to the course of their dialogue which are consistent with his role. This information is largely implicit and can therefore be thought of as comprising a *feedback dialogue* within the main dialogue which is centred largely on what is explicit. The following two examples of feedback dialogue illustrate some of the subtleties. The first is the common form based on a series of teacher questions; the second is the less common form based on a series of pupil questions.

In the first example, the pupil seeks to give as much information as possible on the course and state of his thinking; the teacher makes corrective adjustments to that course by way of information on the significance of ideas and the provision of new information. Thus both focus on error in different ways because of their different roles in the dialogue.

> *Teacher*  How were the Canterbury Plains formed?
>
> *Pupil*    I *think* from bits of mountain. (Emphasis on *think*.)
>
> *Teacher*  What do you mean by *bits* of mountain? How would *they* form *plains*? (Emphasis on *bits* and *they* and *plains*.)

The pupil here assumes that the teacher will enter into a corrective dialogue, that is, he will accept the feedback content of the pupil's answer and react appropriately in his teacher's role. The pupil, in addition to giving an answer to the question, is giving the following information:

1. He is uncertain of his hypothesis. (I *think* . . .)
2. He is uncertain of how to structure a satisfactory answer. (The crudity of the expression *bits of mountain* relative to the question and the ignoring of the significance of *flatness* in the connotation of *plains*.)

The teacher accepts this feedback and provides the following contribution to the feedback dialogue:

1. Your answer *does* convey a worthwhile idea.
2. Tell me more.
3. The really significant idea is conveyed by the word *bits*.
4. Elaboration of what you mean by *bits* will give an answer of more satisfactory structure.
5. Do you see the significance of a relationship between *bits* and the *flatness* of a plain?

In the second example teacher and pupil have partially reversed their roles in that the pupil asks the initial question and is thereafter in the position of supplying feedback on the state of his understanding through successive questions as he plots his course through to understanding. The teacher designs his initial response to be at the level of "primitive intuitive" and thereafter limits his feedback to direct responses to pupil feedback: the onus is on the pupil to set and maintain the course. Thus, using the previous question, but reversing the roles of questioner, the exchange might go as follows:

*Pupil*      How *were* the Canterbury Plains formed?
*Teacher*   They were made from bits of mountain.
*Pupil*      But how could they *possibly* have been made from bits of mountain?

In this case the pupil is providing feedback on the state of his understanding as follows:

1. He is confused concerning the magnitude of *bits*. (He is possibly assuming *bits* to be of the order of billions of tons.)
2. He cannot conceive of a process which made the formation of *plains* possible.

The teacher could then respond directly to this feedback treating it as information on the pupil's state of understanding—and on his readiness for a particular aspect of the total explanation.

The significance of trust in the generation of feedback dialogue will be apparent. However, when pupils have accepted the opportunity to engage in such dialogue, the teacher can improve the efficiency of the dialogue considerably by working within the framework of a set of "ground rules" derived from the logical structure of communication. This will be discussed in the appropriate section below.

## The Structure of Communication

All communication can be regarded as involving description and any particular description can be located on a scale of complexity ranging from the simple enumeration of characteristics to complex networks of concept of principle.

However, some descriptions focus on the *relationships between ideas*— which we shall call *explanations*. Explanations can also be located on a scale of complexity ranging from simple listing of explanatory principles to detailed explications of the relational network.

### THE ORGANISATION OF DESCRIPTIVE EXPOSITION

Exposition must be organised for understanding; and it must be planned not only to make understanding easy, but to assist the reader or listener to get as much meaning from it as he is able. An example of this kind of thinking is involved in the following example of the game of *What am I thinking of?*

(a) Man, dark clothes, black shoes, black hat, gold signet ring, walks rather slowly.
(b) Man, white reversed collar, dark clothes . . . .

If I have *priest* in mind it is obvious that the second clue gives the idea more quickly for most people. This is because the first set of information lacks the kind of organisation in which we are now interested. The idea "white reversed collar" is a highly significant attribute of the specifications of the concept of priest. If a *particular* priest were to be identified, the succeeding items could be added in a more or less systematic way to the composite "picture" being built up—and particularly so if succeeding items are significant attributes of the priest in mind. Thus the player of this game can be *directed* to the identity by the *ranking of the information in order of its importance*. Even if not systematically ranked, incoming information can be assessed for relevance and significance for the idea being built up. Thus, when we know what we are doing or where we are going, everything has more meaning. For example, if I discover that my family is planning a surprise party for me, all sorts of remarks, glances, etc. have meaning which they would not have had if I did not know of their secret.

Compare the examples below after reading them in the order given:

### 1. Ancient Egyptian Agriculture

The ground was slowly turned by oxen-drawn wooden ploughs which could cut only a shallow furrow. Clods were broken with wooden hoes and the seed broadcast by hand and covered by the hooves of goats driven across the field as a kind of living harrows.

Each year flood water was allowed to cover the fields. This water was laden with silt which covered the fields when the water drained away. The silt contained a considerable amount of plant food which restored the fertility lost through the year's cropping.

As the land was flat, water could easily be channelled some distance from the Nile once it had been lifted above the height of the banks of the river and canals. Ingenious machines were invented to manage this, and many men spent all their working days during the growing season, just keeping the water flowing.

### 2. Ancient Egyptian Agriculture

*Thousands of years ago the ancient Egyptians had only crude tools but they had a considerable knowledge of agriculture.*

*Tools were wooden, and power was that of animals and men; yet though these tools were primitive, they were used to carry out the very same operations still considered essential in agriculture today.* The ground was slowly turned by oxen-drawn ploughs which could cut only a shallow furrow. Clods were broken with wooden hoes, the seed broadcast by hand and covered by the hooves of goats driven across the field as a kind of living harrows.

*The fields were regularly enriched by the plant food carried in the waters of the flooding Nile.* Each year flood water was allowed to cover the fields. This water was laden with silt which covered the fields when the water drained away. The silt carried a considerable amount of plant food which restored the fertility lost during the year's cropping.

*The problem of supplying plants with water during the growing periods in such a dry region was overcome with a series of canals and water lifting devices.* As the land was flat, water could easily be channelled some distance from the Nile once it had been lifted above the height of the banks of the river and canals . . .

It will be apparent that the second version better prepares the reader (and particularly the listener) for the relevance and significance of what follows by communicating the ideas to him prior to his receiving details of the communication. Note, for instance, that the first sentence gives the overall idea, and the first sentences of each paragraph the ideas contained in those paragraphs. Put another way, the first sentence is a higher level proposition which subsumes the general propositions of the "topic sentence" of each paragraph, which in turn subsume the propositions (both singular and general) which follow them. The passage can thus be diagrammed:

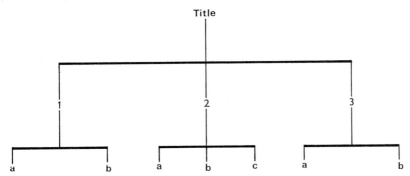

Figure 8.1: Paragraph structure

Thus not only are the relevance and significance of ideas communicated but also information on the classification (meaning in this case the inter-relationships) of the constituent propositions.

The above is not to suggest that such an order is the only or even the best order for a communication, but it does illustrate an essential principle: recognition of levels of generality and of significance of the *process of generalisation* is the basis of economical descriptive exposition. In practice there are many variations of this order which, however, rely on other skills not discussed here.

### PROBABILITY OF RELEVANCE AND SIGNIFICANCE IN COMMUNICATION

If we want to communicate an idea to another person who is familiar with both the context of the idea and our particular viewpoints, we can adopt various shortcuts, such as using big breaks between one idea and another, and still be reasonably sure of a successful communication— the essence of a good telegram.

For example,                    AVAILABLE 9.15 A.M.
                                                 PRITCHARD.

However, in the case of an *unusual* idea the recipient of the communication needs to be prepared so that he can adopt an appropriate viewpoint or attitude for the substance of the communication. For example, look at this story:

> A pilot in the Korean War jumped without a parachute but landed safely by sharing a friend's parachute.

The reaction could well be—tall story! However, compare it with the following version:

> During the Korean War a pilot made an almost incredible jump to safety. He jumped without a parachute but on the way down . . .

There is a very significant difference here. This second communication is designed to take into account the possible incredulity of the recipient after an *assessment of the probability of the recipient adopting the appropriate viewpoint*. The assessment of the other person's probable viewpoint is often critical for the success of a communication.

Teachers thus frequently fail to exploit the creativity of their pupils because they have not taught their pupils the skills associated with probability in communication and are unreceptive to communication which may be faulty in this way.

Here we are concerned with how we manage to give the minimum of information and yet *maintain the thread of understanding* in our audience. Obviously, if we told them every little detail we knew, our audience would be overwhelmed by the sheer mass of information and so would lose the thread of the argument. So we select not only what we shall tell them, but also what we shall *not* tell them—in fact, we leave out whole sets of information so that there are big gaps in the communication. This we confidently expect our audience to bridge the gap with a "*mental leap*" of comprehension. But we can go too far with this—the gaps may be so great that the audience is not able to bridge them. Leaving gaps in our exposition must be balanced by planned linkages between one set of information and another—we shall refer to this as the *principle of coherence* and hence, coherence skills.

"*Mental leaps*" or discontinuities in discourse. The size of the break in the flow of a communication which will still allow the recipient to continue to understand also depends upon probability judgments. If the context of the communication is familiar, big breaks are permissible.

> E.g., green apples; David (age three); sick.

While this is not a conventional communication it is quite adequate in this case because it is assumed that it is sufficiently probable that readers would be familiar with both green apples and small boys.

This skill of judging the permissible gap is particularly evident in the paragraphing adopted by many contemporary writers, Virginia Woolf for an extreme example, and in any case is fundamental to effective paragraphing—particularly in narrative prose.

*Coherence*. When the meaning is not common knowledge and a step by step description and/or explanation is needed, *coherence* is more important than *selective omissions* requiring mental leaps—though the latter still have to be kept in mind.

Coherence consists essentially of learned devices to ensure continuity of the thread of understanding. When the substance of the communication is novel for the intended audience, there is concern to ensure that:

1. The link between the propositions of succeeding sentences is maintained by the use of synonyms for the previous subject, pronouns, explications, etc.
2. The direction of structure of argument is known; e.g., the word "thus" indicates an inference to follow; "however" a departure from the previous line of argument to a new tack, and so on.

The following exercise requires discrimination between coherence devices, the object being to select those which maximise overall coherence.

---

*Exercise:*

Except for the first sentence, the following paragraph has three sentences for every one needed. In each case select the sentence which provides the strongest linkage with its preceding sentence while contributing to overall coherence, and identify all coherence devices.

*The Avoidance of House-fire Risk Caused by*
*Overload of Electrical Circuits*

House electrical circuits can be protected from fire risk which results from overload.

1. (a) At times the wiring of a house has too many appliances for its capacity to carry current.
   (b) When many appliances are connected on the same circuit the wires must carry a large amount of electricity.
   (c) The more appliances in a house the more current must be carried by the wiring.
2. (a) This heavy load of current makes the wires hot and can cause fires.
   (b) Hot wires can cause fires.
   (c) When wires become hot they can cause fires.
3. (a) However, the fuse is a safety device which prevents the wire overheating because it melts before this happens so that it breaks the circuit.
   (b) The fuse is designed to break the circuit before the danger point by melting at a low temperature.
   (c) Before the danger point is reached, the circuit is broken by the fuse which is designed to melt at a temperature below danger point.
4. (a) Control of the amount of electricity in the circuit is therefore a valuable protective device.
   (b) If there were no fuses there would be many more fires because of overloaded circuits.
   (c) Thus the fuse gives protection by ensuring that the amount of electricity in the circuit is within a safe limit.

The correct answers are: 1 (b); 2 (a); 3 (a); 4 (c).

---

## Explanatory Exposition

When communication is intended to produce understanding of relationships, *explanatory* exposition is required. This has a number of logical forms which can be grouped according to the assumptions made about prior knowledge of the relationships involved in the explanation.

*Analogy.* The main purpose of all forms of analogy is to gain acceptance of the equivalence of two relationships. Figure 8.2 shows the structure of the analogy.

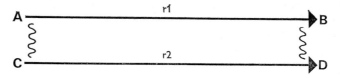

Figure 8.2: Logical structure of an analogy

It proceeds from the known to the unknown on the basis of points of equivalence: C is shown or implied the equivalent of A, D of B, and r2 of r1. Implicitly, the argument runs: C is sufficiently like A, D is sufficiently like B and r2 sufficiently like r1 for r2 to be treated as identical with r1.

Consider the analogy below, where it is assumed that John has asked his father how a steam engine works. John is now at the stage of asking many questions, so his father happens to remember previously explaining why the lid of a full, boiling kettle will chatter up and down with the successive increases and decreases of steam pressure.

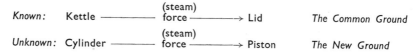

Figure 8.3: Kettle-engine analogy

John's father reminds him of the relationship between the kettle and the lid—as an agreed common ground. He then proceeds to "point up" the common features which exist between the two situations in the diagram, e.g., "The cylinder is like the kettle; the piston is like the lid—in the same way that the steam forced the lid to move, it forces the piston in this cylinder." John is asked, in effect, to accept the two situations as equivalent, the relationship as identical.

While the detailed exposition of an analogy in this way has special value in this circumstance and those analogous to it in the classroom, the greater number are simply communicated by a declaration that the two situations meet the requirements of analogy. The reader or listener is then left to make the appropriate inferences.

Teachers frequently assert that "analogies are dangerous"—meaning they are a frequent source of error. However, awareness of logical construction and sources of common error equip even pupils to cope very effectively with this form of explanation. The following are the most common sources of error:

1. The relationships are *not* equivalent, i.e., (r1 ≠ r2).

2. Either or both of the first and/or second elements (AC and BD of Figure 8.2 above) do not in fact, possess the common feature necessary for equivalence.

---

*Example*
> The *conscious* and *unconscious* are analogous to the iceberg: *there is much more below.*

---

This analogy is valid in so far as the relationship is *restricted to proportionality*. However, if one inferred from the analogy the relationship of *inaccessibility*—what is below cannot have access to the surface—the analogy would be invalid, because the relationships r1 and r2 would not in that case be identical, nor would AC and BD be equivalent.

Thus the above highlights the source of much error—reading more into an analogy than is intended. Care is obviously required in relation to the intended common features of the elements AC and BD (see Figure 8.2) and in the communication of analogy to ensure that the intended relationships are perceived.

1. *Analogies can also be considered weak.* This occurs when the common features of AC and BD are not *parallel*, i.e., not the most significant features of A, B, C and D in the designated context, so that other than the intended features are likely to be identified.

2. *Concrete analogies.* Concrete analogies exploit our preference for tangible or concrete experience as a basis for understanding the abstract.

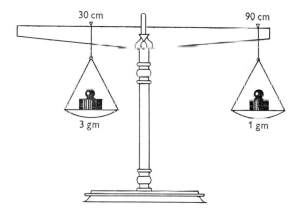

Figure 8.4: A beam balance as a concrete analogy for the principle AB = CD, i.e., the product of the weight and distance from the fulcrum on the left hand side equals that of the weight and distance on the right hand side when the beam is balanced

3. *A nesting of analogies.* In practice the analogy may require too big a step from the context of one relationship to the context of the other (in terms of degree of abstraction) for the person to accept equivalence.

In this case a progression of analogies is used, each becoming progressively more abstract.

4. *Models.* When given analogies are the recognised ways of explaining phenomena in a subject they may be called models. Thus in junior science the *particle model* accounts for all phenomena encountered in that part of the science syllabus; but the *atomic model* is necessary for more advanced science.

Models differ from a simple analogy, in practice, in that *systematically developed* relationships can be identified in the context of the model, which may be either concrete or abstract.

### HARRÉ ON SYSTEMATISED EXPLANATION[3]

1. *Lineal explanation.* In this form of explanation the assumption is made that the reader or listener is already aware of the pattern of cause and effect relationships that are relevant. If this knowledge is not available the explanation fails, because the relationships remain unknown.

In lineal explanation we explain a particular event with a statement about another particular event. For example:

Why has the heater gone off?
The fuse has blown.

It is assumed in this case that the relationship between a heater "going off" and a "fuse blowing" is already known—the situation requires only that its relevance for this particular case be made apparent.

2. *Hyperbolic explanation* (hyperbolic = throwing beyond). This type of explanation also assumes previous knowledge. However, in answer to the question about a particular event, the answer is given in the form of a principle and the reader or listener is expected to identify the appropriate event. For example:

Why has the heater gone off?
The circuit must have been overloaded.

It will be apparent that this kind of explanation is appropriately named—it is a "throwing beyond" what is asked. Nevertheless it is also a *correct* explanation in the sense of identifying the relevant *principle:* even though it leaves more to the recipient who must make the inference as to which particular event is appropriate. In other words he is left to make the lineal explanation himself.

3. *Explanation in detail.* This type of explanation is a combination of lineal and hyperbolic explanations to effect a complete descriptive account of all antecedent events as they relate to subsuming or organising principles. It is assumed that the principles and concepts of the exposition are already known.

## IMPLICATIONS FOR PEDAGOGY

When communication is accepted as the heart of teaching and learning it follows that setting up the conditions necessary for its greatest effectiveness must be given high priority. We have seen that communication involves a transaction between teacher and pupil in which they should be able to alternate roles. It follows that both the teacher *and* the pupil need to be trained in communication skills: how to listen and respond and how to structure communication relative to purpose. If this is to be accomplished, not only will it be necessary to teach the logical structure of communication, but it will also be necessary to develop the psychological abilities which vitalise direct communication between *people*. Thus pupils should be taught to reflect and to engage in feedback dialogue and other forms of clarification. The implication seems clear: as the teacher and pupils need to be *partners* in communication, the pupils must have *inside* knowledge.

In the discussion below this theme is developed from two viewpoints both of which emphasise the cognitive components of communication.

1. The general significance of the theme for class management in terms of organisation and evaluation processes.
2. The significance of the *structure* of communication in improving:
    (a) the likelihood of acceptance of the explicit *content* of communication, and
    (b) the likelihood of successful generalisation.

The affective component will be discussed in the next chapter on interpersonal relationships.

## THE TEACHER SHOULD TEACH HOW HE IS TEACHING

### "Time Out"

The most effective way in which a teacher can change the status of his pupils to that of *partners* seems, in practice, to be to take "time out" from teaching the syllabus in order to *teach how he is teaching*. Such a practice is highly significant in the context of personal interaction but discussion of this will be deferred to the next chapter. Our concern here is with knowledge of the processes and the improvement of cognition.

The discussion below illustrates how a teacher can *teach how he is teaching* in order to improve the quality of thinking in groups.

#### PROFITABLE USE OF GROUPS IN THE CLASSROOM

Individualised programmes and group projects have long been advocated by those concerned about underachievement in classrooms. Primary school teachers have used such methods during and since the heyday of the progressivists, and with sufficient success to consider them essential. But secondary teachers do not appear to have fully accepted these methods, largely, it seems, in the belief that such methods are not practical. Secondary teachers who have attempted group methods, for instance in a project as simple as formulating a generalisation from a given set of facts, have typically found the venture an uneconomic use of time—particularly when preparing a class for examination. However, analysis of attempts to establish group methods of this kind in secondary schools has shown that they have failed because the teacher expected too much of his pupils: *he failed to teach them how to work in groups.* Interestingly, analysis of such groups in primary schools often indicates a similar fault; but the primary teacher tends to be generally oblivious of the inadequacy because of less concern about the quality of the cognitive product. The teacher who accepts that he should *teach how he is teaching* will have a very different view on the value of group methods because he will have given his pupils the means to work in groups. The following points discuss features of how this could work in practice.

1. The teacher would provide a model for group work in part of his teaching of the whole class and seek to give the class an *inside* look at his behaviour as group leader. Subsequently a pupil acting as leader of a group would then be able to act more effectively because he would be acquainted with the specifics of behaviour as group leader. Group members would be able to act more intelligently because they would be able to recognise their cues from discussion of *their* required behaviours in the whole class situation. The idea is, simply, to let the pupils know the rules and the *principles of play* so they can be intelligent participants. To this end the teacher will:

   (a) acquaint pupils with major features of the psycho-dynamics of groups (discussed in the next chapter), and

   (b) systematically take "time out" for the development of a comprehensive set of skills needed for group work. As these are identical with those needed to establish a partnership with his pupils in teaching the whole class, it is a simple matter to establish their relevance for group work.

2. The following illustrates how this might work out in practice for the skill of "handling the fumble".

PART OF LESSON TRANSCRIPT

*Teacher*    We have then, a great block of land that has come from the sea—the Southern Alps—here, and two volcanoes over there, with the sea between. Today, however, the Canterbury Plains fill this gap between the Alps and the now extinct volcanoes of Banks Peninsula. How, in your opinion, were the plains formed?

*Pupil*    I think they were formed from bits of mountain.

*Teacher*    What do you mean by *bits* of mountain? How would *they* form *plains*?

Let us now assume that the above part of the lesson has been completed; the teacher could take "time out" to inform his pupils of the function of this handling of the pupil's answer and ask them to be alert for similar responses in group work so they could handle them similarly.

One way of explaining this handling could be:

Let's take *time out* to look at what we have been doing. When we are learning something we have often to fumble for words and often for the idea—so we express ourselves in a clumsy fashion. However the idea can still be the "right" one and may often be profitably developed. I illustrated one method in this lesson. (Class reminded of exchange above.) Now I asked this final question in this way in order to tell John his answer was on the right track, to tell him which parts of his answer needed to be developed—which, as you know, he did very successfully. What *did* I tell him in the two questions? How was it done? . . .

Pupils explore significance of emphasising *bits* and *plains*.

The teacher finishes the session by asking pupils to act as teacher in response to a prepared set of "fumbles".

In developing the use of the "fumble" the teacher will be making the pupils aware, incidentally, of aspects of the *feedback dialogue* which might later be the specific objective of a "time out" session.

In the same way the need for statements to give a frame of reference, orientation and coherence (see below) and the like, as well as discussion techniques, can be established and skills can be developed.

## TEACHERS AND PUPILS NEED AN EVALUATION VOCABULARY

It is commonplace that the pupil has his essay returned with the briefest of comment or perhaps some effusion on his improved spelling or grammar—but with little reference to his thinking beyond "good thinking", "woolly", or "obscure". The pupil therefore gains little from the exercise. This failure occurs because such evaluative comments do *not permit the pupil to know the dimensions of his success or failure in terms of the skills that went into making the product*. Reinforcement could be given if teachers and pupils had a *common vocabulary* that permitted reference to these more important sub-skills and to qualitative assessment of performance. Such a vocabulary would, of course, have value beyond written work  in fact it could enter largely into the conduct of class discussions and its use could be the occasion for "time out" sessions.

The proposition is that all pupils should be sufficiently familiar with the basic cognitive skills as described in Part II *so that they can understand an evaluation of the product of such thinking in terms of the process*. To achieve this they need to have a vocabulary sufficient to name the skill and significant aspects of the process and product. Thus the pupils should be thoroughly conversant with the minimum vocabulary presented in Figure 8.5.

**Discrimination**
    relevance
    significance

**Classification**
    concept
    set of specifications
    non-instance

                                  selecting

**Generalisation**
    sample—total population        learned probabilities
    selection of sample
    identity-type generalisation      grouping
    adequacy of range
    order in sample             concrete

Figure 8.5: Minimum cognitive vocabulary

I

Figure 8.5—*cont.*

**Communication**
  verbal—non-verbal
  listening—responding
  feedback dialogue
  reflection
  frame of reference

abstract
degree of abstraction

structure

advance organiser

**Description**
  order
  continuity
    "mental leaps"
    coherence

probability and frame of reference

feedback

probability in generalisation

**Explanation**
  analogy
    common and new ground
    "pointing up" the analogy
    concrete analogy
  model
  lineal
  hyperbolic
  explanation in detail

As discrimination, classification and generalisation are *interdependent* skills, a special vocabulary has been found necessary to supplement that of the *names* and nature of the skills themselves. This vocabulary highlights significant features of their products in relation to their use. For example, if a group is taken as constituting a sample for generalisation, the problem arises as to how the generalisation can be related to the sample in terms of its adequacy as an inference from the nature of the sample. The sample vocabulary in Figure 8.6 has been found useful.

Good fit

Too narrow

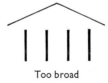
Too broad

Figure 8.6: Examples of evaluation vocabulary
(Where the strokes ⅠⅠⅠⅠ represent the sample and ⌒ the generalisation)

The following example illustrates its use and how it facilitates discussion. Note that the words of the groups are to be taken as representative of sentences, paragraphs, or even sections of a chapter.

What is the best name for each group of words in Figure 8.7?

### To Establish the Vocabulary

In addition to exercises designed to develop the skills outlined in these chapters, it is essential to establish the vocabulary in the evaluation contexts for which it is planned. Thus particular emphasis needs to be given to justification of answers in exercises in terms of the vocabulary: it is not enough to give the "correct" answer.

| | Group | Answer | Evaluation |
|---|---|---|---|
| I | parsnip<br>carrot<br>beetroot<br>swede | roots | A good fit<br>The nature of the sample is accurately represented. |
| II | parsnip<br>carrot<br>beetroot<br>swede | plants | Too broad<br>There are other names which better convey the significant features of this group. |
| III | parsnip<br>carrot<br>beetroot<br>swede | vegetables | Too broad<br>While this is better than the preceding *plants*, it still does not convey the most significant feature. |
| IV | parsnip<br>carrot<br>beetroot<br>pumpkin | roots | Too narrow<br>Ignores the significance of pumpkin as a member of the sample. |

Figure 8.7: Naming groups of words

## NOTES ON SOME EXERCISES TO DEVELOP SKILLS
### Establishing the Vocabulary
#### I. DISCRIMINATION
1. Relevance
2. Significance.

The exercises given in Chapter 5 (pp. 63-64) have usually been satisfactory as a *minimum* set, provided there is sufficient exploration of selection under "control of an idea". The two skills should be introduced as complementary so that discussion of the two exercises can thoroughly explore selection under "control of an idea" in terms of relevance and significance.

At the end of the training session, pupils should be able to select what is relevant and rank for significance in novel exercises and to justify their selection in terms of the "*controlling idea*". Thus, for example, they might be expected to comment as follows:

(1) "That is not *relevant* because it has to do with the *stage of colonial exploitation* whereas we are talking about *national resources*." ("Controlling idea" other than our topic.)

Or again,

(2) "That is not *significant* (i.e. sufficiently significant) because though it is a *resource* there is no known way in which this mineral can be extracted from that rock cheaply enough to be profitable." (Justification of low ranking.)

*Example of an application exercise.* Given the following outline of an essay on the Russian Revolution of 1917, select from Chapter X of your text all those facts you consider relevant for each of the paragraph topics below.

Para. 1. The breakup of the old Russian order was induced by the impact of Western civilisation on Russian civilisation and then precipitated by war, on which process the Bolsheviks acted merely as a catalyst.

Para. 2. The 1917 Russian Revolution resulted from the profound effects of the First World War on a society already racked by the stresses of a transition to Western culture.

Para. 3. The inexorable pressure on the old order was a direct result of Western influence in industrialisation and the demands for a more democratic social structure.

On completion the class would spend time *justifying their selection*, the teacher being more concerned with the quality of this justification (and its use of the evaluation vocabulary) than with the "right" answer.

## II. CLASSIFICATION

Pupils seem to gain from the knowledge that we handle information by *grouping* and that we learn to accept things as belonging to groups in terms of learned specifications which often undergo progressive refinements. There is also value in their knowledge, without being too fussy about detail, that a new concept "is like this group we know" (conjunctive) "or that" (disjunctive) "or that" (relational), i.e. *concepts have certain characteristics in the learning*, and in the pattern of specifications when learned—and pupils are able to verbalise these characteristics.

Undoubtedly the most important exercises here are: (1) the ranking of ideas in terms of degree of abstraction, and (2) the ordering of these ideas into a hierarchy.

*Exercises*

*Arrange in a formal schema to show rank in terms of "degree of abstraction".*

*A.* 1. David recently swore at the Sunday School superintendent.

2. David has been misbehaving during the last few weeks.

3. David pushed his ice cream into his sister's face.

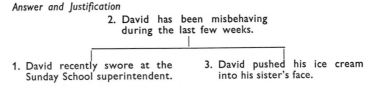

*Answer and Justification*

Figure 8.8: Degree of abstraction

The idea of *misbehaviour* in this set of ideas is more abstract than *swearing* and *aggression*—*misbehaviour* "includes" the others as part of its meaning.

*B.* 1. Man can be so impressed by his own creations that he can lose his sense of proportion.

2. Even small space achievements can cause man to lose sight of the day-to-day world of nature.

3. Technical progress can mean cultural stagnation or even regress.

*Answer:* The third is on the highest rank, the first on the middle rank and the second on the lowest.

In this example the idea of *cultural stagnation and even regress* includes the idea of *losing sense of proportion* (among others) and this in turn includes the idea of *losing sight of the day-to-day world of nature* (as one example).

Note that in the justification of levels of abstraction it is necessary to resort to the idea of *inclusion*.

C. 1. $A.A. + A.B. + B.A. + B.B.$

2. $(3+5)(3+5)$

3. $A^2 + 2AB - B^2$

4. $(A+B)^2$

*Answer:* From most to least abstract: 4, 3, 1, 2. If the reader keeps in mind the idea of *inclusion* he should be able to justify this order if he is familiar with the mathematics.

---

### III. GENERALISATION

Development of skill in generalisation seems to depend critically upon the ability to "fit" the new idea to the idea perceived in the *sample*. To develop skill pupils need to communicate their judgments of "fit".

(The following sample exercise assumes pupils are familiar with the nature of generalisation to the extent that it is "an inference as to the nature of the whole from the nature of a sample".)

---

*Exercise*

From column B select the best generalisation for the set of ideas in column A *and justify your acceptance or rejection of each alternative.*

| A<br>(in a school classroom) | B |
|---|---|
| The teacher went red in the face, his eyes widened, he clenched his fist, and his voice rose to a high-pitched scream. | 1. The teacher is conducting a revivalist meeting.<br>2. The teacher is giving his opinion on racialism.<br>3. The teacher is extremely angry at some misbehaviour. |

*Answer:* 1. Too broad; probability low. (Much more information needed in sample to make this a "good fit".)

2. Too broad; probability low. (As for 1.)

3. Best fit. (The sample "most probably" implies anger. The fact that it is a teacher in a classroom gives high probability in that it is directed at *misbehaviour*.)

## THE VOCABULARY SHOULD INCLUDE THE HIGHER LEVEL SKILLS

The above illustrations of the vocabulary are from the basic processes covered in Chapters 4-8. However, knowledge of mental processes and associated vocabulary can be profitably extended to include higher level skills as included in Bloom's Taxonomy. The argument remains the same: pupils should be aware of the processes involved and have a vocabulary to refer to significant aspects of the product of their thinking. Sanders[4] provides a useful discussion of the skills of the taxonomy which is in sufficient detail for this purpose.

## THE SIGNIFICANCE OF STRUCTURE IN THE IMPROVEMENT OF COMMUNICATION

### Acceptance of Explicit Content

Some of the most significant content of communication between teacher and pupils is lost because the teacher (and the pupil) is unaware of the structural implications of the questions he asks relative to the answers he gets. This is particularly apparent in the domain of explanation and probability of "frame of reference" which are discussed below to illustrate the point.

### ACCEPTANCE OF EXPLANATION

As will be recalled, explanation is regarded here as the description of the relationships between ideas. As such it is of special concern to teachers who wish to have their pupils discover principles inherent in practical work: a principal theme of modern curriculum development. However, when a teacher is unfamiliar with the logical structure of the different forms of explanation, he may cumulatively *suppress* the ideas he seeks. For example, to use an earlier illustration:

*Teacher*   Why did the electric radiator go out?

*Pupil*     The circuit was overloaded.

*Teacher*   That's not what I was looking for.

In this case the teacher was looking for a *lineal* explanation (the fuse was blown) but received a *hyperbolic* explanation which he is unable to accept because it was incompatible with the frame reference governing the discussion at that stage. However, if the teacher realised that he was looking for the *lineal* form of explanation and had received the *hyperbolic*, he could well have responded:

> Yes, that is the *general principle* but at the moment we are looking for the *particular event* . . .

The advantage of such care in the acceptance of explanatory content is that it clarifies understanding by relating a pupil's understanding to the relevant network of ideas and in so doing also avoids the confusions attendant upon a rejection of his contribution. It is all too frequently the case that a pupil may be a little uncertain of his knowledge, so that a rejection of what is, in his mind, a correct idea becomes a setback to his understanding. Cumulatively this can lead him to be reluctant to volunteer ideas and to dislike the "discovery" type lesson.

Another facet of the problem is provided by the case of the pupil answer which takes the form of analogy.

*Example*

Teacher    What does this traditional Japanese music make you think of?

Pupil    It is like a circus.

The teacher here needs to recognise that the pupil is regarding the music as *analogous* to the circus. A teacher who is insensitive to this might well dismiss the idea as absurd. On the other hand he *could* ask for the analogy to be elaborated—and discover a rather stimulating idea. If the pupil has been taught the logical form of analogy he might well be asked to present it systematically to help others perceive it in the same way, i.e., to "point up" the analogy.

Teacher:    (1) What is it about the circus you have in mind?
(The common ground.)
(2) What are the corresponding features of Japanese music?
(The new ground.)

### ACCEPTANCE OF DESCRIPTION

One of the most frequent causes of the rejection of descriptive content is the failure to communicate the *frame of reference*. The teacher (or the pupil) may have one viewpoint with its implicit assumptions and the other party to the communication may be left with another. The significance of what is being said is quite lost without the proper frame of reference.

However, this failure to communicate the *frame of reference* is so prevalent that we develop some skill in determining the probability that it will be one thing rather than another. Such skill is, of course, the product of experience in a particular subject area, so the novice is at a considerable disadvantage. Thus, in the area of creative writing, pupils frequently have original ideas rejected because they are unskilled at assessing the likely frame of reference of the person reading their work. If the teacher becomes aware of this problem he can react more constructively than "woolly idea here" or the like. Assuming he has taught the pupil about *probability* and the *frame of reference*, he can proceed differently: he can ask the pupil to defend himself against the charge of neglecting to assess the probability that the reader will be able to determine the frame of reference. In so doing the pupil may well expose the fact that a "woolly idea" merely appears so because he has failed to introduce it properly. Adjustments can follow; creativity is recognised and developed.

### IMPROVING THE LIKELIHOOD OF GENERALISATION

The nature of the generalisation process is such that when it is expected in the classroom the number of variables involved significantly diminishes the likelihood of success. Consider, for instance, the fact that the teacher's particular orientation to a topic is, in all probability, remarkably different from that of his pupils, and that unless he does something to orient them, teacher and class may well remain at cross purposes so that the significance of questions seeking generalisation is obscured by the differences of viewpoint. Again, a teacher's question may wrongly assume that pupils will recognise the significance of ideas covered earlier in the lesson: the loss of coherence will make the question far too difficult.

Many verbal contingencies are so complex that it seems common sense to prepare for the more important ones. The proposal, then, is that in planning we prepare to set up conditions which will facilitate the kinds of intellectual behaviour a teacher wants. The discussion which follows deals with some of the more important categories which need to be considered in setting up these conditions.

The general conditions to which the discussion gives priority (following the argument on the significance of basic processes) are primarily discipline-centred—a conceptual approach. However, consonant with the wider implications of the nature of the generalisation process and the notion of a developing autonomous self, *modes of inquiry* are a necessary complement. These are not discussed in this part as they fit more conveniently into a later part on the design of Episodes and the Lesson, i.e., the design of the framework of verbal interaction.

## STATEMENTS TO INCREASE THE PROBABILITY OF GENERALISATION
### Statements of Information

If the pupils do not have sufficient information from which to generalise, it should be given. This can be done in the form of a lecturette, reading, slides, film, demonstration and the like. Unfortunately many teachers have been impressed with the dangers of lecturing instead of teaching and consequently ask questions when they should be giving information. For example, in the following transcript of a third form lesson, the pupils knew vaguely where Indonesia was, and nothing else for certain, yet the teacher persisted with the pattern of questions for twenty-eight minutes— finally to dictate to the class, in the last seven minutes, the generalisations he wished them to have on problems to do with population, transport and diversity of language and culture.

#### EXCERPT FROM A LESSON ON INDONESIA

| | | |
|---|---|---|
| T | | What's it [Dutch New Guinea] called now?<br>[Long silence] |
| T | | West? |
| | P | Republic .... |
| T | | No.<br>[Strained silence] |
| T | | West Irian—that's what it's called now. |
| T | | What's this island called? [Timor] |
| | P | Timor [surreptitious use of atlas in desperation.] |
| T | | Why have I divided it? |
| | P | Part belongs to Malaysia. |

| | | |
|---|---|---|
| *T* | | No, long way from Malaysia! |
| | *P* | Part Indonesia. |
| *T* | | What about the other part? |
| | *P* | Holland. |
| *T* | | No, Dutch have no colonies here now. |
| | *P* | Australia. |

and so on.

If, instead, the teacher had assessed *readiness* (pupils had little knowledge) he could have given them the necessary information in the introductory part of the lesson and had them working on a significant set of information to achieve for themselves the generalisations sought.

## Statements of Orientation

As previously stated, teachers and pupils can have different viewpoints on a given topic. Quite apart from the need to ensure that teacher and pupils are cognitively aligned, however, there is the need to consider the pupils' need for autonomy. If the teacher goes arbitrarily from one activity to another the pupils are driven, as it were, in blinkers—never really knowing what is going on nor what is really in front of them. The teacher can anticipate this, and largely overcome it, by a statement conveying the intended orientation. One of the most important statements of orientation is that which conveys information on the function of an activity. For example, a teacher intends to use a quiz at the beginning of his lesson to remind his pupils of significant ideas of the previous lesson. If he plunges into the quiz without explaining its function, his pupils will be likely to define it as a test situation and react in terms of success-failure—and on this feedback the *teacher's* actions will subsequently tend to confirm this. When, however, he *orients* the pupils, they can react differently—and allow him to achieve his purpose. Thus he can say: "Our topic today requires us to remember the main ideas of our introduction . . ." and when the pupils do not answer, the teacher immediately reminds them. The difference in accordance with class expectation, as described, may appear a splitting of straws: in practice the difference is as real as that between the class which knows where it is going and the one which is led by the nose. A further example will illustrate a longer-term orientation. If a teacher is taking a poem, and is aiming to use the poem to crystallise the pupils' thinking on the theme, his assessment of readiness may indicate that differences of opinion are likely—quite apart from levels of thinking. In this case, imagine the result of a teacher who informs his class near the beginning of the lesson (assuming a new class): "We shall in all probability be unable to agree on the meaning of the poem." He is telling his pupils he does not expect them to agree with him or each other—that the truth is many shades of gray and that each may have a part of the truth.

### EXAMPLES OF STATEMENTS OF ORIENTATION

1. Now we want to discover how such a large sector of humanity has such a comparatively small land area.

2. We must now "tie up the ends" of our discussion and relate the generalisation we have on the blackboard to success and survival of the land plants.
3. In this way we are going to build up a model so that we can account for the behaviour of these salts.
4. Our problem now is to decide whether Marcie Hans meant us to stop there or to go on to see some greater truth.

## Statements of Coherence

If a significant idea is not perceived *by the pupils* as part of the sample from which the teacher expects a generalisation, their success is less likely. The teacher, therefore, needs to ensure that significant ideas are accessible at the time he expects pupils to generalise. To achieve this, he needs to use various "coherence devices" which have the general function of ensuring that the "thread of understanding" is not lost; that ideas are in mind when they are needed.

### EXAMPLES OF STATEMENTS OF COHERENCE

1. You will remember in the exercise we did in the first lesson that too many people in the underdeveloped areas had too little land.
2. Keeping *this* in mind . . . .
3. In doing the transformations of the first group we had a name for the final position of a point after transformation. How then . . . ?
4. We know then that under the rules of this transformation . . . .
5. Now when we described the motion . . . .
6. *This* ability of the electrons to leave the lattice. . . . (Repetition following pronoun *this*.)
7. This heavy load of current. . . . (Pronoun followed by *paraphrase* of key idea).
8. However, while . . , in the present case . . . .

## Statements of Bounds

As discussed previously, the probability that a generalisation will be achieved is dependent upon the perception of constraints or bounds within which thinking must be done. Put another way, if criteria of relevance and significance are not communicated in some way, pupils are free to select their own. The consequences for class discusson are notorious: an unproductive meandering which may have a place in a discovery stage but is wasteful when systematic mastery of content is intended.

The function of the statement to set "bounds" is thus similar to that of the statement of orientation. The essential difference however is that while the statement of orientation is concerned essentially with *viewpoint*, that of bounds is to convey the *limits* of the viewpoint while also communicating the criteria of relevance and significance either explicitly or implicitly. The statement of bounds, then, is in effect a delineation of the sample from which the generalisation will be made. It differs also from a statement of information in that it must be more rigorously selective. This is necessary since it is to be followed by a question set designed to achieve a *particular* generalisation.

### EXAMPLES OF STATEMENTS OF BOUNDS

The words in italics are statements of bounds.

1. *Given this set of equations,* what can we say of . . . .
2. What then can you say about the direction of movement, *relative to the desk top* . . . .
3. *Some people say that if there is an increase in government activity in social welfare there will be less active concern by individuals about the plight of those less fortunate than themselves.*
   - How could this be so?
   - Can this view be reconciled with that underlying our tentative definition of the Welfare State? . . . (If so, how?)
4. *In Britain new technology at the beginning of the twentieth century had the effect of relocating industry.*
   - What effect would this have had on declining areas?
   - What possible effects may it have had on the older traditional growth areas which relied on old forms of technology?

*Note:* 3. and 4. above: a statement of bounds before a question increases the likelihood that pupils will think and talk to the point.

5. *Taking into account the national significance of the West Coast timber resources,* make some reasoned suggestions forecasting . . .

*Note:* This statement includes coherence but priority is given to the "bounds" function because of its explicit use in the question.

6. *We must especially ask this question as we look at the following information.*

*Note:* This statement could equally be said to be orienting in function but favouring "bounds", because question assumed to have been explicit.

7.

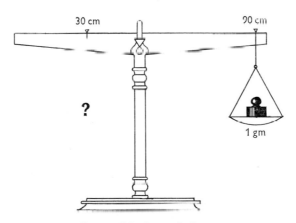

Figure 8.9: Beam balance

*Apparatus:* beam balance as in Figure 8.9. What weight is needed at 30 cms to balance the beam?

*Note:* The apparatus is implicitly a statement of bounds.

A statement of bounds can be more complex than above. In the following case all the conditions of the exercise are a statement of bounds.

---

*Exercise from a creative writing programme.*
*Instructions:*
    1. Fill the gap using 70-100 words. (15 minutes)
    2. Sustain the characters.
*Reminders:*
    Your work will be marked for:
    1. Relevance to the theme you adopt.
    2. Sensibility.
    3. Probability. (Both events and the solution as a whole.)

"No, Robert, you may not go to the pictures on Saturday. Your work has been a disgrace this week. Besides, I have not forgotten your impudence."
    Robert simmered.
    "Vera," ventured Robert's father.
    "Now don't you try getting round me," snapped Robert's mother. "You know very well the boy should be punished."

GAP

The door shut quietly. Robert's parents sat in shocked silence.

---

## Statement of Frame of Reference

It will be apparent that statements of orientation and bounds are both implicitly the statement of a *frame of reference*. However, there are occasions when the frame of reference needs to be delineated with special care—as before a set of questions designed to explore a *sample* from which a generalisation is to be made. In these cases a composite statement which performs both functions meets the requirement.

### EXAMPLES OF FRAME OF REFERENCE
1. Now to move on to more specific information (orientation) about the kinds of products which make up Japan's industrial export (bounds).
2. Well now, when geographers talk of major industrial trading nations, they look at their capacity for making steel, or big steel products such as ships. So we'll look at Japan as a steel-maker and ship-builder compared to these other countries.

## REFERENCES

[1] S. M. JOURARD, *The Transparent Self*, Van Nostrand, New York, 1964, pp. 111-20.
[2] See JOURARD, op. cit.
[3] R. HARRÉ, *An Introduction to the Logic of the Sciences*, Macmillan, London, 1960.
[4] N. M. SANDERS, *Classroom Questions: What Kinds?*, Harper and Row, New York, 1966.

# CHAPTER 9

# Interpersonal Relationships in the Classroom

## EXCERPT FROM REPORT ON THE PLANET EARTH

The Earth people make mechanical facsimiles of their own brains which they call *computers*. By some quirk of their social evolution the characteristics of computer "thinking" have come to represent the ideal for its creators! Thus, these people, who have the potential to live as we do, condition their young to repress all feeling (and to repress all perception of feeling in others) which is in any way an exposure of the self! Thus young children are reprimanded for their fumbling attempts to express their perception of adult motives; yet are not expected to tolerate any other form of frustration! Not surprisingly, they soon become conditioned to expect little help with an ailing self and many suffer from immaturity of character. The schools most favoured by those with "money" are designed to reinforce and confirm the repression of feeling, with severe penalties for those who do not conform. These institutions have programmes designed to produce graduates who are adept at interpersonal "shadow-boxing" wherein they must not make contact with the real self of the other person. What a strange inversion of our society! The schools least favoured by those with "moncy" claim to develop the "total self". However, their conception of this task is so naïve, their teachers so ill-equipped for the task and their pupils so handicapped emotionally and socially by the conditioning of their social milieu that they have little success.

If ever we needed justification for our belief that the *transparent self* is the foundation of mental and social health we have it in the consequences of this rigorous masking. Earth society is sick; its schools appear to be nothing more than a production of mental and social ills.

## INTERPERSONAL RELATIONSHIPS IN THE CLASSROOM

Living is a complex undertaking which taxes our resources.

The assumption of this chapter is that a balanced development of cognitive, affective and social skills is a necessary resource for *survival* in the community—let alone the attainment of such refinements as *self-actualisation*. In this discussion, therefore, we shall beg the question of what constitutes a *balance*; our concern will be merely to examine interpersonal relationships in the classroom in terms of the presence or absence of these resources.

Common sense alone would suggest that the characteristics of learning in the classroom (at least in so far as it involves problem solving) should reflect those of successful problem solving outside it. In any case, there is no evidence to suggest that the capacities of pupils are in some way peculiarly different by virtue of their presence in a classroom.

Consider, for instance, the following representative situations from everyday living:

| Category of resource skills | Task |
|---|---|
| 1. Cognitive | Managing a household budget. |
| 2. Affective | Comforting a daughter who has lost her boyfriend. |
| 3. Social | Joining a party where you know only the hostess. |

Figure 9.1: Skills used in everyday living

Reflection on one's ability to cope with each of these tasks soon brings the realisation that these situations can only be assigned to their respective categories on the basis of a *predominance* of a particular resource. In fact, each of these activities clearly requires resources from other categories for its success: *a deficiency in any category will mean a significantly lower level of success in the tasks*. In other words, affective and social resources must be considered in any assessment of capacity to cope with complex problems. Thus a father may know intellectually what he has to do to comfort his daughter but may find his efforts nullified by lack of affective and social skills. *Failure* to consider the implications of these three areas of resource as pertinent to classroom learning is highlighted by the following from an address by Morris:

> On the timetable it says mathematics, and Mr A is teaching the class. Mr A is a moderately good, perhaps average, teacher, with quite a lot of enthusiasm for his subject; he is very energetic and says he is teaching mathematics. The question I was interested in was what were the children *learning*. There were, I would say, probably about a fifth of them learning mathematics—some mathematics—and learning it quite well. There was another proportion who were learning to dislike mathematics—I should say that it was probably equal in number. There were others again, including those I have just mentioned, who predominantly were learning to dislike Mr A, and it is very likely that a good many of those were learning to dislike the school, and dislike education, and all it stood for. As for the rest, I concluded they were really learning nothing at all; they were going through various motions which kept at bay the worst disasters that might befall them.[1]

Mr A's concern with his *subject*, his typical preoccupation with the *cognitive*, ignores the psychological reality of affective and social factors in learning. He succeeds with one-fifth of his pupils by exploiting the affective and social capital created by the parents and previous teachers of these pupils. He fails with the remainder to the extent that they lack affective and social resources which would enable them to overcome the difficulties generated by his exclusively cognitive approach.

## THE TEACHER'S ROLE IN INTERPERSONAL RELATIONSHIPS
### The Ideal
The ideal teacher, with regard to interpersonal relationships which may appear implicit to the discussion in previous chapters, has been described by Adams and Biddle as:

> the "empathetic" teacher who somehow always seems to appreciate your thoughts, your feelings, your problems so that inevitably your learning is *personally* relevant and meaningful.[2]

Without "empathy", communication is limited; responsibility for emotional and social welfare is a pretence; and control of a class is a repression. But without other qualities this is a hopelessly impractical approach to classroom teaching. The respect for the individual and consideration of his needs that govern this kind of relationship must come to terms with the need for *moral toughness, salesmanship* and *leadership* if it is to be practical.

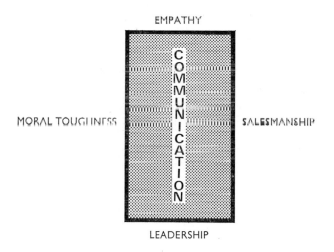

Figure 9.2: Qualities of the ideal teacher in terms of interpersonal relationships

### MORAL TOUGHNESS
The first rule of life applies to the teacher in his classroom: he must survive. Unfortunately, the more he develops empathetic ability, the more pupils he will see who need help and the more he will become aware of

the limitations of his emotional resources and competence to help. Further, he can easily become so involved with the needs of *individuals* that he fails to meet the needs of his class as a *group*. While a teacher must develop empathy in order to *understand* his pupils and to appreciate their feelings, he must develop sufficient moral toughness so that he can accept his limitations. That is, he has to develop the ability to put things "out of mind" until he next reviews his priorities.

Then again, because of the developmental requirements of those who are immature, he must be able to insist on and get compliance even in the face of strong expression of negative feelings. The unpleasant truth for teachers is that though empathy leads to *understanding* it does not necessarily lead to *rapport*. Not all pupils possess sufficient capacity for *insight* and *self-direction* for them to accept the exigencies of a corrective programme. Those of markedly immature or defective character development, for instance, are likely to be characterised by the *acting out* of emotions, attempts to *manipulate* the people about them, and a general outlook which is antipathetic to the kind of interpersonal relationships favoured by the presumably mature, socialised teacher. While, then, the teacher needs empathetic ability to understand such a pupil, he also needs moral toughness to meet his needs.

### SALESMANSHIP

When a pupil cannot be self-directive because of immaturity or defect of character, improving his condition will often mean that he should be required to function within a framework of some degree of coercion. Assuming that the aim is autonomy and insight, this cannot succeed unless the pupil *contracts with his teacher to accept the regimen*. The teacher therefore has to *sell* the programme in terms of his own confidence in its outcome, its credibility in the eyes of the pupil and the pupil's familiarity with the *fine print*—the choices he will face and the consequences of particular decisions.

Salesmanship needs to be a facet of many classroom activities. Its general significance can be stated in terms of the principle that the teacher needs to be able to accept the *obligation* to sell what he is teaching. In other words he must motivate his class in the broadest sense. Thus in one lesson he may *plan* to motivate in terms of Berlyne's *conceptual conflict* but instead he may find it necessary both to recognise the negative feelings of his pupils about the merits of the subject and to undertake *to justify it within their frame of reference*. Such a project requires empathetic competence to identify and understand the frame of reference and *salesmanship* to motivate within its constraints. A situation typical of those requiring the qualities of salesmanship was faced by one teacher when she was told by her class of slow learners in response to her own angry outburst:

> We are dumb! Why should we behave and do work? Everyone *expects* us to play up.

### LEADERSHIP

By virtue of his position the teacher has a leadership role in his class. How he performs this role will be a major factor in determining his success.

While the teacher's role is exercised on the basis of *legitimate authority* and he can reinforce this with *rewards* and *coercive powers*, his success as a leader depends critically upon *interpersonal influence* and *perceived competence*.[3]

Interpersonal influence appears to be a function of the inderdependent factors of the teacher's interpersonal relationships with *individuals* and his management of *group* processes. While both of these depend upon empathetic competence, management of group processes requires additional skills to those involved in relationships between one person and another. A teacher may thus be able to "get on side" in private with Wayne, but finds Wayne "difficult" in the classroom because the teacher cannot "get on side" with Paul.

In this case group processes have added a new dimension. Paul is the natural leader of a group within the class of which Wayne is a member. In exercising this role Paul has contended with other small group leaders for class leadership and in so doing has become "off-side" with the teacher. Paul's lack of rapport with the teacher is reflected in Wayne's response (by a kind of ripple effect), for Wayne gives higher priority to maintaining his role in Paul's group than to maintaining rapport with the teacher.

The conflict between Paul and his teacher is essentially a problem of leadership which poses special problems for the teacher who seeks to reinforce *legitimate authority* with *interpersonal influence*. He must, for instance, resolve his problem with Paul *in front of the other pupils*, for only by so doing can he establish an interpersonal influence that is credible in terms of the group processes of the class he must lead.

Nor will it suffice to aim to gain class rapport through a kind of aggregation of rapport with individuals, for each *individual* in the class changes his frame of reference once he acts as a member of a *group*: he will be seeking to establish or maintain a role which he will accord various degrees of priority depending upon the extent of his autonomy in the sense of self-direction. As Schmuck and Schmuck point out:

> . . . change in the power structure of a classroom cannot be brought about *simply by attempting to change some of the individual students*. Attempts at helping low-power students learn skills in trying to wield interpersonal influence may meet with some short-term success, but only *normative changes in the climate of the entire group* would assure major changes in classroom leadership patterns.[4] (My italics.)

Perceived competence has long been recognised as a major factor in the secondary pupil's liking of his teacher.[5] However, its significance for the individual pupil will vary according to his type of orientation to learning. Two of Ausubel's three learning orientations are significant here:

1. *The satelliser*—the pupil who emotionally identifies with the teacher (from whom he derives a major source of security) and who will tend to accept the suggestions of his teacher regardless of content.

2. *The incorporator*—the pupil whose security is derived almost exclusively from his own performance and who will only accept suggestions

> that do not run counter to his need for ego enhancement; . . . in any event the power of his preceptor to suggest is not derived from a

personal relationship but from perceived superiority in knowledge and experience.[6]

Ausubel also draws attention to the built-in *resistance* to learning that is implicit to the two orientations.

> The satelliser is resistive to the acceptance of new values because such acceptance presupposes a repudiation of prior personal loyalties —a feat which cannot be accomplished without feelings of guilt. Resistance to learning in the incorporator springs from an entirely different source. Guilt feelings do not enter the picture at all since values have never been accepted on the basis of personal loyalty, and hence can be replaced by others without any suggestion of disloyalty. Instead resistance is first elicited by the very fact that the source of the new idea is outside himself. He finds this situation threatening not only because it qualifies his desire for absolute volitional independence, but also because of the obvious implications that others are more adequate and competent than he is.[6]

*The leadership should be appropriate.* So far we have ignored the significance of the teacher's individuality which will be shown, for instance, in his preference for a particular style of leadership. Thus, to use Lewin, Lippit and White's categories, he may favour the autocratic, democratic or *laissez-faire* methods because of complex defensive needs, idealism and conditioning of past experience.[7] Then again, we have ignored the possibility that the teacher's style of leadership may be incompatible with the needs, ideals and conditioning of his class. It is a common enough experience in schools to have, for instance, a teacher who favours the democratic style matched with a class conditioned to need the authoritarian style and to have chaos result.

Dunham suggests below that the function of leadership must be related to a complete group situation in which we seek to understand the nature of the total group and to adopt the *most appropriate* leadership pattern.

> We should operate in other words according to what Tannenbaum and Schmidt have called the principle of appropriate leadership. They suggest that there are three sets of factors which should be taken into consideration by the leader when he is trying to determine what the appropriate pattern of leadership will be in any situation. These factors are (1) forces in the leader; (2) forces in the follower; (3) forces in the situation.
>
> 1. *Forces in the leader will include:*
>     (a) His system of values—for instance how strongly does he feel that individuals should have a share in making the decisions.
>     (b) His confidence in his subordinates.
>     (c) His own leadership inclinations—there are some leaders who seem to act more comfortably and naturally as highly directive leaders while other leaders seem to work more comfortably in a more non-directive way.
>     (d) His feelings of security—some leaders have a greater need than others for predictability and stability and will be less able to tolerate the ambiguity of non-autocratic leadership.
>     (e) His physical and mental well-being.

2. *Forces in the follower will include:*
   (a) His need for independence or dependence.
   (b) His interest in the work and the organisation.
   (c) His expectations of the pattern of leadership—for according to Tannenbaum and Schmidt, "Persons who have come to expect strong leadership and are suddenly confronted with the request to share more fully in decision making are often upset by this new experience. On the other hand persons who have enjoyed a considerable amount of freedom resent the boss who begins to make all the decisions himself".[8]

3. *Forces in the situation will include:*
   (a) The type of organisation—its size, customary leadership patterns, values and traditions.
   (b) The nature of the task.

What then are the requirements for successful leadership? Tannenbaum and Schmidt say: "The successful leader is one who is keenly aware of those forces which are most relevant to his behaviour at any given time. He accurately understands himself, the individuals and the group he is dealing with. But this sensitivity or understanding is not enough. The successful leader is one who is able to behave appropriately in the light of these perceptions. If direction is in order, he is able to direct; if considerable participative freedom is called for, he is able to provide such freedom".[8]

The necessity of considering the appropriate leadership pattern has been indicated by Uris,[9] "Autocratic leadership, in certain situations, will be effective and successful, whereas democratic and free-rein approaches will fail.

"Free-rein leadership under the right conditions will produce more successful results than either of the other kinds of leadership. This, despite the fact that it is usually written off as useless.

"And democratic leadership, also under the right conditions, will give better results than any other method".[10]

The five bases of teacher leadership thus have considerable ramifications and imply a complex repertoire of skills if the teacher is to be an effective leader.

## The Reality

### THE NATURE OF CLASSROOM TRANSACTIONS

Adams and Biddle commented in their study of "real teachers" in "real classrooms":

> . . . less than half of one percent of the time was spent on matters that dealt with feelings and interpersonal relationships. Flanders,[11] in an earlier study that produced similar findings, was prompted to call the classroom an "affectional desert". The current findings suggest that his graphic simile could be recast and that the term "emotional desert" would be equally appropriate.[12]

It will be apparent that they found teacher behaviour to be significantly different from the model described above in that it was almost exclusively cognitive. Of course, their findings must not be taken as an accurate description of all classrooms for there must be teacher eccentrics some-where who interact with their pupils as people: but the evidence is that they are a minority.

### GROUP PROCESSES IN GROUP LEARNING

On the above account teachers are an insensitive lot. But is this necessarily so? The explanation may be simply that the teacher is not trained to cope with group processes and is overwhelmed by the predicaments he faces in the group situation, so he falls back on traditional defensive ploys. As an informal test of this hypothesis, a group of 72 student teachers who had elected a special course in pedagogy, preparatory to a course in counselling, were given a series of group experiences to test their capacity to cope with group predicaments. All students could be assumed interested in doing their best because they had been told that only 48 of them would be accepted for the counselling course and performance in the exercises would be a decisive factor in selection. It was made clear in the introduction to the exercises that the primary objective was to develop a productive group and this would need the efforts and active goodwill of all members. The students were put into groups of twelve without a designated leader, and were expected to manage various group assignments under a fairly high degree of contrived stress. Contrasting with these experiences were two large group experiences: in the first one, the lecturer demonstrated (incidental to a discussion about the course) the acceptance of feeling; and in the second (a structured and highly organised discussion), he demonstrated frequent reflection of the *cognitive* content only of student observations. Each student was required to keep a diary in which he entered his personal reactions to his experiences. Analysis of the diaries led to two groups of findings:

1. *Conditions governing "productivity" of groups*
    (a) The most productive small groups were characterised by:
        (i) leadership which took account of emotional and social factors in the group situation as demonstrated in the ability to listen, to be warm and responsive, to express group feelings and the like;
        (ii) a group of followers who accepted the leader and each other.
    (b) The achievement of productive *leadership* and *followership* is very difficult as it is accompanied by considerable tension because the psychological reality of one individual's group experience is not necessarily compatible with that of others in the group.
        (i) Because of past experience, there were some who had a leader-ship expectation, tended to talk most and saw the group as more successful than did those who were afraid of leadership and talked less. Further, they tended to be unappreciative of the efforts of less forceful members and inhibited their partici-pation.
        (ii) The "non-talkers" tended to have strong negative feelings about the assertion of leadership and to resent the often clumsy attempts to draw them into discussion.

Some "talkers" who persisted in contending for leadership, for instance, were observed to try to involve "non-talkers" by saying something like the following:

"Come on Joan, you haven't said anything yet—what do you think about it?"
OR
"There are some who haven't contributed. I think they should give us the benefit of their ideas."

A cognitive approach to deal with an emotional social problem! On the other hand, one *accepted* leader (whom one observer found difficult to identify because of the degree of mutual acceptance in the group) approached the matter on the plane of feeling. She smiled warmly at a "non-talker" and said quietly: "What about you, Mary?"—and got a response. Later, this same leader was seen merely to raise her eyebrows to another, and on receiving no verbal response but a non-verbal affirmation of involvement, she was satisfied.

(c) Reactions to the contrasting large-group experiences varied through time relative to the small-group experience. Initially most found the small group to be very threatening indeed and the large group to give anonymity and security. This position was reversed for most by the end of the small group series, when all groups had achieved a reasonable working relationship. Most *enjoyed* the session where the lecturer accepted feeling, but could not identify the cause. On the other hand while most appreciated the structure of the second group experience and the skill shown in management of discussion, they did not *enjoy* it as much as the first session.

(d) Nearly all students commented that the small groups would gain in productivity if the leader were able to structure discussion as demonstrated in the large group but without sacrificing his function of attending to the emotional and social factors.

2. *Conclusions on the performance of individuals considering their future leadership roles as teachers*

(a) Over two-thirds of this highly motivated group were unable to contribute to the group in a manner commensurate with the idea of positive leadership implicit to the model of the first section of this chapter.

 (i) Typically they reported themselves so threatened by *others* at the stage when groups were relatively unstructured that they were unable to participate. Significantly only one of the six groups welcomed latecomers to the group.

 (ii) Even when the group had reached what appeared a good working relationship, at least a quarter of each group was unable to cope with group process well enough to make a "positive" contribution.

(b) Those who were most confident in the group situation were generally insensitive to the feelings of those least confident and were clumsy in their attempts to involve them in discussion.

(c) In situations involving high tension, relatively few felt themselves competent to take a positive leading role.

(d) Overall there was marked insensitivity to non-verbal communication.

(e) Initially, when under tension, few listened but when someone did this was greatly appreciated. Later, as tension relaxed, more listened but few were able to reflect.

(f) Unaided, only a few students were able to identify the more significant group processes operating in the large and small groups.

The overall conclusion is that the student teacher is ill-equipped to manage group processes. In the absence of special training it seems unlikely that teachers in general, who must manage groups of considerable diversity of background and orientation, will be any more competent.

The institutional classroom reality is thus markedly different from the theoretical model of the teacher as the prime mover in the domain of interpersonal relationships.

### The Origins of the Teacher's Problem

To undertake successfully the range of interpersonal relationships implied by the above discussion, teachers must cast off some of the conditioning of their own upbringing.

#### COMMUNICATION ABOUT THE SELF IS NOT PERMISSIBLE

Quite early children learn to keep themselves to themselves for fear of being hurt. They learn that to expose their real feelings is dangerously to expose the self. Instead, as Berne would have it, they learn to play games.[13] This defensive make-believe is a barrier to intimacy and the development of autonomy. As Jourard states:

> If I am struggling to avoid becoming known by other persons then, of course, I must construct a false public self. The greater the discrepancy between my unexpurgated self and the version of myself that I present to others, then the more dangerous will other people be for me.[14]

Not surprisingly, teachers display the same inadequacies as the general population *unless they have had specialised training to counteract the conditioning of their upbringing.* Sadly, when student teachers in professional courses come to appreciate the value of communication (and is not this the *real* vision of the younger generation?) they lack the repertoire of skills which alone would make it possible.

#### LIMITATIONS OF BOOKS

Learning from books limits development of personality resources. Teachers, among others, have to have been successful with book learning. Even if they had not already a preference for ideas rather than people, intensive university study and its rewards appear to condition them to expectations favouring such a preference.

There is also an immediacy of reward with book learning which seems

to condition an aversion to dialogue and discussion as being too unpredictable in outcome to be tolerable. From observations of many teachers
with a marked preference for the lecture or monologue as a teaching
method comes the conclusion that they are apprehensive of the unexpected
idea. It seems that it is not so much that they will be caught out "not
knowing", but that they feel at a loss with people who lack their own
facility with words in the expression of ideas. They seem to have been
so conditioned by book learning as to have a low toleration of uncertainty,
so they eschew dialogue and discussion as the embodiment of what they
fear.

Further, it seems that their study and consequent isolation from the
ordinary concerns of people have been so intense that they become
relatively inefficient at managing interpersonal relationships which involve
any subtlety and finesse in the affective and social areas.

Perhaps because of these inadequacies, teachers are over-concerned
with grades and examinations because these focus attention on the cognitive. In this way they can rationalise their failures in terms of something
external to themselves—the pupil's lack of intelligence and his lack of
application to learning the facts.

Then again the immediacy of book learning and the typical urgency
of university courses seem to condition the teacher (as a product of the
system) to lose his awareness of the time needed by others to think, and
to lower his toleration of the silence needed if others are to solve the
problems he sets. Novice teachers typically will wait barely two seconds
after even a really thought-provoking question before prompting someone
for an answer. Book learning seems, then, to have desensitised him so
that his expectations of the thinking powers of others, in terms of time,
are quite unreal; and his own lack of toleration of silence, with its over-
tones of uncertainty, compounds the difficulty.

## IMPLICATIONS FOR PEDAGOGY

If teaching is to be a *personal* service, it seems clear that the teacher
should have the kind of training in which he develops the ability to
manage interpersonal relationships in his teaching so that he and the
*people* involved with him can utilise their full range of resources: cognitive,
affective and social. Such training would appear to have two main
emphases: (1) principles governing the establishment and maintenance
of rapport between two individuals, and (2) principles that should govern
the exercise of the teacher's leadership role. These two broad areas of
training would thus need to be directed to the development of *empathetic*
and *leadership competencies*. We now have a problem of mythology—the
belief that if we can understand something in a book we have mastered the
appropriate skill. This is manifest nonsense; particularly in the case of
affective and social skills. For instance, a student teacher may accept
the notion he should attempt to establish rapport with his class and may
say as his opening gambit:

> My name is John Masters. I would like to get to know you before
> we start on the year's work.

He *says* the above but may well be *communicating*:

> I do *not* want to know you. I shall keep myself at a distance. I believe
> you should keep your proper place—subservient to me.

by virtue of non-verbal signals of voice, gesture, posture and movement.

Until this student teacher becomes aware of how others see him when
he is under tension in front of a group, and until he practises erasing
negative signals and substituting positive signals to confirm his intention,
he hasn't *begun* to develop the requisite skill.

While, then, it is necessary to describe basic principles underlying the
development of empathetic and leadership competencies, *practical exercises
are a necessary condition for the development of skill.*

The following discussion presupposes that understanding of principles
will be complemented by a course of practical training.

## DEVELOPMENT OF EMPATHETIC COMPETENCE

The teacher can so easily exist in the manner described by Waller[15] and
quoted by Dunham:

> as psychologically isolated from the community because he must
> live within the teacher stereotype, which is a thin but impenetrable
> veil that comes between the teacher and other human beings.[16]

But professions which are primarily concerned with *helping* people
necessarily accord high priority to training in interviewing. As Kahn and
Cannell point out:

> As in most communications processes, we have in the interview two
> people, each trying to influence the other and each actively accepting
> or rejecting influence attempts. The end product of the interview is a
> result of this interaction. Therein lie the strengths and weaknesses of
> the interview as an information-getting technique. If the interaction
> is handled properly, the interview becomes a powerful technique,
> capable of developing accurate information and getting access to
> material otherwise unavailable. Improperly handled, the interaction
> becomes a serious source of bias, restricting or distorting the flow of
> communication. Therefore, we must learn to control the interaction
> between interviewer and respondent in order that the purposes of the
> interview can be achieved. This in turn requires that we have some
> insights into the dynamics of the interaction.[17]

In interview training there is a concern for the totality of communication; the interviewer *must* be *client-centred* and therefore cannot afford
to ignore the significance of any information: cognitive, affective or
social, verbal or non-verbal.

Training in basic skills of interviewing seems therefore part of the
professional preparation of teachers, for there seems no valid reason to
expect that teachers *should* operate within the stereotype if they are
equipped to manage outside its constraints. The following three groups
of principles govern the sets of associated skills which together can be
considered basic to empathetic competence and *fundamental to class
management*. This follows from the notion that sound relationships with
*individuals* inside and outside the classroom are a major determinant of

good rapport with the class as a whole: they provide a kind of social oil. However, while the interviewing principles below are considered basic to sound class management, *teachers would need to be trained to apply them in classroom situations because the principles imply a handling of particular events which can be remarkably different from what the teacher himself experienced as a pupil.*

## The Person Being Interviewed must be Treated as an Individual

Biestek describes the essence of the relationship:

> Individualisation is the recognition and understanding of each client's unique qualities and the differential use of principles and methods in assisting each toward a better adjustment. Individualisation is based upon the right of human beings to be individuals and to be treated not just as *a* human being but as *this* human being with his personal differences.[18]

Thus the interviewer must *accept* the respondent, who must be seen and worked with as he *really* is and not as he conceivably might be or should be. Unfortunately, this principle is often viewed askance by those who think it implies that *behaviour is thereby necessarily approved.* They say: "If I accept this boy, I am approving his bullying ways." But the two *must* be separated for unless the bully feels *accepted* we are most unlikely to get to the heart of his problem because of his inevitable defensiveness. They *can* be separated provided the following principles govern the interviewer's behaviour.

1. *The interviewer should recognise the respondent's need to express his feelings freely, especially his negative feelings.*
   This has four purposes:
   (a) The expression of feeling can make apparent what something really means. Often people are incapable of verbalising their problem, but if free to express *feeling* they can provide powerful cues as to its nature.
   (b) The acceptance of negative feelings is an affirmation of the worth of the individual. Because of their potential for exciting hostility, a calm consideration of negative feelings seems to induce a feeling that the listener "is prepared to accept *me* as I really am".
   (c) When negative feelings are themselves the problem, they can be faced once they are "in the open".
   (d) When feelings are a source of insecurity their expression permits the interviewer to give psychological support to lighten the burden —in the sense that something shared and experienced with another is easier to bear.

2. *The interviewer must avoid making judgments in the sense of assigning guilt or innocence, or degree of responsibility.*
   If the interviewer succeeds in this, the respondent is able to accept evaluation of his behaviour which is the outward expression of his problem. When, however, the interviewer appears to judge, he accentuates the feelings of "unworthiness" which are usually associated with

the need to seek help, and thus he generates a defensiveness which will extend to a resentment of evaluation of behaviour.

3. *The interviewer must give the respondent the right and freedom to make his own choices and decisions.*
   If we accept respect of individuality as a governing idea in interpersonal relationships, it follows that it is the *individual* who has the problem who must choose between the alternatives open to him. In this situation the interviewer must:
   (a) help the respondent see his problem more clearly so that he can perceive his alternatives and their implications;
   (b) help him develop his resources so that alternatives are credible to him; and
   (c) avoid persuasion and manipulation.

4. *The interviewer must be prepared to treat what he is told as confidential.*
   When a person gives information about his "inner self" in a situation where he assumes he will get help, it seems reasonable that he should be entitled to respect of his confidences. However, this does not mean in practice that information cannot on any account be passed to others, though the circumstances under which this can occur are a matter of debate. The following, however, are useful guides.
   (a) In *most* circumstances information should not be passed on without the express permission of the respondent.
   (b) The respondent should approve the form in which it is to be transmitted.

---

*Exercise*

*Situation:* Pupil is one of a group which has been making life miserable for a quiet, rather lonely classmate. Pupil has just talked herself into admitting that she "should not do that sort of thing" and that "Dad and Mum would be very angry if they knew".

*Teacher*   Do you mean that you'd like to make things happier for Joan?

*Pupil*   Why should *I* have to? The others do it more than me.

*Problem:* Select the most appropriate teacher response from those below and be prepared to justify it in terms of the principles described above.

*Teacher*

A. Oh! Then what you have been saying is so many fine words! Don't you think you should be acting more responsibly?

B. Surely you want to make amends?

C. Yes—I see your problem. It's not easy to go against your friends is it?

D. What a miserable outlook! But now, I'm sure you spoke without thinking.

E. I don't think your parents would have liked to have
   heard that.

The most acceptable answer is "C" provided it is said in an
*accepting* tone, it accepts negative feelings and recognises the
respondent's right to make his own choice. All other responses are
judgmental and so automatically deny acceptance and individual
choice.

---

## The Immediately Apparent Facts Matter Less than the Reasons People Feel as They Do

Unless one is prepared to treat human problems as entirely unrelated to
all other antecedent conditions, one is forced to accept that underlying
motives and attitudes are more significant in a problem situation than
the problem itself. Put another way: if one can uncover the motives and
attitudes, the *real* problem may be disclosed and dealt with. To achieve
this the interviewer will need to be able:

1. To see an item in a context.
   *Example:* "I hate maths" may really mean "I don't like failing all the
   time"—which implies a quite specific ameliorative programme.
2. To listen for what the respondent is trying to say, does not want to
   say, or cannot say without help.
   Obviously this principle requires a sophisticated reflection of feeling
which can be a severe test of empathetic competence.

## The Interviewer Must Keep in Mind that the Respondent has a Social Context

Both the interviewer and respondent have a social past and social present
of significance to the interview because the way we define our predicaments is substantially influenced by the groups to which we belong. If an
interviewer is unfamiliar with the way the respondent "defines his world",
social differences may make the interview unproductive. Coupled with
this is the possible influence of the interviewer's own feelings and attitudes
which can interfere with the real purposes of the interview.

## THE DEVELOPMENT OF LEADERSHIP SKILLS

Dunham suggests that leadership should be appropriate relative to forces
in the leader, follower and situation.[19] Unfortunately, observation of
classrooms where the level of interpersonal relationship is high, that is,
where the class has developed as a group (say) to the stage of establishing
influence patterns,[20] indicates the teacher needs considerable flexibility
in his exercise of leadership. In other words the needs of the *followers*
may require the teacher to be able to adopt a leadership pattern that is
not his "naturally". The proposition is that teachers in their *training*
should *be sensitised to the subtleties of group processes and be trained to
adopt the full range of leadership patterns*. Further, they should be trained
to diagnose the leadership needs of a particular class in a particular situation and they should be able to prescribe the regimen for any needed
improvement. Difficult—but not beyond the reach of a *profession*.

### Teachers should be Sensitised to Group Processes

The evidence from practical training programmes, such as the one for student teachers outlined above, is that until individuals are made to face the predicaments of leadership under controlled conditions, their habitual behaviour under stress tends to dominate in group situations. Under controlled conditions they can learn:

1. how others see them—negative signals and all;
2. about the *reality* of group experience for others of different psychological make-up;
3. the dynamics of ploys for leadership;
4. the dynamics of different kinds of followership;
5. about the psychological significance of empathy in group processes through an application of the principles of interviewing outlined above; and
6. about the high priority to be accorded trust and reflective skills in communication.

### Teachers should be Trained in the Skills which Facilitate Group Processes
#### COMMUNICATION SKILLS AND LEADERSHIP FUNCTIONS

In order to be effective leaders, teachers need the communication skills outlined in the previous chapter, for a basic quality of teacher leadership is perceived competence. They need also, however, to be able to apply those skills to perform specific leadership functions in the cognitive plane. As Schmuck and Schmuck suggest, they need to be able to perform the following goal-directed tasks:

(a) Initiating; proposing tasks or goals; defining a group problem; suggesting a procedure for solving a problem; suggesting other ideas for consideration.

(b) Information or opinion seeking; requesting facts on the problem; seeking relevant information; asking for suggestions and ideas.

(c) Information or opinion giving; offering facts; providing relevant information; stating a belief; giving suggestions or ideas.

(d) Clarifying or elaborating; interpreting or reflecting ideas or suggestions; clearing up confusion; indicating alternatives and issues before the group; giving examples.

(e) Summarising; putting related ideas together; restating suggestions after the group has discussed them.

(f) Consensus testing; sending up "trial balloons" to see if group is nearing a conclusion; checking with group to see how much agreement has been reached.[21]

They must also be able to apply these communication skills coupled with developed empathetic competence to perform the following objectives—social tasks listed by Schmuck and Schmuck:

(a) Encouraging; being friendly, warm and responsive to others; accepting others and their contributions; listening; showing regard for others by giving them an opportunity or recognition.

(b) Expressing group feelings; sensing feeling, mood, relationships within the group; sharing his own feelings with other members.

(c) Harmonising; attempting to reconcile disagreements; reducing tension through "pouring oil on troubled waters"; getting people to explore their differences.

(d) Compromising; offering to compromise his own position, ideas, or status; admitting error; disciplining himself to help maintain the group.

(e) Gate-keeping; seeing that others have a chance to speak; keeping the discussion a group discussion rather than a 1-, 2-, or 3-way conversation.

(f) Setting standards; expressing standards that will help group to achieve; applying standards in evaluating group functioning and production.[21]

## TEACHERS SHOULD BE TRAINED TO DIAGNOSE LEADERSHIP NEEDS

Individuals have radically different expectations of learning situations and predispositions to particular forms of behaviour in interpersonal relationships with the teachers. Their aggregation into groups, and their past experience with teachers as leaders, will influence their behaviour— they will exhibit various characteristics indicative of types of leadership needed. Thus, in the interests of their pupils, teachers need to have the ability to diagnose this need and to devise a programme to meet it within their own capabilities in the particular leadership role needed.

## TEACHERS SHOULD BE TRAINED TO PROVIDE APPROPRIATE LEADERSHIP

A myth of training courses is that a teacher cannot adopt a leadership role which is foreign to his natural self. This notion ignores the fact that teachers have been playing an unnatural role all along—and often one that violently interferes with their mental health—when they keep within the constraints of stereotype teacher roles. Further, leadership roles (for example autocratic or democratic) as appropriate for the classroom must operate within the constraints imposed by principles conducive to good mental health of both teacher and pupils. What is proposed, then, should not damage anyone's psyche. For example, if the class is in need of a more autocratic (perhaps dominating would be a better word) type of leadership, this needs to be exercised in terms of requiring compliance with rules, firmness of direction and a certain distance in interpersonal relations.

## REFERENCES

[1] B. MORRIS, "The Personal Foundations of Education", *Education*, New Zealand Department of Education, 1960, **9**, No. 6, pp. 162-64.

[2] R. S. ADAMS and B. J. BIDDLE, *Realities of Teaching*, Holt, Rinehart and Winston, New York, 1970, p. 86.

[3] See J. R. P. FRENCH and B. RAVEN, "The Bases of Social Power", in D. CARTWRIGHT (Ed.), *Studies in Social Power*, Institute for Social Research, Ann Arbor, 1959.

[4] R. A. Schmuck and P. A. Schmuck, *Group Processes in the Classroom*, W. C. Brown Co., Dubuque, 1971, p. 34.

[5] See N. L. Bossing, *Teaching in Secondary Schools*, Houghton Mifflin, Boston, 3rd Edition, 1952, pp. 523-27.

[6] D. P. Ausubel, *Ego Development and the Personality Disorders*, Grune and Stratton, New York, 1952, p. 152.

[7] K. Lewin, R. Lippitt and R. K. White, "Patterns of Aggressive Behaviour in Experimentally Created Social Climates", *Journal of Social Psychology*, 1939, **10**, pp. 271-99.

[8] A. Tannenbaum and W. H. Schmidt, "How to Choose a Leadership Pattern", in R. A. Sutermeister, *People and Productivity*, McGraw-Hill Book Co., New York, 1963.

[9] A. Uris, "How Good a Leader Are You?", in R. A. Sutermeister, *People and Productivity*, McGraw-Hill Book Co., New York, 1963.

[10] J. Dunham, "Appropriate Leadership Patterns", *Educational Research*, 1965, **7**, No. 2, pp. 123-24.

[11] N. A. Flanders, "Teacher Influence, Pupil Attitudes and Achievement Studies in Interaction Analysis", *University of Minnesota Final Report, Cooperative Research Project No. 397*, Office of Education, Department of Health, Education and Welfare, 1960.

[12] Adams and Biddle, op. cit., p. 41.

[13] Eric Berne, *Games People Play*, André Deutsch, London, 1966, p. 18.

[14] S. M. Jourard, *The Transparent Self*, Van Nostrand, New York, 1964, p. 26.

[15] W. Waller, *The Sociology of Teaching*, John Wiley & Sons, New York, 1932.

[16] Dunham, op. cit., p. 125.

[17] R. L. Kahn and C. F. Cannell, *The Dynamics of Interviewing*, John Wiley & Sons, New York, 1957, p. vi.

[18] F. P. Biestek, *The Casework Relationship*, Unwin University Books, London, 1957, p. 25.

[19] Dunham, op. cit., p. 123.

[20] Schmuck and Schmuck, op. cit., p. 121.

[21] Ibid., p. 42.

# CHAPTER 10

# A Broad Look at the Additional Conditions of Learning

Part II began with a discussion of Gagné's conditions of learning but concluded that they had limited usefulness in the classroom because they did not allow for concepts that were not rigorously definable. It was suggested that Gagné had been too concerned with the conceptual *product* and that a consideration of conceptual *processes* might be a source of insight. Chapters 5 to 8, therefore, were an exploration of basic processes. Chapter 9 took a rather broad look at interpersonal relationships as these seemed to have a substantial influence upon the efficient operation of basic processes.

Two additional conditions of learning were disclosed which can be described, in brief, as those which are required to allow for (1) probability factors in learning, and (2) the individuality of the learner.

In the following discussion the implications of these two additional conditions are outlined in terms of their general significance for planning and management.

## PROBABILITY FACTORS IN LEARNING: SIGNIFICANCE FOR PLANNING

Probability factors are an integral part of generalisation and communication and hence are significant in all complex learning.

### PROBABILITY IN GENERALISATION

As learning involving generalisation depends upon probability judgments which are based on learned "inferential weightings", it follows that conditions must be contrived in the learning situation which facilitate their retrieval and application.

#### The Significance of the Sample

If the *sample* is adequately representative (a good *selection* and adequate *range*) and is organised to be presented in an *order* which exploits the inferential advantages of proceeding from the known to the unknown, conditions will exist which favour recall of significant probability resources and their most profitable application.

### Information is Needed on the Relationships between Ideas

Generalisation as a process focuses on the *relationships* between ideas: the better the sample in terms of its implicit network of relationships, the more likely it is that learned probabilities will influence cognition to a successful outcome. In order to set up conditions which exploit the learners' probability resources, the teacher needs information on the network of relationships between ideas inherent in the topic, and between the topic and the subject where more general ideas bear on the topic. The *topic analysis discipline* described in the next chapter is designed to provide this information. The assumption is that planning must start with a topic analysis and its explication of the relationships between ideas.

## PROBABILITY IN COMMUNICATION: VERBAL INSTRUCTIONS IN GENERALISATION

The most critical function of verbal instructions in "shaping" generalisation processes, relative to the exploitation of probability resources, lies in the communication of successive frames of reference. This is essential as the exploration of a complex sample frequently requires shifts in the frame of reference as different features of the sample are examined. Unless a teacher communicates these shifts, he is likely to "lose the pupils" so that retrieval and application of probability resources are fortuitous—and his pupils appear far less intelligent than they are.

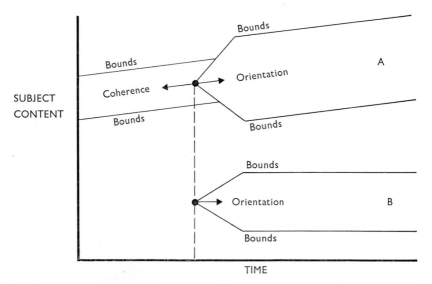

Figure 10.1: Interdependent use of statements of bounds, orientation and coherence in verbal instructions to increase efficiency of generalisation processes and in particular that of the retrieval and application of probability resources

## Communicating the Frame of Reference

Three kinds of statements must be used to cope with the contingencies of communicating the frame of reference: *bounds, orientation* and *coherence*. Figure 10.1 illustrates their relationship at a particular point in time (*x*) when the lesson development is conceived as a grappling with content through time.

Statements of *bounds* convey the limits or range of relevant thinking; *orientation* defines the particular viewpoint or procedural mode; and *coherence* facilitates retrieval of previous findings. In Figure 10.1 the teacher is shown as having choice A, changing the frame of reference by enlarging the bounds but retaining the same orientation, or shifting the frame of reference to B with new bounds and orientation. In both cases, statements of *coherence* would add to the efficiency of the communication.

## IMPLICATIONS WHEN CONCEPTS ARE NOT RIGOROUSLY DEFINABLE

### Selection of the Sample

In all preceding discussion of selection of the sample in generalisation, it has been assumed for the purpose of clarity that the *teacher* does the selecting because of his superior knowledge of the subject. Given information on the network of relationships between ideas implicit to the topic, he should be able to select a workable sample. However, this assumption ignores the difficulties, inherent in the creation of samples for generalisation, of achieving concepts which are not rigorously definable in terms of the subject as an ideational structure. The problem arises from the fact that such concepts must subsume idiosyncratic experience of the learner—we cannot ignore this aspect of the learner's individuality and of the communicability of concepts. The implication seems clear: the more a conceptual product of generalisation must subsume the idiosyncratic experience of the learner, the more its achievement depends upon *his* selection of the sample.

When selection of the sample is the prerogative of the learner there is even greater dependence on communication of verbal instructions, for the frame of reference must provide the means for a considerable degree of independent thinking. To achieve this the teacher must first provide a frame of reference which is credible to the learner in terms of his cognitive, affective and social resources. The teacher is faced, therefore, with the problem of estimating the probabilities that a given frame of reference will be not only understood by his pupils but will also be able to generate the kind of thinking needed for the achievement of his teaching objective. To illustrate this, imagine a class in a school close to the sea which has been set its most dreaded topic as an exercise in written expression—*A Day At The Beach*—in which they are expected to "show some imagination". Looking at their problem solely as one of cognition, their response as measured in terms of the typical product is to be overwhelmed by the amount of more or less relevant events. Their writing seldom shows any

L

sensibility; is usually a humdrum account along the lines: first I did this, then that. The theme provides no realistic frame of reference, is too broad to be relevant to the *personal* response to life which would be necessary for the imaginative response required. However, if the class had been given the same topic but asked to write on the theme *Odd Man Out*, it would have been provided with a frame of reference likely to evoke a personal response from members of the class. This frame of reference would also provide, implicitly, criteria for the selection of relevant experience. This experience must, of course, be organised in such a way that it conveys the meaning that the theme *Odd Man Out* has for each individual. The relevant events must therefore be organised into samples from which what are in effect sub-themes of the given theme are generalised. But the teacher's difficulties in estimating probabilities are illustrated by a few pupils in the particular class who, while able to understand the given theme, did not find it had relevance to their way of looking at life: it was not credible. They were unable to write on the theme even though motivated to do so under experimental conditions.

When, then, learning depends upon *the learner selecting the sample*, the major factor for a successful outcome is the teacher's ability to assess the probabilities associated with a particular frame of reference in relation to pupil resources and intended product. To improve the likelihood of his success, it seems obvious that the teacher must maintain communication with his pupils on all planes: cognitive, affective and social.

### Behavioural Objectives

The content of the sample is unpredictable, as is the outcome of the pupil's exploration of his self-selected sample. (This should be particularly apparent in topics involving aesthetics.) When, then, it is asserted that objectives should be in *behavioural* terms (that a terminal performance should be designated as a valid means by which to infer successful learning) and criteria such as those of Mager[1] are laid down for their evaluation, serious damage will be done to the integrity of a subject unless these criteria take account of the element of the unpredictable when the pupil is learning on the basis of self-selected samples. The significance of this and some suggested modifications to Mager's criteria will be discussed in Chapter 12.

## GENERAL SIGNIFICANCE FOR PLANNING

The need to differentiate the conditions of learning according to the type of conceptual product (which will be apparent from the topic analysis) means that planning must meet the particular conditions needed for each of the topic's major concepts. Accordingly, each major concept needs to become the focus of an organisational unit of the lesson which will allow its special conditions to be met. We shall call this basic unit of the lesson the *episode*—the planning of which relative to the range of appropriate strategies for particular conceptual products is discussed in Chapter 13.

## THE INDIVIDUALITY OF THE LEARNER: SIGNIFICANCE FOR PLANNING AND MANAGEMENT

If a teacher takes into account the individuality of the learner, he must conduct his transactions with his pupils so that he (1) establishes his *acceptance* of each individual, and (2) provides for the exercise and development of *autonomy*—in the sense of self-direction. The first of these conditions has been discussed at length in previous chapters; the second has two implications which warrant special consideration here.

### THE EXERCISE OF AUTONOMY REQUIRES KNOWLEDGE

The basic assumption is simple; if we really do want to promote intellectual development, we must provide pupils with the means to think independently—to exercise autonomy. To that end the following interdependent conditions are assumed to be essential.

1. The pupils must be provided with the knowledge to be self-directive, i.e., knowledge of:
   (a) the more important mental processes involved in classroom learning, and
   (b) the specialised vocabulary without which there can be little evaluation of the products of independent thinking, *either by the teacher or his pupil*.

2. Associated with knowledge of mental process and vocabulary, there also needs to be provision for the exercise of specific cognitive skills to alert the pupil to the significance of relevant mental processes so that he can apply his intelligence to the refinement of a particular skill more effectively.

3. When *understanding* is the aim, classroom learning needs to be pre-structured in the sense of planning the framework of verbal interaction in order to increase the probability that pupils can create their own understanding.

The disciplinary factor implicit to the above conditions has been found to be a necessary condition. In terms of Whitehead's three stages,[2] discipline contributes to the Stage of Precision in two ways: (1) by promoting the ability to be self-disciplining in exploiting the Stage of Discovery, and (2) by providing the external constraints necessary for a mastery of an established discipline. (The argument here is that a substantial part of formal learning is necessarily *reception learning*.)[3]

The words of G. F. Kennan from another context are pertinent:

> It is only through effort, through doing, through action—never through passive experience—that man grows creatively. It is only by volition and effort that he becomes fully aware of what he has in him of creativity and becomes capable of embodying it, of making it a part of himself, of communicating it to others.[4]

There is one further condition which is equally important.

4. The teacher must accept the discipline involved in stating his teaching goals in such a way that *he and his pupils* can evaluate *his* performance.

But *why* the requirement that the statement of objectives in terms of performance or behaviour is to permit evaluation of the teacher's performance? This is because the teacher is responsible for the product—his actions set up conditions and influence pupil performance. Traditionally, however, if a pupil fails to achieve in a lesson it is because of *his* inadequacy, and if he succeeds it is because of the teacher's skill. The case is overstated, of course, but there is a large element of truth in it as teachers have, on the whole, avoided scrutiny of their performance by shifting responsibility to the failing student. Can teachers afford to continue with this and still aspire to professional status? Surely not!

However, there is a further factor. If a teacher tells his pupils what is to be achieved, and the *measure* of that achievement, and accepts lack of pupil achievement as at least partly his responsibility, he is thereby establishing his credibility in the eyes of his pupils for *they have known all along of his responsibility* but have not been able to say anything because of their inferior position relative to authority. Such a teacher is truly a member of a classroom community in that he and his pupils can communicate more directly in the absence of the teacher's traditional barriers of defensiveness. (Pupils would still pass or fail, of course, but under conditions set up to test their ability to think independently *once they have been taught* to do so.)

## THE EXERCISE OF AUTONOMY REQUIRES MATURITY

If a pupil has marked immaturity of character, he cannot exercise that degree of self-direction in learning that is to be expected of his peers. The teacher must therefore give high priority to establishing the conditions necessary to promote his character development. This may even mean that his ordinary, but nominal, progress with the subject matter will have to be abandoned to make way for the requirements of a behavioural programme.

If a *school* were prepared to consider itself accountable for the character development of immature pupils, it might well withdraw them from ordinary classes for a special part-time programme with a teacher specialising in such work: "progress" with subjects being secondary. Either way the education of such pupils requires this priority.

## CONCLUDING NOTE

While it has been convenient so far to separate planning and management into independent categories, it will be apparent that while planning may and in practice usually does originate with the *subject*, the needs of the pupil may require planning to be *pupil*-centred. This occurs in the case where behavioural programming is necessary, but it must also occur when it is necessary to ensure that the pupils can act as partners in communication and when it is necessary for the teacher to teach how he is teaching, to develop cognitive skills, and to communicate with the class as a group on the plane of feeling.

When planning takes into account the individuality of the learner and the conditions implied by probability factors in learning (in addition to those proposed by Gagné), three interdependent areas of decision making must be involved: topic analysis, determination of behavioural objectives and episode design. These will comprise the topics of the chapters of Part III.

## REFERENCES

[1] R. F. MAGER, *Preparing Instructional Objectives*, Fearon Publishers, Palo Alto, 1962.

[2] A. N. WHITEHEAD, *The Aims of Education and Other Essays*, Williams and Norgate, London, 1932, p. 48.

[3] D. P. AUSUBEL, *The Psychology of Meaningful Verbal Learning*, Grune and Stratton, New York, 1963, pp. 15-21.

[4] G. F. KENNAN, "Democracy and the Student Left", *Dialogue*, 2, No. 2, U.S. Information Service, 1968, p. 16. Copyright © 1968 by George F. Kennan. From "Democracy and the Student Left", by George F. Kennan, published by Hutchinson and Company, Ltd. (London).

### PART III

# Principles of Method in Planning

These chapters develop the notion of planning as prestructuring the framework of verbal transactions. Three interdependent areas of decision making are described in the first three chapters: the topic analysis discipline (as a source of essential information); behavioural objectives (disciplined statements of goals); and episode design (the basic unit of the lesson).

The examples of episode design are chosen from subjects and topics to illustrate a range of strategies dictated by matters of conceptual rigour, or considerations of pupil readiness, or teacher preference.

The final two chapters illustrate the effects on planning (and, by implication, management) when planning is *subject-centred* as in the case of a lesson in mathematics, and when planning is necessarily *pupil-centred* in the case of creative writing.

---

### Teaching to a Plan

Though the planning of the following chapters is detailed, this does not imply slavish teaching to a plan, for anticipation of contingencies makes possible a greater flexibility of response as manifested, for instance, in greater sensitivity to pupil fumbles and perception of the state of readiness. However, not only must planning be regarded as *contingency* planning but also as secondary to the need to establish and maintain good conditions of learning in the domain of interpersonal relationships.

---

# CHAPTER 11

# Topic Analysis as a Discipline

Conditions which best facilitate learning require that a teacher know his subject in a much more disciplined way than was necessary for him to pass his examinations. As a learner he would have been conditioned to expect that a teacher would "pick up his fumble" when he attempted to communicate something imperfectly understood. He may even have answered his degree examination questions with anything that was more or less relevant in the frequently realised hope that he would get the benefit of the doubt. In preparing to teach a topic, however, he needs some check on the clarity of his own understanding—he cannot expect his pupils to make good the deficiencies in his understanding. Further, as has been shown, he needs certain information about the topic if he is to set up the conditions of learning.

The topic analysis discipline has been devised to meet these needs. As it is based on the assumption that a topic can be *structured*, it is necessary to look first at some of the implications of this idea before detailing the characteristics of the topic analysis itself.

## THE CONCEPT OF STRUCTURE

A topic is said to be structured when the interrelationships of its inherent ideas are systematically described as clearly and simply as the topic allows. Typically such statements of structure are diagrammed in the form of an hierarchical schema reflecting the fact that the more abstract an idea is, the greater the number of other ideas included in its meaning. The learning structure from Gagné[1] of Figure 3.3 is a typical illustration. The notion of structure can be applied to the subject as a whole, though for various reasons the structure cannot be expressed as a single integrated explication with the same rigour as a topic. Thus, presumably for reasons of philosophical difference, complexity, and advantage of varied frames of reference, the *Biological Sciences Study* authors identified "*seven* conceptual schemes describing modern biological thought and used these to pattern the content of the courses".[2] (My italics.)

## IMPLICATIONS OF DEGREE OF CONCEPTUAL RIGOUR

Subjects vary in the degree of rigour with which the great majority of their concepts are defined, hence not all teachers of comparable mastery in a subject will necessarily agree with a particular statement of structure, and this position is aggravated when different philosophical positions are adopted. Teachers of mathematics, a subject noted for its conceptual rigour, should be able to reach agreement on a statement of the structure of any particular topic, whereas teachers of English may be unable to agree on the statements of structure of many topics because of the idiosyncratic content in the connotation of significant concepts. Thus subjects must be considered as varying in the degree of uniformity to be expected in the structuring of their topics: the more rigorous the conceptual definition generally in the subject, the greater agreement on statements of structure; the less rigorous, the greater diversity. However, while mathematics and English may be considered conceptually in terms of their general characteristics as at either end of a continuum representing structural uniformity and diversity, there will be particular topics in English, such as in grammar, where the structural uniformity of mathematics is possible.

## IMPLICATIONS OF CONCEPT FORMATION

The nature of concept formation is such that the curriculum as a whole needs to be organised "spirally" as well as "lineally".

1. The *lineal* curriculum is organised on the idea of logical inclusiveness—of one concept being included in the meaning of another—in order to facilitate the preparation of sequences to meet Gagné's condition that lower-level capabilities must be established first.

2. *The spiral curriculum* recognises and exploits the following features of the process of concept formation.

   (a) Most concepts develop through a progressive modification of their specifications as more classes of experience within the range of the concept are mastered.

   (b) *Some* concepts are strategically more important than others in achieving the goal of subject mastery because *even with limited specifications they can facilitate generalisation of the concepts they subsume.*

A *spiral* curriculum, following Bruner,[3] is thus one in which these more important concepts, which we can consider *generic*, to use Bruner's term, are "revisited" a number of times during schooling. These encounters are planned to occur at times when the generic concept can best facilitate the formation of other concepts. By exploiting this process a

| English | Geography | Science |
|---|---|---|
| style criticism discrimination sensibility | interdependence cultural appraisal    of resources change | energy transformations equilibrium ecosystem bonding |

Figure 11.1: Generic concepts

teacher makes the opportunity to refine progressively its originally very general specifications.

Figure 11.1 gives examples of generic concepts in various subjects.

### The Hierarchical Interpretation of Structure is of Limited Utility

If a teacher has in mind the sequence in which the subsidiary ideas of a topic need to be taught, a knowledge of the hierarchical organisation is essential. It is necessary, of course, on the grounds that lower level concepts of principles must be regarded as prerequisite capabilities for those of higher levels, as Gagné has established so clearly.

But in teaching we must give priority to understanding, which is a function of that aspect of knowledge expressed as "network of relationships". The typical schematic statement of a "learning structure" conveys relationships only to the extent of subsumption, that is, that this concept is contained within the meaning of that concept and so on. Many syllabuses which claim to be structured may even list concepts in such a way that those of quite remarkable difference in generality appear on the same rank, for example, *ecosystem* and *cell*, as in one official biology syllabus. Such statements of structure are of little value if a "specific" curriculum is in mind because the generic concept which is *at a lower level of abstraction than its true place in the structure* requires a very sensitive discrimination between the relationships inherent in its specification. Faulty selection of the modified specifications and necessary restatement in simpler language can mean that it will be too abstract and/or no longer valid.

Further, it is found in practice that, though teachers may know their subject well enough to structure a topic in the form of the conventional schema (in the sense of inclusiveness), serious inadequacies in their mastery of the topic may remain undetected at great cost to their pupils. This is because, in order to set up the conditions necessary for pupils to generalise these ideas, it is necessary for the teacher himself to be able to verbalise the relationships between ideas. If he cannot do this he cannot be intelligent in the selection of a sample, his management of its exploration and subsequent generalisation from it.

### The Structure must be Explanatory

Conventional schema for the description of learning structures do not provide sufficient information to cover essential conditions of learning. To obtain this information, an explanatory mode of exposition must be adopted which focuses on ideas and the relationships between them. It seems, then, that a topic analysis must combine the advantages of an hierarchical organisation with explanatory exposition.

## CHARACTERISTICS OF THE TOPIC ANALYSIS DISCIPLINE

Given that any subject must be capable of being organised into hierarchies of ideas, that is, can be structured: *a topic analysis is a detailed explication of the more significant ideas and their relationships that are inherent in the topic while being consistent with its relationships with its context of higher order ideas.*

PART I: IDEA CONTEXT

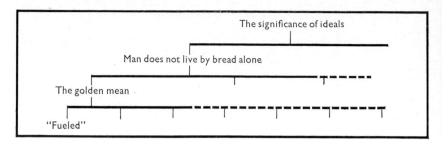

2. *The Poem "Fueled"*

> Fueled
> by a million
> man-made
> wings of fire—
> the rocket tore a tunnel
> through the sky—
> and everybody cheered.
>
> Fueled
> only by a thought from God—
> the seedling
> urged its way
> through the thickness of black—
> and as it pierced
> the heavy ceiling of the soil
> and launched itself
> up into outer space—
> no
> one
> even
> clapped.
>
> Marcie Hans*

PART II: DETAILED EXPLICATION OF TOPIC

A. Technical progress can mean cultural stagnation or even regression.

   I. Man can be so impressed by his own creations that he loses his sense of proportion.

      1. Even small space achievements can cause man to lose sight of the marvels of the day-to-day world of nature.

Figure 11.2: Topic analysis of the poem "Fueled"

* From *Save Me a Slice of Moon,* © 1965 by Marcie Hans. Reprinted by permission of Harcourt Brace Jovanovich, Inc.

## PART I: IDEA CONTEXT

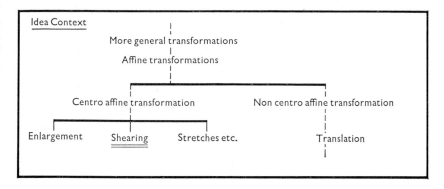

## PART II: DETAILED EXPLICATION OF TOPIC

A. The image of a geometrical figure under shearing can be inferred from a set of information about the points constituting the figure and their images by exploiting invariant properties of this transformation.

   I. The set of information must necessarily permit the inference of the position of the axis, the direction of the shear, and the amount of the shear—all or some of which information, and other derived invariants (including that of straightness), will enable the image to be completed.

     1. Since the axis Is, by definition, a set of invariant points, each point and its image coincide: the image of any point on the axis is thus known.

      (a) The Image of a point on the axis being thus known, it is possible, exploiting the invariance of straightness, to draw the image of a line, given only one point on it, its image, and the point of intersection of the line with the axis.

     2. As the direction of the shear is parallel to the axis, the line joining a point and its image is always parallel to the axis, and this relationship can be used to determine the position of the image of a point relative to the axis.

     3. The length of the line segment joining a point and its image is proportional to the distance from the axis; this, together with the knowledge of the direction of the shear, can be exploited to determine the image of any point in the plane.

      (a) In the case where the distance from the axis is constant, such as on a line parallel to the axis, the length of line segments in this direction is invariant under shearing.

        (i) Because a pair of parallel lines cuts off equal intercepts on lines parallel to the axis, and these Intercepts are thus invariant under shearing, *any* pair of parallel lines must remain parallel under this transformation.

Figure 11.3: Topic analysis of "shearing" In transformation geometry

Note: While the emphasis in the following exposition is upon the analysis of a *subject*, the discipline applies equally to cognitive and affective skills *which must also be analysed to provide the kind of information needed for their effective teaching.*

Figures 11.2 and 11.3 are contrasting examples of topic analysis from English and mathematics to be discussed below in terms of the characteristics of the discipline.

At this stage it is necessary to anticipate two frequent misconceptions.

1. The order of presentation in a topic analysis is not necessarily the order in which ideas will be taught. This is decided in terms of *readiness* and teacher preferences for particular strategies (see Chapter 13).
2. The fact that a teacher has done a topic analysis on (say) the poem "Fueled" does not mean that this interpretation will be *imposed* on his class. Rather, having accepted the discipline of clarifying his own thinking he will be better prepared to see the significance of different ideas. The important principle governing selection of strategy and management of such a lesson is that *where there can be diversity of topic analyses because of lack of conceptual rigour in the topic, the individuality of the pupil response must be recognised in the planning and management.*

The topic analysis discipline has two parts: Part I is the idea context, and Part II is the detailed explication of the topic. Each must comply with the following three requirements: (1) ideas must be expressed in a single sentence, (2) they must be written with an explanatory frame of reference, and (3) they must be organised hierarchically and in a conventional format.

Note: The three requirements above are applied less rigorously to the idea context to allow for such contingencies as inadequacy of overall subject structure and economy of time when the structure is well established. The idea contexts of the topic analyses in Figures 11.2 and 11.3 have been given in note form for reasons of economy of space. For training exercises, however, the idea context would be expected to meet all three requirements—becoming, in effect, a "skeleton" topic analysis displaying relationships between the topic and its more significant higher level ideas.

## PART I: IDEA CONTEXT

Each topic analysis requires that the idea context be identified and the topic clearly related to it. The notion of an idea context is a simple extension of the idea of *structure*, for if a topic is to be justified as worthwhile, it must itself be part of a hierarchy of ideas. The most significant of these higher order ideas must then be allowed to influence the explication of the topic itself for otherwise its full meaning cannot be developed. In the case of *energy transformations* from the idea context of photosynthesis below (p. 160), the topic analysis would obviously highlight a substantially different set of ideas and relationships between them.

The following mathematics illustration makes the same point but also implies the radically different lesson content which usually results.

A teacher is required to teach the Theorem of Pythagoras which states that in the right angle triangle, the square on the hypotenuse is equal to the sum of the squares on the other two sides. However, he may approach this topic with a much more general idea in mind which can be expressed as: the relationship between the square on the side opposite a particular angle and the sum of the square on the other two sides *when the angle varies between acute and obtuse*. With this viewpoint, the Theorem of Pythagoras is seen merely as a special case, that is, the case when the sum of the squares on the other two sides is *equal*, rather than *greater than* (as in the case when the angle is obtuse) or *less than* (when the angle is acute). The subsequent topic analysis must be different from that of the one based on the Theorem of Pythagoras alone. The lesson will also be different and with substantially different learning outcomes.

The reader can establish the point for himself by establishing a different idea context for the poem "Fueled" and writing a new topic analysis.

---

### WARNING
The topic analysis discipline has been found to be best understood by those who attempt it—learning by doing.

---

### Uniformity and Diversity of Idea Contexts
The greater the conceptual rigour of a subject, the greater the uniformity of idea contexts for a given topic; the less the conceptual rigour, the greater the diversity. Thus in the teaching of the topic "*agreement in English*" the idea contexts produced by a number of teachers of comparable competence would display a marked degree of uniformity, whereas those for the topic "*appreciation of English*" would show, in contrast, considerable diversity. The reason, of course, lies in the differences in the communicability of the two concepts.

Thus, in the case of the poem "Fueled" there are probably a number of equally valid but substantially different idea contexts because of the amount of idiosyncratic content in the concepts which may be called upon to convey the meaning of the poem.

On the other hand mathematicians could be expected to produce idea contexts for *shearing* which would display substantial uniformity.

### PART II: DETAILED EXPLICATION OF TOPIC
The detailed explication of the topic must comply strictly with the three requirements mentioned above and detailed below.

## A. Express Ideas in Single Sentences

This is mandatory in order to:

(a) "force" identification of the higher-order or subsuming idea, in the case that a particular idea is not being seen as part of an ideational structure.

A teacher may, for instance, say that he is going to teach *photosynthesis* which one teacher described as:

> a process of using energy, carbon dioxide, water and chlorophyll to build up food for the green plant. Energy is obtained from sunlight. The food manufactured is in the form of simple sugars.

But he failed to identify the higher-order idea of *energy transformations*, awareness of which would lead to an explanation of photosynthesis which could have far greater value for understanding it as a process and its significance for living things in general.

(b) "force" the explicit statement of relationships as distinct from that of implication.

When an idea is not clear in the mind we frequently resort to the practice of stating a number of ideas that are more or less relevant. In the example of photosynthesis above, facing up to the requirement of one sentence would have highlighted the lack of relatedness between the expressed ideas and hence the need for some higher-order idea to provide it.

## B. Write the Topic Analysis with an Explanatory Frame of Reference

"Explanatory" means the description of *relationships* as distinct from description which enumerates characteristics. The topic analysis discipline is a special form of explanatory exposition. Unlike the *lineal* and *hyperbolic* forms, it does not assume understanding of the pattern of relationships but rather seeks to make them explicit. Further, unlike the *detailed* form, it is not concerned with sequential exposition but with *hierarchical ordering of explanatory principles*. Put another way, *it is a systematic explication of the most general explanatory principle relevant to a topic*. However, because of the requirement that the topic analysis be presented in hierarchical form (see below) the explanatory content tends to get "weaker" (more descriptive) as lower levels of generality are reached, that is, as ideas become more specific.

### EXPLANATORY "STRENGTH" AND "WEAKNESS"

The notions of explanatory strength and weakness arise from the need to differentiate between the effectiveness of explanations in terms of:

1. the extent to which relationships holding between the elements of a situation are made explicit, and

2. the need to ensure that the highest relevant explanatory principle is identified and its relationships with the concepts it subsumes are made explicit. (This requirement is related to that of the topic analysis expressed in hierarchical order—see below.)

Exposition can therefore be considered as locatable on a descriptive explanatory continuum as illustrated below.

1. *Abseiling* is a method of descending a cliff using a rope.
   This is *descriptive* in that it merely enumerates some of the characteristics of abseiling. There is no relationship between them.

2. *Abseiling* (a method of descending a cliff using a rope) exploits the forces of gravity and friction.
   This is *weakly* explanatory in that gravity and friction are significant forces in the execution of this skill, but the particular manner of exploitation in relation to descent of the cliff is not made clear. On the other hand in the third attempt, the explanatory content is stronger.

3. *Abseiling* (a method of descending a cliff using a rope) exploits opposed forces of gravity and friction in such a way as to execute a series of controlled falls.

In this third attempt, the explanatory content is stronger because the relationship between ideas is *detailed*, that is:

1. The forces of gravity and friction are now related, i.e., they are *opposed* in a special way over a period of time—so their special application in the case of abseiling is now more specific.
2. The inclusion of *controlled falls* in the statement and the relationship of the forces of gravity and friction to it is a necessary recognition of the *significance of this concept in the hierarchical ordering of concepts relevant to an understanding of abseiling.*

---

*Exercise:* Which of the following is the "stronger" explanation?
1. A crisis in the world population arises when food production is unable to meet the demand.
2. The essential cause of the world population crisis is a population growth increasing faster than growth in food production.

*Answer:*
The sentence whose first letter comes later in the alphabet.

---

However, it should be noted that some topics have very little explanatory content because:

1. they are from poorly designed syllabuses concerned more with factual content than understanding—for example, descriptive biology which is now being superseded; or
2. they are validly descriptive topics in that they are part of much larger topics, the explanatory content of which is apparent in the idea context.

DISTINGUISHING BETWEEN DESCRIPTIVE AND EXPLANATORY EXPOSITION
The following examples are given to highlight the differences between descriptive and explanatory exposition.
1. Is the following *descriptive* or *explanatory*?

In our mass society any tendencies toward individuality or nonconformity are frowned upon or actively discouraged.

M

This is descriptive. Two ideas are mentioned but no detail of a relationship between them: a certain feature of society is said to exist but its *relationship* to past or present society is not stated. For instance, what are its functional relationships with mass society? If it had read:

> Our mass society depends for its existence upon the repression of tendencies toward individuality

the functional relationship would be explicit and the statement explanatory.

2. Is the following *descriptive* or *explanatory?*

> Climatic and other factors of the Canterbury Plains have been utilised and assessed by man. (Topic: Mixed Farming on the Canterbury Plains.)

This is again descriptive. A certain condition is said to exist but nothing about, for example, the *reasons* for its existence. If it had been written in either of the following ways it would be explanatory:

(a) The features of the mixed farming distinctive to the Canterbury Plains arose from the need to renew pastures frequently.
(b) Mixed farming on the Canterbury Plains exploits the need to renew pastures frequently.

## C. Organise the whole Topic Analysis hierarchically and in a Conventional Format

Because the topic analysis is intended as a systematic explication of the most general idea implicit to the topic, it is necessary that its organisation be rigorously hierarchical—a requirement which follows from the notion of *structure*. The formal exposition of the topic analysis is in effect a taxonomy of the conceptual content of the topic. As a result of this and the requirement of an *explanatory* viewpoint, a topic analysis which meets the requirements of hierarchical order displays the following characteristics.

1. There is one subsuming statement (designated the "A" statement).
2. All that is below the "A" statement is an explication of its significant ideas.
3. All ideas indicated by a particular notation are of the same rank, i.e., of the same order of generality.
4. All ideas below a particular idea of a particular level are in fact an explication of that idea—that is, the hierarchical requirement applies throughout the analysis.
5. Numbers do not indicate serial order unless this is stated explicitly.

To facilitate communication and evaluation of a topic analysis, it is presented in the following conventional format:

A
    I
        1
            (a)
                i

where "A" represents the highest level of generality (there is thus never a B or C); I the next level (there is often a II or III on the same rank); 1 the next level—and so on. Thus in Figure 11.4, the schema on the left would be presented as on the right.

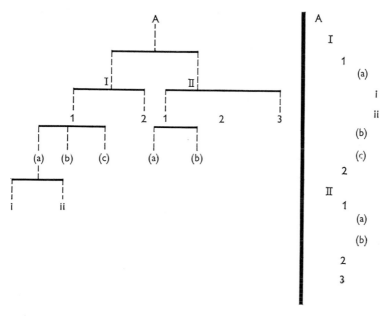

Figure 11.4: Schema and presentation of topic analysis

## EVALUATION OF A TOPIC ANALYSIS

The following schedule has been developed to assist the evaluation of topic analyses.

I  *Idea Context*
1. Is the idea context valid from viewpoint of the structure of the subject?
   (a) Are the ideas listed the most *significant*, relative to an understanding of this topic?
   (b) Are the implied relationships between ideas valid?
2. Is the topic's relationship to the idea context clear?

II  *Single Sentence*
1. Is each idea assigned a specific rank in the hierarchy?
2. Are all the ideas in sentences?

III  *Explanatory Viewpoint*
1. Is the "A" statement valid in terms of subject structure/context as usually understood?
2. Is the "A" statement explanatory and in sufficient degree for the topic?
3. Are the propositions "below" the "A" statement explanatory?

4. Are the relationships between ranks made explicit?

*Note:*

(a) Sometimes the ideas at the first level below the "A" are more explanatory than the "A". If so it is possible that the "A" belongs to the idea context.

(b) As lower levels of the hierarchy are reached, propositions tend to become more descriptive and more so in some subjects than others.

IV *Hierarchical Organisation*

1. What is the main proposition of the "A"?
2. Is the proposition of the "A" the most significant proposition in relation to the idea context?
3. Is this main proposition explicated below?
4. Does the "A" subsume *all* that is below?
5. Is the content of the "A" *adequately* explicated?
6. Is the explication rigorously hierarchial?

    (a) Are all propositions of a given level of *equal* rank?

    (b) Are all such propositions adequately subsumed?

    (c) Are the relationships which exist between ranks made explicit?

---

*Exercise:* Evaluate the following topic analysis (which is given without an idea context) assuming the "A" statement to be valid.

A. Roman social organisation was successful because it had the family as a stable base.

1. The patriarchal nature of the family contributed to its stability.
2. Because the family unit extended beyond the blood relationship, society was complex.
3. The community was united through the heads of the family units.
4. A rigid class structure ensured the stability of the Roman hierarchy.
5. Positions of responsibility were the prerogative of the nobility.

---

#### KEY EVALUATION QUESTIONS FOR THE ABOVE EXERCISE

1. Are the key ideas of the "A" statement explicated in 1-5?
2. Are 1-5 all of the same rank?
3. Are 1-5 subsumed by the ideas of the "A" statement?

#### PART OF A MODEL EVALUATION

1. There are two propositions implicit in the "A" statement: that the *civilisation was successful,* and that this was *due to the stable base* provided by the family unit.

(a) None of 1-5 are an explication of the first proposition.

(b) 1 and 3 are part of an explication of the second proposition.

2. 1-5 are not of the same rank. For example, 4 is a generalisation embracing the whole of Roman society, i.e. is much broader than *the family as a stable base.*

3. Not all statements 1-5 are subsumed by "A", for example, 5 is not implicit to the "A".

The general conclusion is that there are serious faults—the topic analysis excerpt lacks hierarchical rigour. These inadequacies mean that 1-5 *do not provide an adequate sample of ideas from which to generalise "A".*

*Note:* A complete evaluation would cover the weaknesses in explanatory exposition, i.e., that relationships between ideas are not made explicit.

---

Further examples are given in Appendices C, D and E.

---

## REFERENCES

[1] R. M. GAGNÉ, *The Conditions of Learning*, Holt, Rinehart and Winston, New York, 2nd Edition, 1970, p. 263.

[2] P. D. HURD, *New Directions in Teaching Secondary School Science*, Rand McNally and Co., 1969, p. 79.

[3] J. S. BRUNER, *The Process of Education*, Harvard University Press, Boston, 1961, p. 52.

# CHAPTER 12

# Behavioural Objectives:
# A Disciplined Statement of Goals

## INTRODUCTION

Given that the topic analysis of a subject provides a sufficient basis to prestructure the framework of verbal transactions, its *use* will depend upon the specification of goals. At present there is considerable controversy on the specification of goals which are in the form of what are called *behavioural or instructional objectives*, but the position adopted here is that teachers who are professionally accountable must accept, with Mager, "goal specification as an unavoidable, practical problem requiring hard-headed solutions".[1]

Such specification is, of course, of a terminal performance or behaviour from which it will be possible to infer validly that learning has taken place during a given episode lesson, or unit of instruction. Thus, as Popham puts it:

> an instructional objective describes a future behavioural response in the learner's repertoire that the instructor plans to promote. . . . The essential quality of an . . . instructional objective is that the response that reflects the satisfactory attainment of the objective is thoroughly explicated.[2]

Leading proponents of behavioural objectives are uncompromising on the need to specify instructional objectives. For instance, in reaction to the claim that it is more difficult to identify measurable pupil behaviours in fine arts and the humanities, Popham states:

> Sure it's tough. Yet, because it is difficult in certain subject fields to identify measurable pupil behaviours, those subject specialists should not be allowed to escape this responsibility. Teachers in the fields of art and music often claim that it is next to impossible to identify acceptable works of art in precise terms, but they do it all the time. In instance after instance the art teacher does make a judgment regarding the acceptability of pupil-produced artwork. What the art teacher is reluctant to do is put his evaluative criteria on the line. He has such criteria. He must have to make his judgments. But he is loath to describe them in terms that anyone can see.

Any English teacher, for example, will tell you how difficult it is to make a valid judgment of a pupil's essay response. Yet criteria lurk whenever this teacher does make a judgment, and these criteria must be made explicit. No one who really understands education has ever argued that instruction is a simple task.[3]

Perhaps the most contentious issue between proponents of behavioural objectives (such as Mager,[4] Gagné,[5] Glaser,[6] Popham,[7] Bloom et al.,[8] Gerlach and Ely[9]) and their critics is that of their demand for *operationalism* and *specificity* to ensure communicability and replicability of objectives. Briefly, operationalism refers to the defining of constructs such as intelligence, comprehension, appreciation and understanding (which lack precision in their usual definition through the use of synonyms) by the *operations* one can perform to measure them. As Gerlach and Ely put it:

> Operationally, then, "intelligence" might be defined as "a person's score resulting from the administration of the California Test of Mental Maturity." The shift in meaning between the two statements that follow illustrates the key difference between the definitions. "A person received a score of 130 on the California Test of Mental Maturity because *he is intelligent*." In this non-operational statement, the descriptive concept "intelligent" is being used as an explanatory word; that is, intelligence is given as the reason for the performance. "A person is considered intelligent because he *received a score* of 130 on the California Test of Mental Maturity." In this operational statement, "intelligent," a descriptive word, is being defined by the person's performance on a given task. While one may disagree, no latitude is left for different interpretations of the term. Thus, whenever the psychologist uses the word "intelligence" in his work, the reader has been apprised of the exact and limited meaning that can be properly attached to the construct. Further, anyone wishing to replicate the psychologist's findings can exactly reproduce the construct in other samples because the method for measuring it has been spelled out, and can be followed like a recipe in a cookbook.[10]

Specificity refers to the detail required in explication to meet the criteria for a good behavioural objective.

Both, in the view of the critics, damage the integrity of the subject, and also the teaching and learning processes. Raths, for instance, is reported by McAshan as saying that:

> the specificity now being demanded by curriculum workers and teachers in the writing of behavioural objectives runs contrary to their values of humanism and intellectualism.[11]

Eisner is more explicit. He suggests that *expressive objectives*, which he considers the type that teachers most frequently use, are the *outcomes* of an encounter or learning activity planned to personalise learning.

> An expressive objective describes an educational encounter. It identifies a situation in which children are to work, a problem with which they are to cope, a task in which they are to engage; but it does not specify what from that encounter, situation, problem or task they are to learn. An expressive objective provides both the teacher and the student with an invitation to explore, defer, or focus

on issues that are of peculiar interest or import to the inquirer. An expressive objective is evocative rather than prescriptive.

The expressive objective is intended to serve as a theme around which skills and understandings learned earlier can be brought to bear, but through which those skills and understandings can be expanded, elaborated and made idiosyncratic. With an expressive objective what is desired is not homogeneity of response among students but diversity. In the expressive context the teacher hopes to provide a situation in which meanings become personalised and in which children produce products, both theoretical and qualitative, that are as diverse as themselves . . . .

Statements of expressive objectives might read:

1. To interpret the meaning of *Paradise Lost*.
2. To examine and appraise the significance of *The Old Man and The Sea*.
3. To develop a three-dimensional form through the use of wire and wood.
4. To visit the zoo and discuss what was of interest there.

What should be noted about such objectives is that they do not specify what the student is able to do after he engages in an educational activity, rather they identify the type of encounter he is to have.[12]

As Eisner explains, he sees instructional or behavioural objectives and expressive objectives as performing complementary functions: "instructional objectives emphasise the acquisition of the known; while expressive objectives its elaboration, modification and, at times, the production of the utterly new".[13] It is not surprising that Eisner cites Whitehead's "rhythm of the curriculum"[14] and goes on to suggest provision for an alternation of the two kinds of objectives in the curriculum.

The view developed in previous chapters of this book is that planning must not only be *subject*-centred but also *pupil*-centred if it is to avoid damage both to the integrity of the subject and to the development of independence in the learner. This view rests on the grounds that if basic processes of mind are to be exploited to the full in learning, provision must be made in teaching for a *necessary* autonomy of the learner. Thus, for instance, generalisation which is basic to the achievement of new ideas depends on *samples* selected by teacher or pupil according to the communicability of the constituent concepts. Thus the autonomy of the learner has a significance which is ignored by those on the behavioural objective bandwagon and which justifies the concern of critics such as Eisner[15]—though on rather different grounds. The difference is important. Eisner justifies, in effect, the need for *expressive* objectives on the grounds that the learner needs to exercise autonomy *once he has the tools*, if he is eventually to educate himself (in the fullest meaning of *educate*), whereas the view developed here is that the exercise of autonomy is also a necessary condition for the *acquisition* of the tools.

Eisner's viewpoint is, of course, compatible with that of the *progressivists* of the '30s and '40s and has the same weakness in practice: it all too easily promotes *busywork* which is the inevitable characteristic of learning encounters undertaken without the requisite skills. Popham reacts typically to the implicit danger:

> I am afraid that too many teachers would have an excessive proportion of instructional activities related to unassessable objectives . . . it's easier for a teacher to go into a classroom and ask the question "What shall we do?" than to ask the question "What will the learners become?" I'm afraid that even if a teacher accepted a dual emphasis on instructional activities related to operationally stated objectives and activities related to unassessable objectives, the proportion of the latter would quickly predominate.[16]

Eisner's claim that "expressive objectives are the type that teachers most frequently use" is, if true, more a justification of Popham's fears than a reason for adopting expressive objectives. Nevertheless Eisner makes an important point: there must be a place for expressive objectives if the "rhythm of the curriculum" is to be maintained. Further, we just cannot afford to exclude from our lessons all that cannot be defined operationally (we would be left with the bare bones of our culture); nor do we know enough of complex learning to warrant committing ourselves to such an exclusive doctrine as enunciated by Popham. A compromise seems necessary, for surely *professional* training designed to develop specific competencies should allay Popham's fears. We need, then, some way:

1. to differentiate between objectives appropriate for teacher *or* pupil selection of samples in generalisation, and
2. to provide for the need to maintain the "rhythm of the curriculum" by allowing for what Eisner calls the "expressive objective".

If examples of *expressive* objectives are examined in the context of processes of generalisation, it will be apparent that they merely represent *different degrees of freedom* to select and explore samples and determine the direction of cognition. The greater such freedom, of course, the greater the pupil autonomy. But even in the learning of complex ideas which are *operationally* definable there must be *some degree of freedom* to utilise learned probability judgments or the learning is more difficult than it should be. The *instructional* objective (as expressed by Popham) and the *expressive* objective (proposed by Eisner) may therefore *represent only poles of a teaching objectives' continuum*—which we may as well continue to call behavioural objectives.

## THE GENERALLY ACCEPTED CHARACTERISTICS OF GOOD BEHAVIOURAL OBJECTIVES

The following characteristics of a good behavioural objective are adapted from Mager[17] and Gerlach and Ely[18]:

1. It must specify it is the *learner* who performs the behaviour or produces the product.
2. It states an observable *behaviour or product* from which it is possible to infer that learning has occurred.

3. It states the *conditions* under which the behaviour or product is to occur.
4. It states the criteria of an *acceptable performance*.

---

*Examples*

The following are examples of behavioural objectives which have the above characteristics.

*Example 1*

On completion of this section of the course the trainee will reassemble the Bren [light machine gun] while blindfolded, in a time of two minutes, the parts to be mixed and placed a few inches apart after blindfolding and located within easy reach.

*Outline Analysis*

I *Learner specified:*
the trainee

II *Observable behaviour or product:*
reassemble the Bren (light machine gun)

III *Conditions under which the behaviour or product is to occur:*
the parts to be mixed and placed a few inches apart and located within easy reach in front of him after blindfolding

IV *Criterion of an acceptable performance:*
in a time of two minutes

*Example 2*

The pupils will understand the theme of the poem (Marcie Hans: "Fueled") so that they can identify it in four of six examples in a set of eight public issues.

*Outline Analysis*

I *Learner specified:*
the pupils

II *Observable behaviour or product:*
identify

III *Conditions under which the behaviour or product is to occur:*
six examples in a set of eight public issues (identification)

IV *Criteria of an acceptable performance:*
four of six

---

## CRITERIA OF A BEHAVIOURAL OBJECTIVE

### The Learner Specified

This first characteristic is essential, given acceptance that it is the *learner* who must create his own understanding. The important thing here is for the teacher to ensure that he does not confound his own actions and those of his pupils—perhaps because of a tacit assumption that the *teacher's* actions necessarily result in learning. The following statements of teacher actions do not indicate what the *learner* is to do or be able to do.

1. Create a picture of life in Japan so that pupils have a background for the lesson on *Japan as a trading nation*.

2. Give the class understanding of the redox reaction.
3. Analyse the structure of the novel as a genre so that pupils will have a basis for criticism.

## A Learner Behaviour or Product

Assuming that the teacher does not read minds, he needs an *observable* behaviour or product from which to infer that learning has occurred.

### AN OBSERVABLE BEHAVIOUR

Something the learner does in his mind is only known to us indirectly— a cause of widely different interpretations. This point is made by comparing the two lists below from the viewpoint of having to identify behaviour from the evidence likely to be available. List A comprises behaviours which are only *indirectly* observable; List B comprises behaviours which are *directly* observable.

| *List A* | *List B* | |
| --- | --- | --- |
| to know | to write | to find |
| to understand | to recite | to gather |
| to understand really | to identify | to make |
| to appreciate | to differentiate | to specify |
| to appreciate fully | to solve | to relate |
| to grasp the significance of | to construct | to justify |
| to enjoy | to list | to estimate |
| to believe | to compare | to infer |
| to have faith in | to contrast | to deduce |
| | to explain | to predict |

We can only infer the existence of the behaviours in List A from outward signs which are open to a variety of interpretations. For instance, the glint in Frank's eye *may* signal understanding but it could be embarrassment, grit in the eye or even tears at the teacher's ineptitude. List B on the other hand gives behaviours which are not only observable but open to fewer interpretations. It should be noted that many observable behaviours would not be suitable as terminal performances because they also have too many interpretations. For example, the following:

> To develop an appreciation of Bach's "Brandenburg Concerto No. 2" so that the pupils *sigh in ecstasy.*

To sigh in ecstasy is an observable performance but it is also a behaviour open to other interpretations, such as boredom, sadness, pain, joy and asthma.

### AN OBSERVABLE PRODUCT

The product of behaviour is frequently more significant as evidence of learning. In the case of the reassembly of the light machine gun in the first example of behavioural objectives, the trainee will have to *select* parts in certain order and manipulate them in certain ways to achieve the product—the reassembled weapon. Again, in the case of the selection of examples of the theme of the poem in the second illustration above, the act of selecting is a learner behaviour, but the product of that behaviour is of greater significance.

## Conditions must be Stated

The inference that learning has occurred depends not only on observing a significant behaviour or product but also on observing it under specified conditions. If this is not done, the objective may be accepted as fulfilled by any of several levels of competence. For example, the reassembly of the light machine gun could be done with full vision and with the use of a manual and unlimited time; without a manual and in limited time but with the parts systematically laid out; and so on. Each would represent a different level of competence. Stating the conditions for the behaviour or product ensures that a particular level of behavioural competence is in mind prior to the learning, and that this alone will demonstrate that learning has taken place. Mager gives a helpful list of examples of statements of conditions which can usefully *precede* the statement of the behaviour or product:

> Given a problem of the following type . . .
> Given a list . . .
> Given any reference of the learners' choice . . .
> Given a matrix of intercorrelations . . .
> Given a standard set of tools . . .
> Given a properly functioning . . .
> Without the aid of references . . .
> Without the use of a slide rule . . .
> Without the aid of tools . . .[19]

The following example uses one of the above and then specifies further conditions. Identify the behaviour or product and all the conditions.

> *Example*
> Without the aid of tools, locate the source of an intermittent fault in the high tension lead made by a loosely fitting coil connection.
> *Answer:* The behaviour/product is *locate*; all the rest specifies conditions.

## A Standard of Performance

If we are to exercise objectivity in the inference of learning, some standard by which the quality of the performance can be assessed often needs to be stated. In the case of the reassembly of the light machine gun, the *time* element is validly considered an important measure of quality so the criterion of performance is a reassembly *completed in two minutes*. In the second example the quality of the performance is given by the criterion *four of six* of the examples in the set of eight. However, by itself this may in fact *not* be an adequate standard of performance because relevant sets of examples of public issues may have a wide range of difficulty. The problem is the same as that of the teacher of mathematics who specifies he wants 80% of a set of ten problems solved. The solution is the same in both cases: the teacher must realise that each element in the set must be examined to ensure that it represents the intended level of difficulty and that it is a product from which it is valid to infer that the specified learning has taken place. (A detailed example from mathematics is given in Chapter 15.)

## A BEHAVIOURAL OBJECTIVES CONTINUUM

### THE APPROPRIATENESS CHECK

If, however, we accept that the instructional and expressive objectives represent only poles of a continuum (see page 169) then each behavioural objective has a place in this continuum according to the degree of rigour in the concepts to be mastered. But the behavioural objective can also be located in a second place—always towards the expressive objective pole of the continuum—in terms of the topic's place relative to the "rhythm of the curriculum". For instance, a topic may only involve operationally defined concepts, but, because prior capabilities have been established it may be structured at the teacher's preference in terms more of an *expressive* than *instructional* objective. This would then provide a legitimate opportunity for the exercise of a greater degree of autonomy.

The usual characteristics of behavioural objects must then be modified to conform to the conditions of learning. This can be effected in terms of an *appropriateness check* which serves to indicate the necessary modification of particular components. Having outlined the usual components of behavioural objectives, we must next detail the appropriateness check which puts the concept of behavioural objective in a more realistic perspective.

If the notion of a disciplined specification of objectives is to remain credible to class teachers, the usual criteria of behavioural objectives will need modification. This may be done in terms of a model in which

1. all behavioural objectives may be located upon a continuum ranging from *instructional objectives* at one pole to *expressive objectives* at the other. In this continuum instructional objectives represent the greatest degree of conformity with the behavioural objective criteria described above, and expressive objectives demonstrate the greatest degree of variation.

    The differences in degree of conformity with the four characteristics described above derive from the fact that the greater the degree of pupil autonomy, the less outcomes can be predicted. Thus an objective at the expressive objective pole of the continuum

    (a) would not contain a stated behaviour or product, but would instead have additional and compensatory *conditions* (see below), and

    (b) would not necessarily contain performance criteria but if it did the most valid criteria would be those nominated by the pupil.

2. each objective can be located in *two* places on the continuum:

    (a) the first is *mandatory*—it occupies its place by virtue of the communicability of the concepts which are involved in mastering the topic (the degree of conceptual rigour) and hence by the *degree of pupil freedom* to select and explore samples for generalisation and to direct cognition generally.

(b) the second is *discretionary*—it is located towards the expressive objective pole of the continuum from its mandatory position—as determined by teacher preference. The purpose of this discretionary type of objective is to provide for discovery learning of various degrees (and hence for the "rhythm of the curriculum") but is necessarily conditional upon prior capabilities having been established.

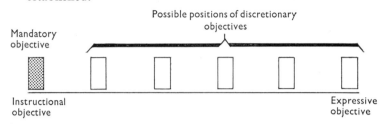

Figure 12.1: Mandatory position of a particular topic in mathematics and range of possible positions of discretionary objectives

In order to ensure that each behavioural objective measures up to the criteria appropriate for its place on the continuum (mandatory or discretionary) it must be checked against additional criteria. This we shall call an *appropriateness check*. Figure 12.2 below illustrates the two sets of criteria: (1) the four characteristics of a strictly-defined instructional objective as described above, and (2) the four categories of the appropriateness check. Satisfaction of these latter justify, in effect, the amount of variation that a particular behavioural objective may have from the four criteria of a strictly-defined instructional objective. The appropriateness check is discussed below.

## A. Which Objective?

Given the information on his topic that is supplied by a topic analysis, a teacher must then decide between a *mandatory* or *discretionary* behavioural objective.

### CRITERIA FOR MANDATORY OBJECTIVES

Objectives located at various points on the continuum are locatable in terms of the conceptual rigour of their topics as determined by examination of information contained in the topic analysis.

1. Those topics which involve concepts that are operationally definable as, for instance, in mathematics, will be towards the instructional objective end and must conform to four criteria described above: (1) learner behaviour; (2) behavioural or product outcome; (3) conditions; and (4) standard of performance.

2. Those topics which would be considered as belonging to aesthetics and feature a highly personal or idiosyncratic response would be towards the expressive objective pole of the continuum and

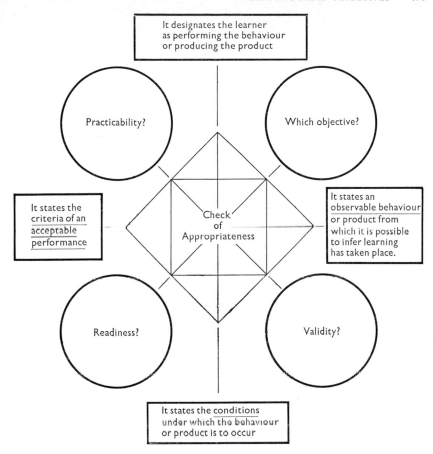

Figure 12.2: Behavioural objectives: characteristics and appropriateness check

(a) would only state the behavioural or product outcome in the most general terms—if at all; and

(b) would therefore not specify the conditions as a further definition of the behaviour or product, but would necessarily detail the "bounds" of the encounter. This would be only after due cognizance of the probabilities that the range of outcomes would show a profit on the investment of time and effort relative to the previously established capabilities and their presumably higher-level generalisation. Thus, for instance, to ask the pupils to

examine and appraise the significance of *The Old Man and The Sea* [Eisner's example above]

(i) designates that a learner has to do something; (ii) only *implies* a product; and (iii) does not detail the conditions under which the product will be produced, *but does set limits or bounds to the activity in designating that this encounter* with *The Old Man and The Sea* will be an examination and appraisal. However, unless the pupils in this case have a complex repertoire of skills or knowledge, the probabilities of "success" would be low as the "bounds" are so ill-defined that only the sophisticated student would be capable of creating an adequate frame of reference. The problem is analogous to that of the pupils asked to write on *A Day at the Beach*—discussed above—they do not have the means to structure the situation and can therefore only exercise autonomy at a low level of cognition.

Assuming that the pupils had an insufficient repertoire of skills to cope with the bounds set, the following instruction would increase the probability of a profitable outcome:

> Appraise the following statement in terms of your understanding of and feelings about *The Old Man and The Sea*: the old man *failed*!

Such a behavioural objective is, of course, closer to the instructional objective pole of the continuum than the first because of the greater constraints of the set bounds, but it still does not state the nature of the behavioural or product outcome.

Again, for pupils who were considered as not yet ready for even this degree of freedom, the behavioural objective might be written with even closer bounds:

> In our discussion of *The Old Man and The Sea* we agreed that he had failed yet we also noted that we felt "sympathetic". Account for this . . .

The success of an expressive objective is therefore in the profitability *for the learner* in the exercise of his autonomy; this will depend on adequacy of requisite skills and *bounds* to provide him with a frame of reference within his capacity. Its particular location will decide the degree of constraint to be set by the "bounds".

3. Those objectives which would be considered as towards the middle point of the continuum would be characterised by a topic analysis which included concepts of some degree of rigour in the sense of communicability so that its various alternatives could be identified within limits although the behavioural or product outcome had some degree of diversity. Thus the significant difference of the behavioural or product outcome would be a range of alternatives which could be specified or implied. In the case of the poem "Fueled" (see p. 156), therefore, it is necessary to amend the statement of the objective to meet this modification of the second criterion. It would now read:

> The pupils will understand the theme of the poem (Marcie Hans: "Fueled") so that they can identify it in a set of eight public issues at *their level of understanding*—two of each of the three levels of the topic analysis being represented in the set.
>
> (see page 213 for topic analysis)

In this case the alternatives which are envisaged are dictated by performance levels.

Thus the conditions and standard of performance are amended to allow for the autonomy of the learner, which in this case is considered likely to be satisfied in formulation(s) of the theme corresponding to one, two or three levels of the topic analysis.

For practical purposes it is convenient to restrict the number of places on the continuum and thus to be able to refer to Types 1, 2 and 3 as in Figure 12.3.

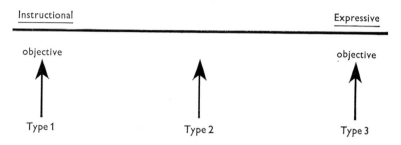

Figure 12.3: Behavioural objectives, continuum and location of Types 1, 2 and 3

Thus the example of topics in mathematics generally would be *Type 1*; the first example of *The Old Man and The Sea* given by Eisner would represent *Type 3*; and the example from the poem "Fueled", *Type 2*. The criteria for each type can be summarised as in Figure 12.4.

| BASIC CRITERIA OF BEHAVIOURAL OBJECTIVES | TYPE | | |
|---|---|---|---|
| | 1 | 2 | 3 |
| 1. Learner specified | √ | √ | √ |
| 2. Behavioural or product outcome | √ | Range of alternative behaviours or products | Only by implication |
| 3. Conditions | √ | √ plus "bounds" | Not specified but "bounds" set with rigour inversely proportional to readiness |
| 4. Criteria of performance standard | √ | Relaxed to suit different alternatives | NIL |

Figure 12.4: Criteria for three types of behavioural objectives

## CRITERIA FOR DISCRETIONARY OBJECTIVES

The criteria for a *discretionary* behavioural objective are necessarily those of the corresponding mandatory objective: Type 2 or Type 3.

N

However, a discretionary objective is not appropriate *unless* two requirements are met:

1. The pupils must be known to possess the resources to act independently in the proposed situation at a level which justifies the investment of time and energy for their stage of development.
2. The pupils must be at a stage in the development of the idea that *discovery* is necessary. In terms of Whitehead's three stages there are *two* occasions for this: the first, the Stage of *Romance* (relatively unsystematised and uninformed discovery), and the third, the Stage of *Generalisation* (when discovery is more systematic in that it is on the basis of knowledge).

Thus even in mathematics the *discretionary* behavioural objective may legitimately be Type 3 when it is the introductory stages of an idea for which there is nevertheless sufficient knowledge for at least unsystematised discovery—to be followed by Whitehead's Stage of *Precision*.

Finally, at the risk of being considered facetious, there is surely at times a place for the discretionary objective to be justified on the basis of "fun"?

## B. Validity

The ability to throw a ball is not demonstrated by the ability to kick it—it would not be a valid test. Before, then, a behaviour or product is chosen as a source of inference that learning has taken place, it must be checked against the following criteria to ensure its validity.

1. *Logical consistency with topic analysis.* This means that if the analysis of the topic indicates it has certain logical characteristics, the behaviour or product belong to the same logical category. If the teacher has done a topic analysis on addition he must not test it in terms of subtraction. Thus, if a teacher has the topic *metals* and *non-metals* to introduce to a junior class, the topic analysis would show that the *real* topic is one of *classification* so the behavioural or product outcome should involve *classification*. Again, if the topic is essentially one of understanding a concept, principle or theory, then the behaviour or product must involve thinking which demonstrates its effective use relative to readiness.

2. *Level of behaviour or product.* If a complex idea has just been met for the first time, its specifications may have to undergo considerable modification through further learning before it can cope with applications in any context (cf "spiral" curriculum). It is therefore important that the level of thinking required to achieve the behaviour or product be decided with this in mind. Thus, in terms of Bloom's taxonomy,[20] *evaluation* against internal criteria would probably not be suitable for a first behaviour or product whereas application probably would. The caution is necessary because the standard of performance set may be inappropriately high. Thus all too frequently a set of problems in mathematics has too many problems which require competencies extraneous to the idea to be tested.

Kibler *et al.*[21] have provided a useful guide to the level at which a behaviour or product is set in a table giving infinitives and direct objects for each category of Bloom's[20] and Krathwohl's[22] taxonomies. These are reproduced in Appendices A and B.

## C. Readiness

Essentially the concept of readiness means the learner has sufficient capability to exercise that degree of autonomy which is appropriate to the chosen type of behavioural objective. If, for instance, it is principle or rule learning, he must have mastered all the constituent concepts so that, in effect, he is on the preceding rung of the ladder. Similarly, he must possess the cognitive skills to produce the behaviour or product—if he does not have these skills, they must be taught first.

In class teaching, the above is the counsel of perfection—teachers necessarily have to compromise and do what is expedient because of numbers. However, it is one thing to do this after weighing the odds; it is another to ignore all consideration of readiness—for this is to be defeated at the outset.

## D. Practicability

A teacher should only do what is practicable in terms of resources of materials, time and effort as measured against the significance of the topic in the curriculum or the personal development of the pupils in terms of considerations of socialisation (affective and social skills). In the case of curriculum significance, thoroughly-mastered generic ideas *save* learning and thus time. In the case of socialisation, some development may improve class climate and motivation and save the teacher from developing ulcers or beating his wife and children.

## REFERENCES

[1] R. F. MAGER, *Preparing Instructional Objectives*, Fearon Publishers, Palo Alto, 1962, p. v.

[2] W. J. POPHAM and E. I. BAKER, *Systematic Instruction*, Prentice-Hall, Englewood Cliffs, 1970, p. 21.

[3] W. J. POPHAM *et al.*, *Instructional Objectives*, (AERA Monograph 3), © by Rand McNally and Co., Chicago, 1969, pp. 49-50.

[4] MAGER, op. cit.

[5] R. M. GAGNÉ, *The Conditions of Learning*, Holt, Rinehart and Winston, New York, 2nd Edition, 1970.

[6] R. GLASER, *Teaching Machines and Programmed Learning II*, Department of Audio Visual Instruction, National Education Association of the U.S.A., 1965.

[7] POPHAM *et al.*, op. cit.

[8] B. S. BLOOM *et al.*, *Handbook on Formative and Summative Evaluation of Student Learning*, McGraw-Hill, New York, 1971.

[9] V. S. GERLACH and D. P. ELY, *Teaching and Media: A Systematic Approach*, Prentice-Hall, Englewood Cliffs, 1971.

[10] Ibid., p. 49.

[11] H. H. McASHAN, *Writing Behavioural Objectives*, Harper and Row, New York, 1970, p. 6.

[12] ELIOT W. EISNER, "Instructional and Expressive Educational Objectives: Their Formulation and Use in Curriculum", in W. J. Popham *et al.*, op. cit., © 1969 by Rand McNally and Company, Chicago, p. 15.

[13] Ibid., p. 17.

[14] A. N. WHITEHEAD, *The Aims of Education and Other Essays*, Williams and Norgate Ltd., London, 1932, p. 48.

[15] EISNER, op. cit., pp. 1-18.

[16] POPHAM *et al.*, op. cit., p. 134.

[17] MAGER, op. cit.

[18] GERLACH and ELY, op. cit., p. 49.

[19] MAGER, op. cit., p. 26.

[20] B. S. BLOOM (Ed.) *et al.*, *Taxonomy of Educational Objectives—the Classification of Educational Goals, Handbook I: the Cognitive Domain*, David McKay, New York, 1956.

[21] R. J. KIBLER *et al.*, *Behavioural Objectives and Instruction*, Allyn and Bacon, Boston, 1970, p. 180.

[22] D. R. KRATHWOHL *et al.*, *Taxonomy of Educational Objectives—the Classification of Educational Goals, Handbook II: the Affective Domain*, David McKay, New York, 1964.

## RECOMMENDED READING

GERLACH, V. S. and ELY, D. P., *Teaching and Media: A Systematic Approach*, Prentice-Hall, Englewood Cliffs, 1971.

KIBLER, R. J., BARKER, L. L. and MILES, D. T., *Behavioural Objectives and Instruction*, Allyn and Bacon Inc., Boston, 1970.

MAGER, R. F., *Preparing Instructional Objectives*, Fearon Publishers, Palo Alto, 1962 (recommended as a very useful introduction to the writing of behavioural objectives).

## RECOMMENDED RESOURCE BOOKS

BLOOM, B. S. (Ed.), ENGLEHART, M. D., FURST, E. J., HILL, W. H. and KRATHWOHL, D. R., *A Taxonomy of Educational Objectives: Handbook I: the Cognitive Domain*, Longmans, Green Co., New York, 1956.

BLOOM, B. S., HASTINGS, J. B. and MADAMS, G. F., *Handbook on Formative and Summative Evaluation of Student Learning*, McGraw-Hill, New York, 1971.

KRATHWOHL, D. R., BLOOM, B. S. and MASIA, B., *A Taxonomy of Educational Objectives: Handbook II, the Affective Domain*, David McKay, New York, 1964.

SANDERS, N. M., *Classroom Questions*, Harper and Row, New York, 1966.

CHAPTER 13

# *Prestructuring the Framework*
# *of Verbal Transactions:*
# *I. Episode Design*

For the sake of clarity this introductory discussion will be concerned with
the mastery of the subject through the creation of conditions which
facilitate *conceptual* processes, on the assumption that the principles
underlying *skills* learning can be fairly readily abstracted. Further, the
episode, as the organisational unit of the lesson, will be the focal point of
planning. However, the relationship of episode to lesson must be kept in
mind throughout although it will not be illustrated until Chapter 14.
First, a lesson is considered to comprise a logically coherent set of episodes
—and so may range from one episode to the more usual three (one each
for *introduction, development* and *conclusion*), to say four or five where
those beyond two form the development. As each part of a lesson has a
distinctive function, its episodes must be designed accordingly.

1. The introduction must be designed to establish the credibility of the
   major frame of reference for the lesson (readiness and motivation).
2. The development must establish and manage the conditions of learning.
3. The conclusion must evaluate the teaching, i.e., show that learning
   has taken place.

While it is necessary to talk as if the general characteristics of episodes
are as above, their design to perform a particular function in a lesson
must allow for the incorporation of special features, or variation of the
general criteria. Finally, it must be emphasised that planning, as discussed
below, is concerned only with prestructuring the *framework* of verbal
transactions; it is not concerned with routine or other "housekeeping"
matters.

## THE DESIGN OF PARTICULAR EPISODES
MAJOR CONSTRAINTS ON DESIGN

The design of any particular lesson or constituent episode must conform
to broad specifications which are determined after examination of the
structure of the topic and the conditions necessary to master it, given a

particular state of readiness. The primary concerns and direction of this decision making are outlined in the flow diagram of Figure 13.1 and are discussed below.

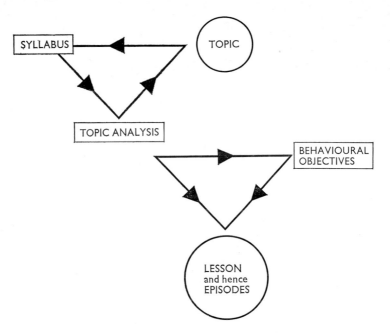

Figure 13.1: Flow diagram of decision making in the planning episodes of lessons

### Topic and Syllabus

First it is necessary to locate the topic in the syllabus in terms of its relationships to higher level ideas. If a topic cannot be located in such a *structured* syllabus it may mean that the *real* topic is not apparent. This is because many syllabuses have been organised *historically*, so that many topics have been accorded an importance which is not warranted relative to mastering the topic. For example, the topic of metals and non-metals in elementary science is really, on analysis, only a particular example of the general problem of *classification* in science; the lesson has more value in terms of transfer if structured accordingly. Alternatively, a topic may be trivial and so better grouped with other topics or simply not taught at all.

### Topic Analysis

The topic analysis is the first step of planning in order to obtain the necessary information about relationships and, by implication, the criteria for selection of relevant and significant facts for the *samples*. It should be noted that topic analysis is time-consuming at first, so that initially one's time is most profitably invested in the more important ideas of the syllabus;

on this basis at least a loosely structured network of relationships is available for planning purposes. The content of the topic analysis sets limits to the choice of behavioural objectives and is a source of information on the range and significance of the ideas in samples necessary to achieve particular ideas. Thus the content of topic analysis influences design indirectly through the behavioural objective, and directly through determination of the content of particular episodes.

## Behavioural Objective

The type of *mandatory* behavioural objective must next be determined relative to the structural rigour exhibited in the topic analysis, or a substitute *discretionary* objective decided if this is preferred and found appropriate. The choice of a particular type of behavioural objective imposes certain restraints upon design of the lesson. For example, a Type II requires a design which permits *alternative* outcomes whereas Type I nominates a single outcome. Again, Type III permits a wide range of outcomes but requires careful specification of "bounds" if it is to be productive.

## SELECTION OF TYPE OF DESIGN

The design of a particular lesson must therefore be restricted to a limited number of options because of the priorities to be accorded the topic analysis and behavioural objective. Further constraints must be accepted before even a *type* of design may be chosen, for the type of behavioural objective (in relation to the cyclic pattern of learning) limits strategy options even more. As quoted previously (see page 49), Whitehead suggested that though learning was cyclic it could be considered as passing through three stages in each cycle: (1) Romance, (2) Precision, and (3) Generalisation. As the salient characteristic of both the stages of Romance and Generalisation is *discovery* in the sense of self-direction of learning, these stages will be referred to as Stage I Discovery and Stage III Discovery respectively, in order to highlight their significance for the exercise of autonomy in learning.

Figure 13.2 illustrates the range of strategy options available for a particular type of behavioural objective when these three stages of the cyclic development of learning are given the priority they deserve.

## Strategies of Stage I Learning (Discovery)

Stage I is essentially an exploration of the topic by the learner on the basis of his already-existing but presumably unsystematised knowledge. As such it is open to behavioural objectives of Type II (see p. 177) because of the range of possible outcomes, and to Type III if undertaken for *fun*. The typical strategy of this stage is represented by [1] in Figure 13.2, the characteristics of which will be discussed below with those of the other strategies. However, some lessons and episodes may start with the intuitive discovery of this stage but proceed to Stage II—(precision) learning of behavioural objectives of Types I or II. These strategies are represented by [7] in Figure 13.2.

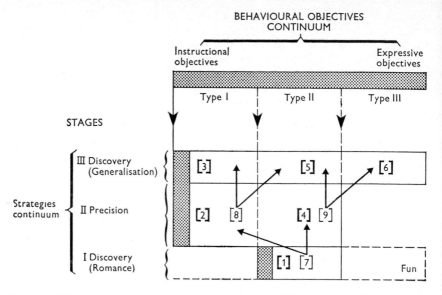

Figure 13.2: Strategies continuum in terms of: (1) behavioural objectives continuum and (2) Whitehead's three stages in the cyclic development of learning. (The Arabic numerals represent episode types—discussed below.)

## Strategies of Stage II Learning (Precision)

Stage II, in terms of Whitehead's proposal of cyclic development of learning, is primarily a coordination of the discoveries of the preceding stage of intuitive discovery.[1] However, in Ausubel's terms it has the characteristics of *reception* learning[2] in that the teacher *gives* information and ideas commensurate with the pupils' ability to incorporate them into already existing networks of ideas. The two viewpoints will be seen as complementary if it is kept in mind that they are both primarily concerned with the understanding of ideas. Strategies compatible with behavioural objectives of Types I and II are possible at this stage, but not Type III because of the degree of learner autonomy necessary for Type III. The typical strategy of Type I is represented by [2] and that of Type II by [4] in Figure 13.2. The numbers [8] and [9] represent the composite strategies of this stage which exhibit the characteristics of both Stages II and III.

## Strategies of Stage III Learning (Discovery)

This is Whitehead's stage of *Generalisation*;[1] it is primarily *discovery* but unlike Stage I is based on systematised and adequate knowledge. As such it is open to the behavioural objectives of Types I, II and III; typical strategies are represented by the numbers [3], [5] and [6].

## CONSTRAINTS ON THE SELECTION OF EPISODE STRUCTURE

Given that the strategy selected will have its general characteristics determined by the chosen behavioural objective type and learning stage, the *general structure* of a particular episode can then be decided in terms of the generalisation continuum of Figure 13.3. The *specifics* of the structure will be determined from consideration of conditions which facilitate concept and principle learning tested in the check list below.

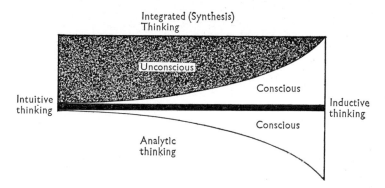

Figure 13.3: Generalisation continuum

## Appropriate Characteristics for Strategies

### STAGE I LEARNING (DISCOVERY)

As this type of discovery learning is primarily *intuitive*, the characteristics of its generalisation must place it towards the *intuitive* pole of the continuum of Figure 13.3. The better informed the learner, the closer this strategy will be towards the inductive pole and generalisation characterised by *analytic* thinking. In the case of a composite strategy such as [7] in Figure 13.2, the lesson or episode design must allow for the needs of Stage II Learning and for the transition to it (discussed below).

### STAGE II LEARNING (PRECISION)

This stage is characterised by analytic and integrative thinking and thus its generalisation processes are located towards the inductive pole of Figure 13.3. Necessarily, the strategies compatible with behavioural objectives of Type I, [2] and [8] of Figure 13.2, involve generalisation located closer to the inductive pole than that of Type II, [4] and [9].

### STAGE III LEARNING (DISCOVERY)

This learning, characterised by discovery on the basis of adequate information (whether for behavioural objectives Types I, II or III), may thus feature generalisation from any point in the continuum. This is permissible under the constraints implicit to the type of behavioural objective. Thus Type I allows least freedom because of its designated outcome and Type III allows greatest freedom because it lacks a designated outcome.

## THE STRUCTURE OF STRATEGIES RELATED TO GENERALITY

Ideally the conceptual content of an episode is explicated in a topic analysis. To achieve the particular conceptual goal of the episode it is therefore necessary to explore the ideas below it in the hierarchy, for these comprise the set of ideas of its most significant sample. However, a topic analysis is not always sufficiently explicated, so the ideas of the sample must be inferred from the proposition expressing the conceptual goal. For example, given the following proposition from a topic analysis on the *Economy of the West Coast of New Zealand*[3] (see Appendix C):

> I. Continued heavy dependence upon exhaustible natural resources rather than diversification of the economy has led to a substantial reduction in regional income following a decreased market for coal and timber.

and assuming no further explication in the topic analysis, the following could be inferred as significant ideas of the sample.

1. Relative to other sources of income, Westland *was* in the past heavily dependent upon natural resources.

2. Other provinces
    (a) have since diversified their economies over the period of time under review;
    (b) now earn relatively less from the exploitation of natural resources.

3. In terms of amount of income, Westland's relative dependence on natural resources remains.

4. The market for coal and timber has decreased.

5. Regional income has decreased.
    (Factual material would therefore be needed from the Census on Occupations, value of productivity of primary and secondary occupations over the chosen period of time.)

These, of course, are not arranged hierarchically; but should be because of the variation in intrinsic difficulty relative to the reading of relevant tables. However, assuming that each proposition is treated as of equal rank, the set could be coded in terms of the assumed level of generality implicit to the questions to be devised to achieve them. Thus if $q$ is used for the 5 questions of the sample and $Q$ for the question to achieve the generalisation, the structure of *this* episode could be represented by:

$$q$$
$$q$$
$$q$$
$$q$$
$$q$$
$$Q$$

thus indicating the two levels of generalisation by use of upper and lower case letters and two different columns. But episodes may be more complex than this—especially when the sample must be recognised as containing ideas of different levels of generality. The convention illustrated in Figure 13.4 is sufficient to cope with most situations:

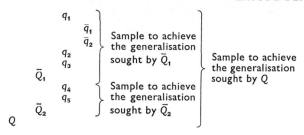

Figure 13.4: Conventional code to represent levels of generality implicit to questions of an episode, where $\bar{q}$, $q$, $\bar{Q}$, $Q$ represent questions requiring an increasingly higher order of generality

## The Nine Basic Strategies

With the above code it is now possible to illustrate a possible structure for each of the nine basic strategies appropriate for different stages of learning and types of behavioural objective. Figure 13.5 illustrates strategies [1]-[6] along with various alternatives. Strategies [7]-[9] are discussed below.

| STRATEGY NO. (Figure 13.2) | STAGE I LEARNING (DISCOVERY) | | | |
|---|---|---|---|---|
| [1] | $Q^{INT}$ (where the use of questions to get an *intuitive* response is indicated by the superscript *INT*.) | | | |
| | STAGE II LEARNING (PRECISION) | | | |
| | Integrative | | Analytic | |
| [2] | (A) $\quad q$ $\quad q$ $\quad q$ $\bar{Q}$ | (B) $\quad q$ $\quad q$ $\bar{Q}$ | (C) $S^I$ $q$ $\bar{q}$ $\bar{q}$ $q$ $\bar{q}$ $\bar{q}$ | (D) $S^I$ $Q$ $q$ $q$ $q$ $Q$ $q$ |
| [4] | | $q$ $q$ $q$ $\bar{Q}$ $Q$ | Note: where $S^I$ states the given generalisation | $q$ $q$ $q$ |
| | STAGE III LEARNING (GENERALISATION) | | | |
| [3] [5] [6] | $Q^{IND}$ (where the use of a question to get an *inductive* response is indicated by the superscript *IND*.) | | | |

Figure 13.5: The structure of strategies appropriate for each stage of learning and type of behavioural objective, described in terms of level of generalisation implicit to the sequence of questions

Though Types [2] and [4] strategies may be called either *integrative* or *analytic*, they must be understood to be so only on the basis that the name gives the organisational priority allocated to that particular mode of thinking. This priority is *necessarily* complemented by thinking of the other mode because of the nature of the generalisation processes.

It should be noted that the illustrations of strategies [2] and [4] of Figure 13.5 merely *represent* the possibilities. For example, the first example of the *integrative* thinking version might have six ($q$) and that of the first analytic example three ($q$) and no ($\bar{q}$). However, the *direction* of the thinking in terms of *level* of generalisation must remain as given. In the case of the second example of the analytic strategy therefore, the strategy would involve the following sequence:

1. Giving a statement of the proposition ($S^I$).
2. Asking for an inference at the next (lower) level of generality, ($Q$).
3. Then exploring the answer to that systematically in three successive ($q$)'s . . . and so on.

### Composite Strategies

The composite strategies are simply an addition of the higher-level strategy to the lower following the use of appropriate statements of orientation, coherence, and bounds as a frame of reference. While the particular form these statements will take will depend upon the stage of learning, the statement of a changed frame of reference *must* be given.

#### CONVENTIONAL CODE FOR STATEMENTS USED IN PRESTRUCTURING VERBAL TRANSACTIONS

The code used to indicate the main types of statements used in the question set of an episode is as follows:

$$S^I \qquad \text{Statement of information}$$
$$S^O \qquad \text{Statement of orientation}$$
$$S^C \qquad \text{Statement of coherence}$$
$$S^B \qquad \text{Statement of bounds}$$
$$S^{EM} \qquad \text{Statement of explanatory model}$$

#### COMPOSITE STATEMENTS

Each of the above can be used in association with other statements for specific purposes, of which stating the *frame of reference* is the most important.

$$S^{O/B} \qquad \text{Statement of frame of reference.}$$

$$\left.\begin{array}{l} S^C \\ S^{O/B} \end{array}\right\} \quad \text{Statements indicating a change in the frame of reference.}$$

When a statement is designed to perform several functions the *primary* function is indicated first. For example $S^{C/B}$ is a statement which performs the function of facilitating coherence and setting bounds, giving greater priority to coherence.

---

*Statements and questions*
The success of the teacher is critically dependent upon his ability to communicate an initial frame of reference and any subsequent changes that are necessary.

Intrinsically good questions are frequently unprofitable because the frame of reference is a matter of conjecture. The teacher must remember that until the learner is thoroughly familiar with a subject area, *he lacks knowledge of probability necessary to create the requisite frames of reference.*

A good question ordinarily requires a frame of reference. This may be in the form $S^{O/B}$ immediately preceding the question; or may be understood to govern the thinking of a set of succeeding questions; or may simply be a $S^B$ before the question with the $S^O$ preceding the set.

---

## CHECK LIST FOR EPISODE DESIGN

Part A below briefly summarises the sequence of decisions on design which has been discussed. Part B of the check list is provided as a reminder of the more important features of the basic processes which are not incorporated in the principles of episode design already covered, but which need to be reviewed constantly when considering the details of episodes and the lesson plan as a whole.

*PART A*
I    Where is the topic in a *structured* syllabus?
II   Topic analysis?
III  Behavioural objective?
IV   Strategy options?
V    Episode design options?

*PART B*
I    1. Is the sample adequate factually and conceptually in terms of:
        (a) relevance and significance,
        (b) range,
        (c) sequence relative to probability?
     2. (a) Is there adequate exploration of the sample in terms of provision for perception of the more significant ideas and the relationships between them?
        (b) Is there opportunity to verbalise
             i. relevance,
             ii. significance,
             iii. probability judgments?
     3. Is there adequate variety in terms of:
        (a) communication media,
        (b) perturbation of feedback through at least accommodation to the interpolation of an event likely to be perceived initially as incompatible?
     4. Is there adequate support for generalisation?
        (a) Are the following types of statements properly used in the approach to, and exploration of, the sample for pupils at this stage of readiness and with these cognitive, affective and social resources?
             i. Orientation
             ii. Coherence
             iii. Bounds

      iv. Frame of reference
      v. Information
      vi. Explanatory model (such as analogy)
      vii. Advance organiser
  (b) Are the questions devised with the learner's capacity for abstract thinking in mind?
      i. Are the steps from concrete to abstract appropriate (in terms of difficulty for *these* learners)?
      ii. Is the *known* sufficiently explored to provide a sufficient basis for exploration of the unknown?

II  Should there be provision for an episode designed to develop specific cognitive, affective or social skills as a prerequisite for the learning of a subsequent episode?
1. Basic mental processes. (see page 113)
2. Higher mental processes.[4]

III  Should there be provision for an episode on some topic of the theme that we should *teach how we are teaching*?
1. Communication processes?
2. Management processes?

## GENERAL CHARACTERISTICS OF EPISODES

In common with the lesson as a whole, the episode has an introduction, development and conclusion.

### Introduction

While there are many devices proposed in methods books to achieve motivation as a characteristic of a good introduction, in terms of pre-structuring verbal transactions the introduction must communicate a frame of reference, which may be a change from a preceding frame of reference. Further, in order to ensure that proper care is given to matters of readiness, more specifically that prequisite capabilities are known, the introduction of an episode will frequently contain a readiness section in which the learners are asked to identify instances of significant concepts *and to verbalise their grounds for identification.* This is to ensure that the concepts *are* known and to *make knowledge of probability accessible in the mind, ready for the new learning to follow.*

### Development

The development of all episodes is structured according to the design principle of the chosen strategy and modified where necessary to incorporate special features selected from the check list.

### Conclusion

Like the lesson as a whole, this episode has a behavioural objective which should be achieved in the conclusion. There may be, however, differences in rigour which are forced on the teacher because of the necessity to economise with time.

    One of the greatest temptations a teacher faces under pressure of time is to accept one pupil response as indicative of the understanding of the class. The alternative has usually been assumed to be a time-consuming written response. However, the following procedure is a more satisfactory solution.

Provided that the teacher has established trust and knowledge of the technique, here is a suitable alternative.

1. The teacher receives the pupil's correct response *non-committally*, that is without the usual verbal and non-verbal cues of acceptance and confirmation of its being correct. However the pupils are expected to play *their* role by communicating non-verbally whether they understand or not.

2. If these non-verbal signals indicate that many do not understand, the teacher interpolates an exploratory discussion designed to highlight the areas of difficulty. Thus he may turn to the pupil who has given the correct answer (still without any indication of its correctness) and ask him to justify it *in terms of the sample*. This should then be followed by a request for other viewpoints and similar justifications and general discussion with cross-talk (pupil to pupil) a major feature. Given that the discussion is directed initially towards the highlighting of difference relative to the inferences made in exploration of the sample, the teacher can then introduce a supplementary episode to make good any deficiencies that cannot be resolved in the discussion.

3. When the non-verbal signals indicate *general* understanding, the teacher thereupon introduces the *confirmation* part of the episode in which the pupils have to identify novel instances of the concept and verbalise their justification. This stage can now be covered on the basis of a show of hands to indicate support for a particular aspect of the justification. The confidence a teacher may have in the show of hands will have been established by responses during the previous stages.

   The behavioural objective for the episode may thus be considered as achieved in terms of a judgment of the class participation in the confirmation segment of the conclusion. Thus a behavioural objective for an episode may indicate a certain generalisation to be achieved under conditions of *class discussion* and to a standard implicit in the general confirmation technique described above. Such a modification, however, is only acceptable if the teacher's control of the discussion is through a competent use of appropriate statements, especially bounds, and if the class has the opportunity to evaluate the inferences made in the exploration of the sample and any generalisations from it.

## EXAMPLES OF EPISODES

The examples which follow illustrate a selection of strategies from several of the subjects of the school curriculum. The topics have been chosen as representative of those of everyday teaching; the designs are within the competence of anyone with adequate grasp of basic principles.

The first example from chemistry is given in more detail because the basic principles illustrated are common to all topics for which this example's behavioural objective-type strategies are appropriate. It should be noted that planning on the basis of strategies [2] and [4] of Stage II Learning (Precision) is the most profitable in terms of flexibility and teacher readiness to cope with difficulties. Thus, if a teacher has at hand the preparation of [2] and [4] of Stage II Learning (Precision), he will be adequately prepared to assist if pupils have difficulty with espiodes designed according to strategies [3] and [5] of Stage III Learning (Discovery).

## CHEMISTRY

### Redox Reactions

*Note:* Only sufficient detail is given of the topic analysis and introductory and concluding episodes as is necessary for understanding the elaborated episode of the development.

1. Topic Analysis
    Part I

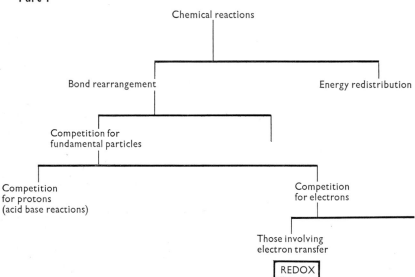

Part II
A. The characteristics of redox reactions depend upon the direction of transfer of electrons between the chemical species which is itself determined by the relative attraction the species have for these electrons.
    I   The substance that shows the greatest attraction for electrons (the electron acceptor) is known, for now outmoded reasons of causality, as the *oxidising agent*.
    II  The chemical species with the least attraction for electrons becomes the electron donor or *reducing agent*.

Figure 13.6: Topic analysis of redox reactions

## 1. Topic Analysis

### Part I

The weakness of this form of idea context is that the coordinating and explanatory principle of chemical equilibrium is not identified. If ideas were in sentences this principle would be needed to make explicit the relationships between the two highest levels of this idea context. This would have implications for the explication of lower level ideas.

### Part II

AI and AII are only adequate as notes for this, as they only partially illustrate the relationship between *characteristics* mentioned in A. The acceptance or rejection of electrons needs explication.

o

2. Behavioural Objective (Type I)

The pupils are (1) to give a general explanation of the redox reaction in terms of the atomic model (see A of topic analysis) and (2) to demonstrate their understanding by describing in words the electron transfer in each of the following redox reactions (not met during the lesson):

(1) $Ca + \frac{1}{2}O_2 \longrightarrow CaO$

(2) $2Na + \frac{1}{2}O_2 \longrightarrow Na_2O$

(3) $HgO \longrightarrow Hg + \frac{1}{2}O_2$

(4) $MgCl_2 \xrightarrow[\text{current}]{\text{electric}} Mg + Cl_2$

(5) $CuCl_2 \text{ Soln} \xrightarrow[\text{current}]{\text{electric}} Cu + Cl_2$

(6) $Cu + Cl_2 \longrightarrow CuCl_2$

Introduction

$S^O$    (1) Over the past year we have done work on burning and other related reactions ... today ... take a fresh look ... and attempt to explain them *in terms of modern theories.*

(2) I am going to demonstrate one of these reactions so that we can refresh our memories of its characteristics.

$S^B$    (Demonstration of magnesium burning in air and oxygen.)

$Q_1$    Can you describe what is happening in this reaction?

$q_1$    What is the name of the original substances?

$q_2$    What has happened to them?

$q_3$    What is the name of the substance formed?

$q_4$    What is the significance of this name as a description of the preceding chemical reaction?

$q_5$    How did we know that oxygen was added to the magnesium? (Increase in weight.)

$\bar{q}_1$    What evidence did we have?

Behavioural Objective

      1. Adequate for a Type I objective when used with a strategy of Type [4] in the development for a topic of this degree of difficulty, i.e., the formulation of an explanatory principle and its use to *interpret* the symbols of the *given* redox reactions.

      2. A class judged to be capable of higher-level thinking could be given a set containing non-instances of redox reactions and be asked to justify in each case acceptance or rejection of each as an instance.

Introduction

$S^o$        Communication of the special viewpoint of this lesson, and *implication* that present understanding may be inadequate.

$S^D$        A statement of bounds; all questions which follow relate to what was observed in the reaction.

    $Q_1$        As this is revision, a fairly open question to get range of answers which will indicate how readily earlier work can be recalled.

      $q_1$-$q_9$        Simple recall but quiz of this nature ensures systematic coverage of essentials and improves its accessibility for all pupils in subsequent development of topic.

      $\bar{q}_1$-$\bar{q}_3$        Interpolated as part of a concurrent theme of *consciousness of processes* of scientific thinking.

$\bar{q}_2$        Is this sufficient evidence to reach this conclusion?

$\bar{q}_3$        How should we refer to our conclusion so that we indicate this probability?

$q_6$        What was the special name for reactions of this type where oxygen was added to a substance?

$Q_2$        How then can we now describe what is happening in this reaction?

$S^{o/c}$        We can now look at the *complete* reaction for so far we have only looked at it from *one* viewpoint—that of the *gain* of oxygen.

$q_7$        What other reaction always occurs at the same time as oxidation?

$q_8$        What does *reduction* mean?

$S^B$   $q_9$        In this aspect of the reaction—which substance is reduced?

$S^B$   $Q_3$        Keeping *both* aspects of the reaction in mind—how can we describe what is happening in this reaction?

*Note:* Other examples given to confirm pupils can identify the *two* aspects of the total reaction and describe it in terms of gain or loss of oxygen.

Final example, the heating of lead oxide on a carbon block is used as a behavioural objective in which pupils must (1) each label the reaction as below

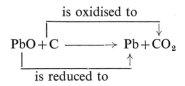

(2) verbalise it:

The carbon removes the oxygen from lead oxide and *reduces* it to lead—
and is thereby—
oxidised to carbon dioxide.

$Q_2$      Exploration of answers to this repeat question should establish readiness or need for urgent fence-mending.

$S^{o/c}$      *Orientation* and *coherence* are particularly important—in association with $S^B$ of demonstration they constitute a *change of frame of reference.*

$S^B$   $q_9$      The *bounds* indicate how the frame of reference applies . . .

$S^B$ $Q_3$      The bounds reiterate the significant features of the continuing frame of reference.

Note:  It is essential that the class demonstrate ability to apply the idea to interpret typical equations and to verbalise oxidation and reduction correctly. This should be written under time pressure—the verbalisation should probably be done as a *completion* exercise.

Development

$S^C$    We have seen that we can get lead from lead oxide by reducing the lead oxide with carbon.

$S^I$    There is, however, another way we can reduce lead oxide to lead—by first melting it, then passing an electric current through it.

$\left.\begin{array}{c} S^O \\[1em] S^B \end{array}\right\}$    In this demonstration, look for evidence that this chemical reaction has taken place.
(Demonstration.)

$q_1$    What indicates that a reaction has taken place?

$q_2$    At which electrode did the silvery substance form?

$q_3$    What is this silvery substance likely to be?

$q_4$    What test would verify this?

$S^B/Q_1$    Assuming this reaction to be true of all instances when an electric current is passed through molten lead oxide—how can we describe it?

$\left.\begin{array}{c} S^C \\[2em] S^O \\[4em] S^B \end{array}\right\}$    So far we have considered only what could be observed directly—the macroscopic world.
It is now necessary to move to the microscopic world of the atomic model if we are to find an adequate explanation of the reactions we are considering, because so far we have examined only reactions which fitted our explanatory model of oxygen gain or loss.
Keeping this in mind, and considering only the electric current,

## Development

Behavioural Objective Type I (with confirmation), i.e., to hypothesise AI and AII of Topic Analysis.
Strategy [4] Type (B) Integrative

$S^C$    Recall of most significant finding relative to development of this episode.

$S^I$    —

$\left.\begin{matrix} S^O \\ S^B \end{matrix}\right\}$    With $S^C$ above establish *change in frame of reference.*

$q_1$-$q_4$    Note (1) *order* of these questions,

(2) $q_3$ is *not* a member of this sample and would be better following $Q_1$ and with its own $S^O$ to establish it as a basic fact for subsequent development.

$S^B/Q_1$    The $S^B$ is again a part of the special concurrent theme of awareness of processes of scientific thinking.

$\left.\begin{matrix} S^C \\ S^O \\ S^B \end{matrix}\right\}$    Change of frame of reference.

$q_5$     How can we describe the electric current in the wires connected to the battery?

$S^{B/C}$     Keeping in mind the fact that the electric current in the wires is a stream of electrons and that the negative electrode has excess electrons—

$q_6$     How can we write the "word equation" to describe what happened?
(lead oxide + electrons $\longrightarrow$ lead) *Note*: oxygen ignored.

$\left.\begin{array}{l} S^O \\[14pt] S^B \\[14pt] S^C \end{array}\right\}$     We shall now have to explain the part played by these electrons in the reduction of lead oxide to lead.
As electrons are parts of atoms, our explanation must describe what is happening in terms of atomic theory.
We noted earlier in the demonstration that solid lead oxide is not a conductor of electricity, yet molten lead oxide is.

$S^{C/B}$     Now, remembering your past work on the structure of solids—

$q_7$     What kinds of particles must be present in the molten lead oxide if it is to conduct an electric current?

$q_8$     What changes must have occurred?

$S^B$     Keeping in mind that unlike charges attract one another—

$q_9$     Which ions will travel to the negative electrode?

$S^{O/B}$     But we can see lead accumulating around the electrode—

$q_{10}$     Which ions produce lead?

$q_{11}$     What charge would lead ions have?

$Q_2$     How do you suggest the lead accumulated at the electrode?
$\left\{\begin{array}{l} \textit{Record:} \\ \text{Lead positive ions + electrons} \longrightarrow \text{lead} \end{array}\right\}$

$q_5$        Recall of significant theoretical fact.

$S^{B/C}$        Further definition of frame of reference and recall of significant facts . . .

$q_6$        Application of "microscopic world" or atomic model theory to "macroscopic world" observations. (Additional work necessary if class not successful, as this is a crucial meeting point of observation and theory upon which subsequent development depends.)

$\left. \begin{array}{l} S^O \\ S^B \end{array} \right\}$        In association with $S^{B/C}$ above, a further *change of frame of reference*.

$S^C$        Coherence—recall of significant findings facilitates application to important problem.

$S^{C/B}$        Coherence and bounds—this statement has a dual function.

$q_7\ q_{11}$ This sample is designed to get a carefully sequenced recall of *lineal* type explanation (which might elicit *hyperbolic* type) and therefore requires for its success a sound understanding of the requisite theory. If it is apparent the class lacks this understanding, a revision episode would be imperative at *this* point.

$S^{O/B}$        Narrowed frame of reference.

$Q_2$        *Complete* type explanation required.

$S^I$        Lead ions have two positive charges,

$$(Pb^{++}+2\bar{e} \longrightarrow Pb).$$

$S^C$        So when lead oxide is reduced to lead, lead ions gain electrons to form lead atoms.

$Q_1$        How, then, would you describe *reduction* in terms of the electrons?

## Confirmation Procedure

$S^{C/O/B}$        But lead oxide is electrically neutral as is shown by this electroscope, so other ions must have been present.

$q_{12}$        What were they?

$q_{13}$        What charges would these oxygen ions carry?

$q_{14}$        In what direction would these negative ions travel?

$S^B$        Keeping in mind that negative ions have excess electrons—

$Q_3$        What will happen when the negative oxygen reaches the positive electrode?

$$(O^{\bar{\bar{e}}\bar{e}} \longrightarrow O+2\bar{e})$$

$S^I$        As very little oxygen is produced we cannot identify it on this small scale . . . but we saw bubbles . . . we shall have to assume this was *probably* the oxygen. (Repetition of demonstration if necessary.)

$\left.\begin{array}{c} S^C \\ Q_2 \end{array}\right\}$        We agreed earlier that reduction was the gain of $\bar{e}$— How would we describe *this* process?

## Confirmation Procedure

$S^I$            Given to avoid distraction of quiz-type guessing procedure frequently adopted.

$S^C$
$Q_1$ $\Big\}$           Generalisation of idea of reduction in terms of electron transfer.


## Confirmation Procedure

Interpolate *confirmation* procedure here to ensure level of *class* performance is adequate.

$S^{C/O/B}$        Composite statement to state a *changed frame of reference.*

$q_{12}$-$q_{14}$ Recall of relevant theoretical facts and their application.


$S^B$            Use of bounds increases probability $Q_3$ will be successful. Could be omitted and thus give higher status to $Q_3$ but there is risk of a confusing digression at a critical point in this development.

$Q_3$            Generalisation from $q_{10}$-$q_{11}$ sample.


$S^I$            Given to avoid distraction from development.


$S^C$
$Q_2$ $\Big\}$           Generalisation of oxidation in terms of electron transfer.


## Confirmation Procedure

As above.

Conclusion

$S^O$            Let us see how these new ideas fit with our earlier description of *oxidation* and *reduction*.

$S^C$            Remember our earlier ideas were on the basis of the macroscopic world and these new ideas are of the microscopic or atomic world.

$S^{O/B}$       Let us now take our ideas from the atomic world and apply them to the earlier reaction of magnesium burning in air or oxygen—

$$\text{That is:} \quad \overset{\displaystyle \overset{\text{is oxidised to}}{\big\downarrow}}{\underset{\underset{\text{is reduced to}}{\big\uparrow}}{Mg + O_2 \longrightarrow MgO}}$$

$q_{17}$      What happens to the magnesium atoms?

$q_{18}$      What happens to the oxygen atoms?

$S^B$            Bearing in mind the atomic structures of magnesium and oxygen—

$Q_1$      Can you suggest reasons why the magnesium atom would tend to lose electrons and the oxygen atom gain them?

$S^{C/B}$      Now we have agreed that oxidation and reduction can be described in terms of the loss or gain of electrons.

$Q_2$      Should the name oxidation be applied, then, to cases where this kind of reaction occurs without oxygen being present?

$S^B$            Keeping in mind the need for explanations to cover all cases and assuming our limited sample to be adequately representative—

$Q_1$      How would you explain the characteristics of the redox reaction?

Confirmation Procedure

Conclusion

$\left.\begin{array}{l} S^o \\ S^c \\ S^{o/B} \end{array}\right\}$      *Change of frame of reference*
Coherence important to ensure significance of present change relative to development of lesson as a whole.

$\left.\begin{array}{l} q_{17}\text{-}q_{18} \\ Q_1 \end{array}\right\}$ Application of notion of electron transfer to example described earlier in terms of gain or loss of electrons. (First step in achievement of behavioural objective.)

$S^{c/B}$      Change in frame of reference; $S^o$ is implicit.

$Q_2$      Second step in achievement of behavioural objective.

$S^B$      Returns to concurrent theme of consciousness of scientific thinking.

$Q_1$      Seeks a complete explanation. (Could be written by each pupil, following class verbalisation.)

Confirmation Procedure
Behavioural Objective: set of problems.

### Development (Alternative Episode 1)

$S^C$        Earlier it was implied that our theory to explain redox reactions was dubious because the reactions observed had been carefully selected to fit—and that we would need an atomic model to satisfy requirements of generality.
Now we have seen that we can get lead from lead oxide by reducing the lead oxide with carbon.

$S^I$        There is, however, another way we can reduce lead oxide to lead—by first melting it, then passing an electric current through it.

$S^O$        This demonstration has been chosen as exhibiting various features from which it is possible to create a theory to account for all redox reactions.

### Demonstration

$S^B$        Keeping in mind (1) the need for an atomic model explanation, (2) *that the lead oxide solid was a non-conductor*, and (3) accepting this example of the demonstration as adequately representative of all redox reactions—

$Q^{IND}$        How would you explain the observable characteristics of redox reactions?

$Q$        What would be a better name for the reaction?

### Development (Alternative Episode 2)

(As above as far as the demonstration, then the following.)

$S^I$        One theory states that the observable characteristics of redox reactions:

## Alternative Episode 1

> *Note:* The behavioural objective would still be Type I but strategy
> would be Type [3] (integrative).
>
> The class (a senior class recently started on chemistry) is
> assumed to have a sophisticated grasp of the atomic model
> and to have developed ability in hypothetic-deductive
> thinking.

$\left.\begin{array}{l} S^C \\ S^I \\ S^O \\ S^B \end{array}\right\}$    Special care with frame of reference and the delineation of
"bounds" to increase probability of successful outcome.
See Figure 12.4, p. 177.

$Q^{IND}$    The learner is required to select his own sample to achieve
the generalisation.

## Alternative Episode 2

> The same conditions must apply as for the Alternative 1
> if this strategy, strategy [3] (analytic), is to be appropriate.

depend upon the direction of transfer of electrons between the chemical species which is itself determined by their relative attraction for these electrons.

$S^B$      Given that this demonstration is adequately representative of the reaction and sufficiently exhibits the necessary characteristics—

$Q$      Can the statement be justified in terms of this demonstration?

---

The examples which follow illustrate various strategies in physics, English and geography. With the exception of the first example, in physics, they are presented without commentary.

---

## PHYSICS

### Distribution of Electric Charges

*Note:* The class has previously observed the behaviour of charged bodies and has hypothesised that they may have either a positive or negative charge. Further, it has hypothesised that an *uncharged* body may be *attracted* to a charged body even though, when charged from the same source, it was repelled.

This episode explores the *distribution* of the electric charge on a body. It is assumed that the concepts of conductor and non-conductor are known and that carbon and rubber can be identified as a conductor and non-conductor respectively.

### Episode of the Development

Behavioural Objective Type I; Strategy [3] (integrative) type, with confirmation procedure.

Pupils to achieve the following generalisation from Part II of a topic analysis.

A. The distribution of an electrostatic charge on the surface of a body is dependent on the body's conductivity.

It should be noted that though the strategy is described as *integrative* it is so only because the final hypothesis is provided and thus all generalisation is within the given constraints. However, *within* those constraints there must be a considerable amount of *analytic* thinking as successive hypotheses concerning trial samples of the data are tested for consistency with the overall given hypothesis.

P

I. If the body is a non-conductor the charge remains located at the charging surface.

II. If the body is a conductor the charge is distributed over its surface.

---

$S^C$

We know that some bodies can be given an electric charge by friction.

$S^O$

We have now to discover how this charge is distributed over the surface of the body.

$S^B$

Keeping the area of the charging surface (the area rubbed with the wool) as the point of reference,

$Q_1{}^{IND}$

Can you account for the behaviour of the two balloons in the demonstration? (See Figure 13.7.)

$S^C$

With the same frame of reference as above, and with reference to the demonstration (or group, or individual experiment) of Figure 13.8—

$Q_2{}^{IND}$

Can you account for the behaviour of the two carbon coated polystyrene balls after *one* is charged?

$S^B$

Assuming the two examples of behaviour of charged bodies is adequately representative of that of conductors and non-conductors—

$Q^{IND}$

What is the general rule for the distribution of the electric charge relative to the location of the charging surface?

Confirmation

$S^C$
$S^O$ } Changed frame of reference (presuming a previous intro-
$S^B$     ductory episode).

$Q^{IND}$

The assumption is that the pupils have a sufficient grasp of the idea of attraction and repulsion of charged bodies that they can select their own *samples* from the data available in the demonstration (or individual or group experiment).

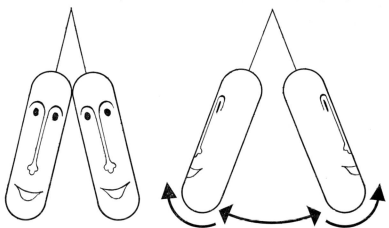

Figure 13.7: Two balloons with faces on surface suspended with cotton. Positions before and after charging.

DEMONSTRATION

(The two balloons are held in position and the faces rubbed with wool. On simultaneous release they move apart and rotate to face outwards.)

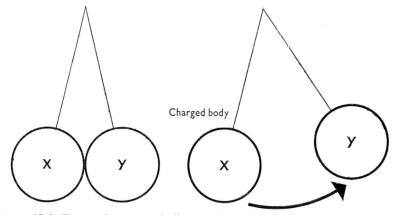

Figure 13.8: Two polystyrene balls coated with carbon and suspended with cotton. Positions shown before charging and after charging of one ball (x).

DEMONSTRATION

(The two balls are at rest before charging. After x is charged, (y) is repelled.)

Alternative Episode

Behavioural Objective Type I, Strategy Type [7] (from (1) to (2))

| | |
|---|---|
| $S^C$ | We know that some bodies can be given an electric charge by friction. |
| $S^O$ | We now have to discover how this charge is spread over the surface of the body. |
| $Q^{/NT}$ | Can you account for the behaviour of the balloons in the demonstration? |
| $S^B$ | Keeping in mind the region of the charging surface as the point of reference— |
| $q_1$ | What happened? |
| $q_2$ | How can we account for the balloons moving away from each other? |
| $q_3$ | How can we account for the rotation? |
| $S^{E/M}$ | We have here two boys facing each other, palm to palm and with elbows bent (Figure 13.9). (Demonstration.) |
| $S^B$ | $\bar{q}_1$    If they simultaneously push, what do we see happen? |
| | $\bar{q}_2$    To what part of the balloon behaviour does this demonstration correspond? |
| $S^{E/M}$ | If we now have the two boys face each other with a left palm to right palm only and elbows bent (Figure 13.9 )— |
| | $\bar{q}_3$    What happens when they simultaneously push? (Move away and rotate.) |
| $q_4$ | Can you use the explanatory model to account for the rotation of the balloons? |
| $S^B$ | Keeping in mind that rubber is a non-conductor— |
| $Q$ | Why, then, did the balloons take up a position so that the faces were directly outwards from each other? |

Confirmation

Answer must be "read on to" the explanatory model.

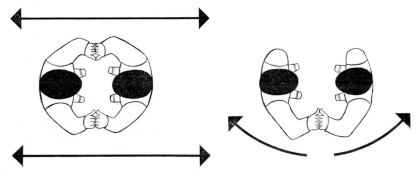

Figure 13.9: Explanatory model for movement of balloons

## ENGLISH
Poem "Fueled" by Marcie Hans

### INTRODUCTORY NOTE

The topic analysis is as in Figure 11.2, page 156, which points to the deleterious effects on man when he loses his appreciation of the wonders of nature. The behavioural objective, as on page 170, requires pupils to identify the theme of the poem in examples of public issues and to justify their selection against *their* understanding of the theme.

### Introduction

| | |
|---|---|
| $S^O$ | . . . continue with our series on "Great Ideas". |
| $S^C$ | Remember what men believe in can greatly enrich or impoverish their lives in terms of the satisfactions they get over a lifetime, and that the attitudes each of us adopts on important issues will reflect our beliefs—whether they are fixed or are being formed. |
| $S^O$ | As an exercise in committing oneself to a viewpoint and being able to discuss and perhaps modify it, we shall start with . . . one viewpoint on an aspect of man's existence: |
| $S^B$ | Given, then, the following statement: |
| | Man has long been a pawn of nature, now *he* says how the game will be played. |
| | (Meaning interpreted if necessary.) |
| $Q^{INT}$ | What do you think? (No attempt to resolve divergent viewpoints.) |

### Development
Strategy [7], (1-4).

| | |
|---|---|
| $S^C$ | We have then the following points of view: (listed). |
| $S^C$ | But here is a poem by someone who feels very strongly about this idea—(the statement of the introduction). |
| $S^B$ | The poem (read to class—individual copies or blackboard copy available.) |
| $Q^{INT}$ | Whose side is Marcie Hans on in our argument? |
| $S^O$ | We'll now look at this poem systematically to clarify our thinking. |
| $q_1$ | Do the two verses give the same "message"? |
| $q_2$ | What *is* the theme of each verse? |
| $\bar{q}_1$ | What *feeling* do you have after reading the second verse? |
| $\bar{q}_2$ | $\begin{cases} \text{Why do you feel this way? i.e.,} \\ \text{What situation produced it?} \end{cases}$ |
| $\bar{q}_3$ | Is this feeling produced by awareness that the seedling was unappreciated—or is it more to do with the *contrast of feeling* between the two verses? |

$S^B$      In the poem Marcie Hans notes that people cheer in the first verse but that no one even claps in the second.

$q_3$      What is the significance of the difference?

$q_4$      What effect would lack of awareness of the world of nature have on a particular man?

$Q_1$      What then is Marcie Hans suggesting as the effect of man's technological success?

$S^B$      Given that the majority of a society had thought this way for a long time—

$Q_2$      How would you expect it to be apparent to a foreigner visiting that country?

$S^C$      Remember we held the following views in the original statement: (List).

$q_5$      What do you think now?
(No suggestion that all must agree—but only that pupils must be prepared to change viewpoint in face of superior argument.)

$Q$      What, then, is Marcie Hans' view relative to the first statement and our present views?

$q_6$      What do you think *she* would say of the statement?

### Confirmation

Supporters of various views asked to establish the validity of their viewpoints relative to given frames of reference.

### Conclusion

Designed to achieve the behavioural objective as outlined on page 170.

### Alternative Episode
### Behavioural Objective Type III, Strategy [6]

$S^O$      This poem . . . has been considered by some to crystallise feeling about a theme of contemporary significance—others think its treatment of this theme superficial.

$S^B$      Read the poem (*not* read to class to avoid communication of bias); decide on your own viewpoint about its worth and justify your position in a statement of not more than 200 words, making detailed reference to at least two major events of world significance.

*Note:* The *ideas* of the poem are in question, not its *structure* as a poem.

*Note:* With this type of strategy the bounds must be carefully elaborated to compensate for limited delineation of the product sought. (See Figure 12.4, p. 177.)

GEOGRAPHY

The Economy of the West Coast, New Zealand

INTRODUCTORY NOTE

The following is an example of Strategy [9] (with Type II behavioural objective) applied to this topic. The episode is assumed to be the first in the development of the lesson. The pupils are assumed to be familiar with the kind of research required and to have a sufficient grasp of the requisite concepts to take the research through to a statement approximating that of the topic analysis—see Appendix C.

Behavioural Objective: Type II

Each pupil to nominate at least three categories of significant information that he needs to make further progress in the assigned research; significance to be considered adequate if the information required has relevance to any of the propositions of the teacher's topic analysis. The topic analysis, however, is not to be available to pupils until they have completed the assignment.

$S^C$        In our study of Northland, New Zealand, we concluded that the economy had been transformed by the injection of capital and the application of new technology.

$S^O$        1. In this study of the West Coast you are required to do the necessary research to make a systematic and comprehensive statement of the status of its economy comparable with that we made for Northland. (Topic analysis format.)

             2. You will all begin with the same information (below) but thereafter will be supplied only with the information for which you ask, provided it is available.

$S^B$        Keep in mind that the context of this study is as indicated by Figure 13.10—

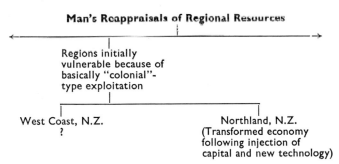

Figure 13.10: Part II of a topic analysis on the West Coast of New Zealand— reappraisal of resources

       Examine Tables 13.1, 13.2 and 13.3[5] below and prepare a list of additional information you will need for the next stage of your research. Applications for additional information must be supported by a brief justification. To receive *any* information you must ask for at least three categories of significant information.

*Note:* If the information is not available in the class set you will have to tackle the problem another way.

TABLE 13.1

| CLASSIFICATION OF EMPLOYMENT BY INDUSTRIAL GROUPS 1966 CENSUS | | | | | |
|---|---|---|---|---|---|
| Census | Totals | Percentages | | | |
| Industrial Group | West Coast | West Coast | New Zealand | Buller County | Westland County |
| Agriculture, forestry, etc. | 1,631 | 12·0 | 13·3 | 18·0 | 32·0 |
| Mining and quarrying | 1,721 | 13·0 | 0·6 | 27·0 | 1·0 |
| Manufacturing | 2,502 | 19·0 | 26·8 | 16·0 | 19·0 |
| Construction | 1,223 | 9·0 | 9·4 | 8·0 | 13·5 |
| Electricity, gas, water, etc. | 225 | 2·0 | 1·3 | 1·0 | 2·0 |
| Commerce | 1,676 | 12·5 | 17·7 | 7·0 | 5·0 |
| Transport, storage, etc. | 1,712 | 12·5 | 9·6 | 9·0 | 8·5 |
| Services | 2,712 | 20·0 | 21·3 | 11·0 | 20·0 |
| Totals | 13,402 | 100·0 | 100·0 | 100·0 | 100·0 |

Source: Department of Statistics, 1966 Census of Population and Dwellings, Supplement No. 7: Marlborough, Nelson and Westland Statistical Areas, Government Printer, Wellington, 1967, p. 5 (Table 7).

TABLE 13.2

| WEST COAST COAL PRODUCTION | | | |
|---|---|---|---|
| Year | Production (tons) | Percentage of New Zealand Production | Men Employed |
| 1930 | 1,268,637 | 50 | n.a. |
| 1950 | 1,093,825 | 41 | 2,617 |
| 1955 | 925,312 | 37 | 2,006 |
| 1967 | 670,898 | 28 | 1,536 |

Source: 1930, 1950, 1955, 1967 Mines Statements in the Appendices to the Journal of the House of Representatives, C.2, Government Printer, Wellington.

TABLE 13.3

| WEST COAST BUTTER PRODUCTION * | | | | | |
|---|---|---|---|---|---|
| Year | Karamea-Westport | Reefton | Greymouth | Hokitika-Harihari | Total |
| 1954-5 | 733 | 378 | 275 | 1,246 | 2,632 |
| 1962-3 | 867 | 425 | 317 | 1,663 | 3,272 |
| 1966-7 | 961 | 431 | 351 | 1,737 | 3,480 |

Source: New Zealand Department of Agriculture, 1956, 1964 and 1968: Lists of Creameries, Factories, Private Dairies and Packing Houses. Government Printer, Wellington.
* All figures in tons.

## REFERENCES

[1] A. N. WHITEHEAD, *The Aims of Education and Other Essays*, Williams and Norgate, London, 1932, p. 48.
[2] D. P. AUSUBEL, *The Psychology of Meaningful Verbal Learning*, Grune and Stratton, New York, 1963, pp. 15-21.
[3] D. W. F. BROWN and J. Y. MACAULAY, "Topic Analysis in the Teaching of Geography", *Proceedings of the Sixth N.Z. Geography Committee*, 1970, II, p. 85.
[4] See B. S. BLOOM, *Taxonomy of Educational Objectives—Classification of Educational Goals, Handbook 1: the Cognitive Domain*, David McKay, New York, 1956, and N. M. SANDERS, *Classroom Questions: What Kinds?*, Harper and Row, New York, 1966.
[5] Tables taken from Brown and Macaulay, op. cit., p. 81.

# CHAPTER 14

# Prestructuring the Framework of Verbal Transactions: II. A Lesson Plan in Mathematics

This example of planning is representative of those subjects, or parts of subjects, which can be rigorously structured. As such it represents one extreme of the structure continuum. The final chapter illustrates one kind of programme planning appropriate for a loosely-structured topic at the other end of the continuum.

## BACKGROUND NOTES

Although mathematically unsophisticated readers may not get much benefit from the content of the box below, they should profit from a study of the elaborated lesson plan which follows.

Transformation geometry is an alternative approach to the study of elementary plane geometry in Forms 3 to 5 in New Zealand. The transformations are restricted to "affine" transformations—that is, to those in which parallelism is preserved. The isometries (principally translation, reflection, rotation), enlargement, shearing, one-way stretches, and combinations of these constitute the extent of the study to the level of the School Certificate Examination. If, in addition to parallelism being invariant, at least one point is also invariant (i.e. a "centro-affine" transformation), the transformation is capable of being represented by a 2 x 2 matrix, and thus a link with algebra is possible at this level. The treatment throughout transformation geometry to Fifth Form tends to be informal, rather than rigorously deductive or axiomatic.

With a class of average ability, this particular lesson would be suitable for the middle of the Fourth Form year. This is the first in a series on shearing, and it is assumed to have been preceded by a thorough study of the isometries and enlargement. Subsequent lessons would consider the construction of images when the invariant line does not intersect the object figure, the transformation applied to the whole plane (as against a subset of it), combinations of shears, the use of coordinates, representation by matrices, the measurement of a shear, and the invariance of area under shearing.

> *Note:* It must be emphasised that shearing is restricted, for the purposes of the syllabus, to "centro-affine" shearing to enable later representation by a $2 \times 2$ matrix. This is thus a narrower interpretation than that of everyday life, or of the geographer, and this requires comment and clarification in Episode I.

---

*Shearing* is a topic of *transformation* geometry. The distinctive feature of transformation geometry is that argument can be at times very much less formal than traditionally deductive Euclidean geometry—theorems and all that! Further, the methods of transformation geometry are much more concrete than traditional geometry, to the extent that at times it can involve the imagined manipulation of shapes. Shearing as a topic, therefore, involves the study of the geometry associated with all those distortions of shapes which correspond to the behaviour of a stack of books pushed horizontally by a ruler pivoted about a point located at a bottom edge of the stack.

## THE LESSON PLAN

### TOPIC ANALYSIS

The topic analysis of this lesson has been detailed in Chapter 11, p. 157. To assist the reader, the objective from the topic analysis is stated at the beginning of each episode, a simplified version being added where necessary for the mathematically unsophisticated.

### BEHAVIOURAL OBJECTIVES

*For the lesson as a whole* (Type I). Pupils will demonstrate their under standing of the concept of shearing by:

1. (a) Having been given the first fish of Figure 14.1, devising a procedure for drawing the second fish accurately.

   (b) Justifying the procedure in terms of properties of shearing as a basis for the biologist's hypothesis.

2. Solving twelve progressively more difficult problems with (say) 50, 65 or 80 per cent success according to ability group. These problems, which are detailed at the end of this lesson plan, have been devised to require, as a set, the application of all the principles covered in the lesson.

*For each episode.* The behavioural objective for each episode is not formally elaborated as it has been found tediously repetitive when the objective is confined to the achievement of a principle explicated in the topic analysis. Further, given the prestructuring of the verbal transactions being illustrated coupled with the confirmation procedure outlined in Chapter 13, *both the criteria of conditions and performance are reasonable for practical classroom purposes.* The relevant principle, or generalisation, is usually cited by the conventional notation, e.g., A II 1 (a).

## INTRODUCTION

### Behavioural Objective

A preliminary understanding of the concept of shearing which is sufficient for an intuitive recognition is the objective. Pupils should note at least that: one line is fixed; points move parallel to it; straight lines remain straight; but the shape is altered.

### Strategy Type [2] (Integrative)

$S^o$    So far we have been looking at transformations such as translation, reflection, rotation and enlargement, which all have certain properties in common. Now we will look at a transformation which differs from all of these in one important respect. It will, for example, explain how the biologist's drawings in Figure 14.1 are related to each other, and how the biologist can discover whether there is an evolutionary link between the two fish. Note for the present that the biologist is prepared to assume a link if it can be shown that *all features of the second fish are uniformly displaced when compared to the first.*

Figure 14.1: Biologist's fish problem (shown with overhead projector)

However, this is a complicated example to start with, and so we will look at a simpler problem which uses the same ideas (and return to the fish later on).

Figure 14.2: "MATH" problem (drawn on blackboard)

The problem in Figure 14.2 is that we want to change the style of printing "M" and "A" to that shown for "T" and "H" so the word will be *strictly in the same style.* (This is really very like the biologist's problem of Figure 14.1 because all features of "M" and "A" *must be uniformly displaced* relative to the displacement of "T" and "H".) Our new transformation has produced "T" and "H"—what will "M" and "A" be transformed to?

Initially we shall have a broad look at this transformation to enable us to recognise and distinguish it from those already met.

$S^B$     Here is a pile of books of different shapes and sizes. The new transformation has the effect of doing the action shown on the right hand side of Figure 14.3.

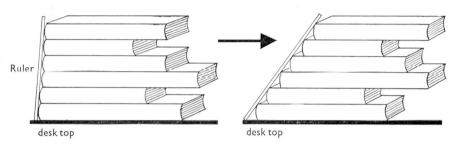

Ruler     desk top       desk top

Figure 14.3: "Shearing" of pile of books

$S^O$     Now let us discover the characteristics of this kind of transformation—the nature of the particular change in the original pile of books.

$q_1$     Which book moves most?

$q_2$     Which book moves least? (Repeat with other examples.)

$S^B$     Keeping these observations in mind—

$Q_1$     What can you say about the *bottom* book in *all* these examples?

$S^O$     Now let's transfer our attention to another feature.

$S^B$     Watch the "path" of the top book.

$q_3$     What can you say about its *height* above the desk?

$q_4$     What about *this* book? And *this?* etc.

$S^B$     Relative to the desk top—

$q_5$     How would you describe the *direction* of movement of all the books under this transformation?

$S^B$     Again relative to the desk top and thinking of the *general case*

$Q_2$     What can you say about the direction of movement under this transformation?

$q_6$     What is the significance of using a ruler in each example of this kind of transformation?

$S^I$      This kind of transformation is called SHEARING.

$S^C$      Remembering the isometries and enlargements met so far—

$Q_3$      How does shearing differ from them?

$Q$      What is shearing (i.e., what are its chief characteristics)?

## Confirmation

$S^O$      To see whether we can recognise shearing—

$Q_4$      Which of the drawings in Figure 14.4 are examples of the shearing transformation? (include "T" and "H" of Figure 14.2.)

$q_7$      Why?

---

# COMMENTS ON INTRODUCTION

## Introduction

$S^O$      The value of this kind of introduction is that it provides a practical application of the topic of the lesson and, in the case of the "MATH" problem, a means whereby the *coherence* of a complete type of lesson can be maintained. As will be seen, each new idea is used to take a further step in the solution of the problem.

The remainder of this episode conforms to a Strategy [3] (integrative).

## Confirmation

It should be noted that the items in the confirmation section (to check on intuitive recognitions) are merely the focal points of the confirmation *procedure* which is designed to check the performance of the *class*.

## Alternative Episode

Instead of strategy [2] (integrative) use a variation of strategy [7] from first $S^B$ onwards, as follows:

$S^I$      This is what we call *shearing*.

$S^B$      Given that (1), (3) and (5) of Figure 14.4 are also examples of shearing—

$Q^{INT}$      Are (2) and (4) examples of shearing?

$S^I$      They are not.

$Q^{IND}$      What then, are the characteristics of shearing?

*Note:* Giving examples of the new concept with *significant non-instances* increases the probability of success. Additional non-instances could be given to highlight that the base (axis) does not move, and that movement is parallel.

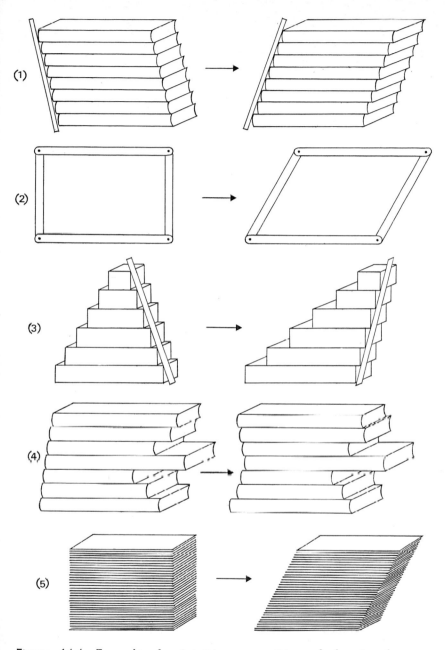

Figure 14.4: Examples for intuitive recognition of shearing (correct answers 1, 3, 5, T and H; (2) varies height; (4) movement not uniform)

## DEVELOPMENT EPISODE I
### Behavioural Objective (A I 2)

As the direction of the shear is parallel to the axis, the line joining a point and its image is always parallel to the axis, and this relationship can be used to determine the position of the image of a point relative to the axis.

OR

As the movement is parallel to the fixed base line, the line joining a point in the original "shape" and its eventual position (image) are always parallel to the base (axis) and this relationship can be used to determine where the image should be.

$S^O$      Now that we can recognise shearing, we need to look more closely at what happens to points (and *sets* of points, i.e. lines) under this transformation to be able to complete the lettering (Figure 14.2). So that we can consider further the properties of shearing in isolation, let us represent them in a diagram in Figure 14.5:

Axis of shearing

### Figure 14.5: Properties of shearing

$\left.\begin{array}{l} S^C \\ S^I \end{array}\right\}$      First, remember that the bottom line remains in the same position after shearing—it is, therefore, invariant, and is known as the invariant line, or the *axis of the shear*. Because it is the only line which stays put, it is a useful reference line.

$S^O$      Now let us see what happens to points under shearing relative to this reference line—the invariant line, or the axis of shearing.

$S^B$      Going back to the books—

     $q_1$      What will happen to this chalk mark during shearing? (Chalk mark is made on a book within the pile.)

     $q_2$      And this? etc.

     $q_3$      And this point *on the diagram?*

     $q_4$      And this? etc.

     $Q_1$      How would you describe the movement of all points above the axis?

$q_5$    What transformation previously studied does the movement of each individual point remind you of?

$S^B$    In terms of this transformation—

$q_6$    How could you describe the motion of all these points under shearing?

$S^C$    Remembering previous kinds of transformation and the special name we had for the final position of a point after a transformation—(given if not remembered)—

$Q_2$    How could you describe the effect of shearing on these points using this term?

### Confirmation

$S^O$    Let's see if we have understood this sufficiently to help with the "MATH" problem. (Figure 14.2.)

$S^I$    Assuming the invariant unchanging line runs along here . . .

$q_7$    How are this point (x) and its image related to the invariant line? (Figure 14.6.)

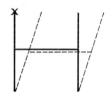    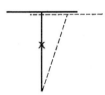

Figure 14.6                          Figure 14.7

$q_8$    Where would the image of this point be? (Figure 14.7.)

$S^{O/B}$    Turning now to the "M" and "A",

$q_9$    What can we say about the images of these three points? (Figure 14.8.)

Figure 14.8: "MATH" problem, continued

$q_{10}$    And the image of *this* point? (Figure 14.9.)

$Q$

Figure 14.9: "MATH" problem, continued

*Q*          Now that you have seen these cases of what happens under a shear, can someone summarise this for *all* points?

---

## COMMENTS ON EPISODE I
### Development (Episode I)
Strategy [2] B (integrative)
#### CONFIRMATION
The focal points only of the confirmation—the full procedure would involve complementary questions.

### Alternative Episode
Strategy [2] C (analytic)

$S^B$        Given that the direction of shear is parallel to the axis and the line joining a point and that its image is always parallel to the axis—

$Q^{IND}$    Where are the images of each of the points in Figure 14.10 below?

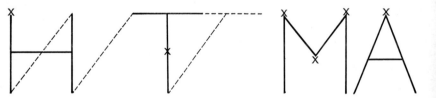

Figure 14.10: "MATH" problem, continued

$q_1$        Where is the axis of shear? (Plus questions of original episode.)
$q_2$        (If necessary.) What is the direction of shear for each point?

---

## DEVELOPMENT EPISODE 2
### Behavioural Objective (A I 3)
The length of the line segment joining a point and its image is proportional to the distance from the axis; this, together with the knowledge of the direction of the shear, can be exploited to determine the image of any point in the plane.

$S^C$    We know, then, that under shearing, points are translated parallel to the axis,

$S^B$ $\begin{cases} q_1 \\ \\ q_2 \end{cases}$ But do we know enough to locate the exact position of the image?

What else is needed, in addition to direction, to describe the translation completely?

$S^O$    Back to the pile of books.

$S^B$    Compare the motion of a point here (top book) with points, say, here ... (about one-quarter, one-half and three-quarters of the way up the pile).

$q_3$    How is the motion similar?

$S^B$    Keeping in mind that the motion is in the same direction—

$q_4$    In what way do they differ?

$Q_1$    On what does the amount of the translation depend?

$q_5$    What happens to points further away from the axis?

$q_6$    What about a point on a book at the top of a stack 100 feet high?

$Q_2$    How, then, can we describe the movement of points on books relative to distance from the axis?

$S^{O/B}$    We have been talking about books, but we express the general case in terms of points and lines. Using our findings to da'e—

$Q$    How can we most economically describe the motion of a point under shearing?

**Confirmation**

$S^B$    Given the "MATII" diagram—

$q_7$    What confirms our finding?

$q_8$    Can you predict where the image of this point (x) Figure 14.11(a) will be, compared with the image of this point (x) in Figure 14.11(b)?

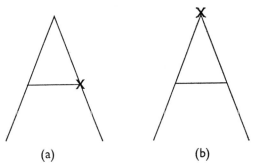

(a)                              (b)

Figure 14.11: "MATH" problem, continued

## DEVELOPMENT EPISODE 3

### Behavioural Objective (A I 1)

Since the axis is, by definition, a set of invariant points, each point and its image coincide: the image of any point on the axis is thus known.

$S^0$        As a test of our understanding so far:

     $q_1$     Where is the image of a point on the axis?

     $Q_1$     Why?

$S^B$        Referring now to the "MATH" problem—

     $q_2$     Can you apply this idea to give reasons for this (pointing) being the axis?

     $q_3$     Can you describe the position of the images of any other points in the diagram?

     $q_4$     Name the invariant line in diagrams (a), (b) and (c) of Figure 14.12.

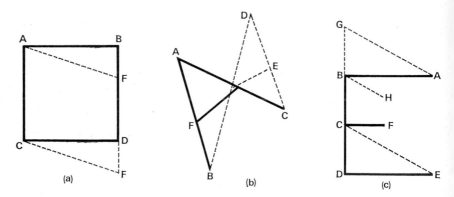

Figure 14.12: "MATH" problem continued

(Correct answers: AC, BC and AE respectively)

## DEVELOPMENT EPISODE 4

### Behavioural Objective (A I 3 (a))

In the case where the distance from the axis is constant, such as on a line which is parallel to the axis, the length of line segments in this direction are invariant under shearing.

$S^{0/C}$      Returning to the "MATH" problem (Figure 14.2), you will remember that though images of points on the topics of letters are in a line parallel to the axis, we do not know the *amount* of translation for points "M" and "A".

$S^B$        Considering points A and B in Figure 14.13—

     $q_1$     How do their distances from the axis compare?

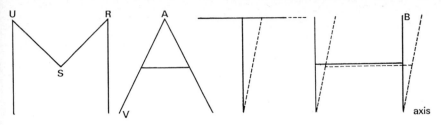

Figure 14.13: "MATH" problem, continued

$S^C$      When we described the motion of a point under shearing, we found that the further a point is from the axis, the greater the amount of its translation.

$Q_1$      What does this mean for the displacement of A compared with the displacement of B?

$q_2$      Where is the image of R?

$S^B$      To find the image of S—

$q_3$      What do we know about its image relative to S and the axis?

$q_4$      What *else* would we need to know?

$q_5$      Where could we get this information?

$Q_a$      How then can we describe the translation of points equidistant from the axis?

**Confirmation**

$q_6$      What then can we say about the length of the image of any line segment parallel to the axis?

## DEVELOPMENT EPISODE 5
### Behavioural Objective (A I 1 (a))

The image of a point on the axis being thus known, it is possible, exploiting the invariance of straightness, to draw the image of a line, given only one point on it, its image, and the point of intersection of the line with the axis.

$S^0$      We can now look at a further property to complete the image.

$S^B$      In the "MATH" problem (Figure 14.13) the images of "T" and "H" are drawn. Note that the lines of the image appear to be straight.

$Q_1$      Can you justify straightness or otherwise?

**Confirmation**

$q_1$      What is the result of applying this idea to one of the legs of the "A" such as AV in Figure 14.13?

$q_2$      How do you draw the complete image of the "A"?

DEVELOPMENT EPISODE 6

Behavioural Objective (A I 3 (a) i)

$S^0$ You may suspect that we now have enough to solve the "MATH" problem. This is so. However for many problems one additional property is useful.

$S^{C/B}$ This property is that lines which are parallel remain parallel after shearing.

$Q_1$ Can you justify this, referring to the parallel lines of the "H"?

$q_1$ How do we draw the image of the "M"?

$q_2$ How about finding the image of the point S if we make it higher than in the original diagram, for example (Figure 14.14)?

(Prompt: "parallelism" for an intuitive solution.)

Figure 14.14: "MATH" problem, continued

## CONCLUSION EPISODE

$S^0$ Now we are in a position, having seen what happens to lines and points under shearing, to summarise.
(Class demonstration as lesson summary, with *class* prompting. Logic to solve shearing problems is outlined.)

$S^B$ Using the same method—

$q_1$ Find the images of the figures (in Figure 14.15).

*Note:* Class is required to verbalise solutions for three of the first ten of these problems.

*Note:* In these questions the axis is shown as a dotted line. $A^1$, $B^1$, ... are the images of A, B, ... The paper must not be rotated to solve these problems.

$S^B$ Given the biologist's problem of the fish (Figure 14.16)—

$q_2$ Can you suggest a possible way in which the biologist can demonstrate that the two fish are linked?

$S^c$    Remember there must be uniform displacement of all features.

*Note:* Pupils to sketch solutions freehand.

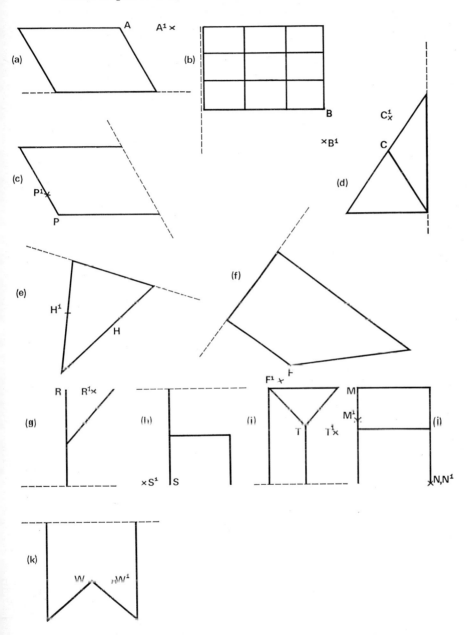

Figure 14.15: Exercises in shearing

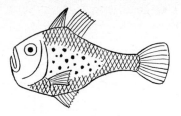

Figure 14.16: Biologist's fish

## HOMEWORK

(a) In Figure 14.17 (a) pupils are required to list the principles used to draw the image, in order of use. $P^1$ is the image of $P$.

(b) In Figure 14.17 (b) pupils are required to find the image of ABC, given that $D^1$ is the image of D and that BC is the axis of the shear.

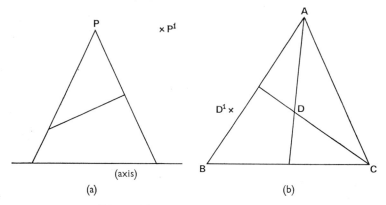

(a)                                                (b)

Figure 14.17: Homework exercises

---

## GENERAL COMMENTS ON DESIGN

### Episodes of Development

These may also be designed according to strategy [3] C and D (analytic) along the lines indicated for the alternative episode of the introduction.

### Note on Conclusion

The set of exercises is graded in difficulty and is designed to require application of each of the principles.

### ALTERNATIVE DESIGN FOR LESSON

An interesting alternative would be to present the set of problems (Figure 14.15) and their solutions as examples of shearing, immediately after the introduction of the above lesson and to require the class—organised into groups of (say) four—to "discover" all the principles.

---

# CHAPTER 15

# Prestructuring the Framework of Verbal Transactions: III. A Programme in Creative Writing

This chapter illustrates the principles of planning applied to the design of a programme to develop creative writing ability—an objective which, in terms of the communicability of its concepts, must be located towards the other end of the structural continuum from mathematics.

Although the programme is designed to develop creativity in *writing*, it can also be regarded as a design analogue for a programme to develop creative aspects of scientific thinking. This is valid once the emphasis is put on the *processes* of scientific creativity rather than on the systematised, structured end product.

Creativity is essentially an exercise in autonomy: originality needs independence of thinking, feeling and behaviour. Thus those who sought to develop creative writing in schools following the stimulus of the ideas of the New Educational Fellowship of the 1930s, established the credo that the child must be free of external constraints in order to write as an individual; his *personal* response to experience must be the primary purpose of the exercise.

The teacher's model and the agonised attempts of his pupils to emulate it were seen as suppression of creativity; the old *composition* gave way to free expression. The result was a quite dramatic improvement in quality, judged as the expression of individual pupils, and an equivalent improvement in fluency, judged by the amount written. But the improvement in creativity has not been as great as expected, though brilliant individual performances are occasionally cited as if they established the general case.

Neither freedom to write nor stimulating experiences to "evoke creative response" have proved sufficient to bring about the expected flowering of creativity. So it is not surprising that teachers generally seem to have accepted that pupils are not capable of much more creativity than is achieved at present. However, when creative writing is examined in the light of the principles developed in this text, it is apparent that pupils

233

have considerably greater potential than is generally realised, and that teachers will need to modify present practice substantially if their potential is to be realised.

## CREATIVE WRITING AND METHOD

### STAGE II LEARNING (PRECISION) NEEDED IN CREATIVE WRITING PROGRAMMES

Whitehead suggested that learning ideally went through three stages and consisted of cycles of these stages.[1] Significantly, present practice provides for the two stages of Discovery in terms of this text (Stages of Learning I and III), but does little about the second stage: that of *Precision*. The flaw in such practice is only too apparent; for example, in elementary mathematics when pupils are given structured Cuisenaire rods to make their own intuitive level discoveries, and are then expected to move directly to Stage III learning without passing through a stage of precision.

At this stage, of course, the teacher should assist in the coordination and integration of the pupils' independent discoveries in order to establish a sound base of systematised knowledge for generalisation at the higher level of discovery of the third stage. *Mathematics learned without the intermediate stage of Precision soon degenerates into rote learning*, for the pupils lack the cognitive resources to function effectively. They lack a sufficient knowledge, for instance, of the interrelationships of ideas to be able to make sound judgments of relevance, significance and probability.

The position is the same in the area of creative writing: unless teachers interpolate a stage of precision, the pupils must take the easiest way out to cope—in this case, responding with what is more or less relevant to what the teacher appears to be wanting—a kind of generalised rote response. As was argued in an earlier chapter, pupils can easily be overwhelmed by the wealth of experience because they lack an ordering principle. As was suggested, some sort of constraint (or *bounds*) is needed to help them order their experience to best advantage.

The pupils, therefore, lack the cognitive resources to function at the higher level which is necessary if they are to exploit their independent discoveries of the intuitive stage. A stage of *precision* is needed.

It will be apparent that the strategy options must not only be of the Stage II learning, but also are limited to those which permit Type II behavioural objectives. This is because, though the degree of structural rigour implicit to creative writing will place it at the other end of the structural continuum from mathematics, the degree of precision needed makes the constraints of Type II essential.

### SENSIBILITY

Judgments on the merits of creative work are notoriously difficult. However, if we are to define the goals of a programme to *develop* creative writing, we must know at least how to *recognise* it. At the risk of being simplistic, the view adopted here is that writing is "creative" when it has something that marks it as original expression of the writer: this "something" is the communication of *sensibility*.

For this context, sensibility is regarded as perception of the subtleties of meaning which are below the surface of experience, and their communication (explicitly or implicitly) through the described speech, thoughts, and actions of people. The pupil, therefore, who is writing creatively is looking and responding to the totality of his experience of thinking, feeling and behaving; he speculates about the part of the iceberg that is hidden, and the swirl upon the surface of the water, for he knows they are a part of reality too.

The following representative example was written by a ten-year-old, of above-average intelligence, after the programme described below. It has numerous examples of sensibility, and in terms of the view of creativity adopted here, it appears to be far more creative than is usually expected of the average secondary pupil's work.

## THE FIRST TIME

Joe was shaking. He was wondering what to say. It comforted him to think it would all be over tomorrow. Tomorrow he would laugh about it; but not today. There were only three people in front of him. What should he say? Two middles? No?

One person gone. His brother would be mad if he went back to ask.

A voice broke his thoughts.

"Yes?"

"Oh, uh, two that cost one and three, please."

"One and threepennies?"

"Oh yes. That was it! One and threepennies!"

"Whereabouts?"

"Uh, well I think it's the middle, but . . . Yes, middle," Joe said, and thought:

"So that's all you say! I should have known." He put his shoulders back and his chest out and walked smartly over to his brother. His feet burrowed deep into the carpet. My it was soft! Funny though, he was still shaking. Maybe it was not all over. Maybe there was still something else. Probably just the memory, he thought.

"Did you get them?" his brother said.

"Yeah."

"What did you say?"

"But-but what do you want to know for?" He was worried.

"It might be interesting."

"Phoocy! What could be interesting about it?" Joe laughed a silly, uneasy little laugh.

"You didn't know what to say," said his brother maliciously.

"B-but how did you know?"

"I could see you were all red, and you were stuttering. Now, what did you say?"

"Uh, well, first I think I said two that cost one and three, or something, but I'm not quite sure though."

He closed his ears to his brother's laughing.

"She asked me if I meant one and—well, whatever it is. Then she said whereabouts? I said I thought it was middle but I wasn't sure. And she gave me middle."

"Ha ha. Hee hee! Wait till I tell the kids at school!"

"Won't affect me," said Joe. "You go to a different school than me."

"I know. But John's brother is in my class."

John was Joe's worst enemy!

All through the pictures Joe worried about it. He nervously fingered the tickets he had bought. He gritted his teeth as his brother laughed louder than anyone when Joe's favourite filmstar rode a bike into a ditch full of muddy water.

"It probably hurt. He hasn't got any sympathy for anyone," he thought. "*He* wouldn't like it."

Joe walked home because he didn't want his brother to bar* him. He went a different way, too.

When he got home, his brother was telling his mother about it.

Joe hid because he couldn't listen, but he could still hear laughing. It was not from his mother. At least someone was on his side, he thought. Then something made his ears prick up.

"So what? You did the same thing." It was his mother.

Joyously, Joe crept to the door, poked his head round it, and said, "Wait till I tell the kids at school!" and galloped away as his brother made a lunge at him.

## Pupils have a Hidden Talent

Each society has taboo words. At an early age children learn that it is not wise to incur the wrath of their parents in this matter. Thus *sex* for an earlier generation was part of the language of the unmentionable—so that many today suffer from feelings of guilt resulting from childhood conditioning. In the same way it appears that the communication of sensibility is conditioned negatively; the young learn quite early that it is not a permissible communication. What parent does not, at some time, suffer from the penetrating insight of a young child? But how few are able to *accept* the observation and thus confirm sensibility as part of the domain of permissible communication! Parents, therefore, train their children to be non-perceptive to the subtleties of thought, feeling and behaviour by withholding reward for communication in these areas. Teachers, unless they take specific kinds of action, merely reinforce early training. On this argument then, creative writing in schools is largely a sham because teachers do nothing to overcome the effects of this negative training, to tap this hidden pool of talent. If creative writing is to fulfil its purpose, *the teacher must establish sensibility as a permissible communication.*

### THE SIGNIFICANCE OF TRUST

In the chapters on communication and interpersonal relationships in the classroom, it was argued that the teacher is a highly significant ego. As well, the *efficacy* of much of his teaching depends critically upon his managing interpersonal transactions so that he establishes a feeling of mutual *trust.*

If the teacher is to break down the barriers to communication of sensibility, he needs this trust, as children have to be brought to a new valuation

* "To bar": colloquialism meaning to give another a ride on the bar of your bicycle as your passenger.

of the communication of *real* thoughts, feelings and behaviour. Further, they need to be supported while they overcome their apprehensions, and they need to learn to accept communication as a rewarding experience, which enriches knowledge of the human condition.

## PREPARATORY PROGRAMME

This programme is designed to provide Stage II Learning (Precision) in the development of creative writing (as explicated informally in the first part of this chapter) from a topic analysis on creative writing. As a programme outline it provides the rationale for the kinds of exercises which are considered most appropriate; it does not detail any lesson plans.

It is necessary to emphasise that the programme as designed will not be successful unless it follows a stage of free-writing corresponding to Stage I Learning (Discovery). Ideally, it should be introduced when the pupils no longer show improvement in the free-writing programme: this is usually apparent by the repetition of thematic content.

Following an intensive programme along the lines described below, which may last for three or four weeks, pupils would go on to a Stage III (Discovery) programme to exploit the learning of Stage II (Precision). The story quoted above—*The First Time*—is an example of one such exercise, where the pupil selected his own theme, but wrote under the constraints of characterisation learned in the previous stage; that is, Behavioural Objective Type II.

After further experience, the pupil should be set an assignment with constraints suitable for a Type III Behavioural Objective, on the assumption that he has a sufficient expertise to use that amount of freedom with profit.

### ESTABLISHING THE CLIMATE

The communication of sensibility is conditional upon a climate based on mutual trust; the teacher must therefore establish that he is a person who *accepts* ideas, feelings and behaviour in the everyday verbal transactions with his class.

### THE CONCEPT OF SENSIBILITY

For pupils to know the objectives of the programme, they must understand the concept of *sensibility* which will be the principal reference point in evaluating their work.

A particularly effective way to communicate this concept is to read an example of writing which displays sensibility (such as the example *The First Time*) and to explore class reactions to it in comparison with an attempt on the same topic which lacks sensibility, written by an anonymous writer from another class. Examples of sensibility are usually identified by the class as points which make the attempt superior. These can be called examples of *sensibility in writing*.

Sensibility involves perception of what is below the surface of behaviour, appreciation of this substrata as an integral part of the presenting (or surface) behaviour, and communication in writing of the totality through the speech, thoughts and actions of people both explicitly and implicitly as appropriate for the meaning to be conveyed. Thus, pupils should be able to identify examples of sensibility and to identify the meaning it conveys, and the means, both explicit and implicit, by which this is achieved. Naïve pupils will probably need examples that are fairly obvious, and help from illustrations of analogous experiences.

Above all, the examples must be credible to the pupils *in terms of the way they view their world*. The topic chosen to introduce sensibility must, therefore, be chosen relative to the concerns of the children considering the cultural background of the particular class *and it must exhibit values which are acceptable to them*. The value of the example given is that it illustrates a universal predicament, and it can easily be translated into predicaments that are of immediate concern to particular individuals or even groups.

## THE USE OF MIME AND ROLE PLAY
### Developing Sensitivity
When communication of sensibility has not been permissible and thus has been generally unrewarded, individuals may have become relatively insensitive to the nuances of meaning in interpersonal relationships. Sensitivity training must, therefore, play an important part in developing creative writing. Mime and role playing are valuable as an introduction to such training.

### MIME
The most important feature of the use of mime must be that it is a *talking point* and not a performance. Teachers who are experts on mime have failed to achieve the purpose of its use in this programme simply by placing themselves too far "above" the pupils in competence and by changing the focus of attention from the *communication of meaning through mime*, to performance. The situations mimed must be within the domain of the direct experience of the class, so that when the mime is discussed:

> How did he show his uneasiness?
> Where were his eyes? etc.
> Would we all react this way?
> How would *you* have felt?
> How would this have been apparent to us if we were watching you?

the discussion is about what matters to them. It is real.

Mime situations suitable for a beginners' programme can be devised to illustrate basic emotions, such as love, guilt, hate, anger, pride, shame and anxiety. The exercises must require that the expression of these emotions is consistent with the social constraints inherent in the given situation. For example, the topic is *pride*—and the situation to be mimed is the reception of a prize in front of the school. In this case the expression of pride is limited by the possibility of censure if it goes beyond certain bounds.

## ROLE PLAY

The remarks about the use of mime in this kind of programme apply equally to role play. The role play should deal with predicaments which are real to the class; talking should be more about what was attempted than the quality of the performance.

### Establishing Sensibility as a Permissible Communication

The teacher must not only establish a general climate of trust as has been previously described, but he must also establish sensibility as a *permissible communication*. A major barrier for the pupil is the teacher's traditional role as a person remote from the real concerns of this world—hence the quip: What county of England is most like the teaching profession? Middlesex!

The teacher is not usually a person to whom one communicates sensibility—he wouldn't understand and, if he did, would moralise!

If the teacher is prepared to participate in mime and role play activities and discussion *at the class level*, giving his own thoughts and feelings as he expects the pupils to do, he steps off his traditional pedestal. Further, if he is prepared to accept comment about the *significant adults* in the pupil's world, he becomes someone with whom his pupils can communicate about real life.

## AN EVALUATION VOCABULARY

If the programme is to deal with the Stage of Precision in learning, evaluation of the written work will need to be explicit. The evaluation vocabulary associated with the basic cognitive processes (described earlier, see Chapter 8) is essential, and it should be established before embarking on the exercises below.

## UNDERSTANDING BASIC COGNITIVE PROCESSES: PARAGRAPHING

Many pupils are handicapped in writing about events because they do not realise the significance of discontinuities of discourse—where we expect the recipient of a communication to bridge the gap with a "mental leap" (see Chapter 8, p. 106). As a result, pupils become lost in the trivia of their experience as they attempt to give it in sequence.

A device necessary to train some classes in the ability to make selective omissions in discourse is to provide comic strips and ask for the removal of as many frames as possible, without making it impossible to "fill in" the story—a kind of "pictorial telegram" writing.

A further device helps with the application of the principle of selective omissions to paragraphing. If each pupil is given a paper divided into four numbered squares, and told that the *third* square contains an illustration of (say) a kitchen in which someone has his hand in the cake tin, he can then be instructed to fill in the other frames with pictures which will complete a story *that is extended in time*. That is, each picture must represent a group of events separated by time, yet together illustrating one coherent event. For example, one ten-year-old gave the following solution: (1) a broken window; (2) a burglar who had been working at a safe for a time; and (4) Father, poker in hand, apprehending the burglar.

Further developments can involve writing captions, the theme of each picture (hence of a paragraph), and then paragraph writing.

# EXERCISES

## ACCEPTING BOUNDS

The first step in writing is to get pupils to accept the constraints of "bounds".

Thus they may be asked to write upon their experiences in a dentist's waiting-room without referring to *anything* that is not apparent within its four walls—"bounds" with a physical context.

To facilitate the writing of sensibility, the miming of a waiting-room predicament—there is a pretty girl alone when a boy enters; where does he sit, and why—is a useful cue. What is the probability of different actions? Pupils are instructed not to write on the situations mimed.

They would be instructed, in addition:

> Your work will be assessed for sensibility; the relevance and significance of the events you describe to the mime you are developing; and your care with probability in communication. Finally, if you refer to anything not apparent in the waiting-room, or seriously offend the principle of probability, you will fail completely—like getting a calculation wrong in mathematics—and you will have to make an entirely fresh start.

### Evaluation

The teacher communicates evaluation of sensibility by underlining the significant phrases, and indicating an appraisal rank by one, two or three vertical strokes in the margin. A useful system for the pupils understand that *one* stroke means the teacher has noted the *explicit* communication of a thought or feeling of significance; *two* strokes mean that it is *implicit* to the behaviour described, and of some subtlety; and *three* strokes mean that it is a perception usually expected of adults. Lack of care with probability in communication can be shown by a question mark—the matter of degree by one, two or three strokes—the latter indicating the point of failure, and the necessity for a new attempt if the pupil cannot successfully defend what he has written.

### A Progression of "Bounds" Preparatory Exercises

The following instructions illustrate two types of exercises which should follow.

1. You have been called to the Principal's office, for an unspecified reason. However you have a guilty conscience.

   Write on what happens outside his office from the moment he answers the door and greets you, but shuts it on hearing the phone, to the moment later when you know the purpose of the summons.

   Your work will be assessed in terms of sensibility, relevance and significance of content to your theme and probability.

2. A picture is provided which illustrates a human predicament, such as a wife in a hospital bed, visited by her husband and adolescent son.

Husband is unashamedly glued to the football programme on the television, the son is obviously uneasy, and the wife has a high head of steam. The class is instructed:

Identify with someone in the picture and describe what is happening. You may only write about events which are immediately relevant to those of the picture, and you must accept the painter's communication of the situation (expression on face, posture, etc.).

Your work will be assessed in terms of sensibility, relevance and significance of content to your theme and probability.

## WRITING WITHIN RIGOROUSLY DEFINED BOUNDS

This kind of exercise is designed to "force" the exploitation of understanding human behaviour in its reorganisation at a higher conceptual level to find a solution to the problem set. Each of the following exercises represents a stage of development: the first (or "gap filler") is the one which best characterises the aims and purposes of the programme as a whole—that of precision; the others are representative of a "weaning" process towards the autonomy of Stage III Learning (Discovery).

### The "Gap Filler"

The following three examples demonstrate precision.

*Instructions.* Fill the gap using 70-100 words; sustain the characters and remember your work will be evaluated in terms of consistency of behaviour with character; sensibility; relevance and significance of content to the theme you adopt and probability.

No. 1 "You're late—as usual," said George with a strangely uneasy grin. It gave me a stab of anxiety which I promptly forgot in the face of having to make decisions.
"Well, we can start now," I said.
"The plan we agreed on is to raid old Simpson," said Tom with a cold glance at me—his usual dislike quite apparent. "I propose we go through the gap in the hedge at Brooke's farm."

GAP

"I don't care if I never see you again," I shouted. "You can keep the gang. I don't want it."

No. 2 She surveyed him thoughtfully. "He needs a haircut, but then Jenny and the others think him dreamy. I suppose for a brother he's not too bad—and he certainly never wants for a girlfriend! Wish I attracted boys the way he does girls! . . ."
"I wonder what he'll say when he finds out what I've arranged. Jill will be arriving any minute now. He *must* like her, he just must . . ."

GAP

"Brothers!"

R

No. 3 "Aw, do I have to go?"
"Of course you do. Aunt Mary would be very disappointed if you didn't."
"But to a *girls'* party!"
"Now, listen, John. I told your Aunt that you were going to Helen's party and you're going."

### GAP

As they heard John arrive, John's parents looked up apprehensively.
"Well?" asked his father.
"Yes, very well," grinned John.

Simple exercises like these would be followed by exercises where character was delineated with greater subtlety.

## Open Enders

The following two examples demonstrate intermediate, "weaning" exercises.

*Instructions:* Complete the "story" using 70-100 words, sustain the characters and remember your work . . .

No. 1 The class filed out until there were only three boys left in their desks and the teacher collecting her books together on the table.
Sam gazed too casually out of the window, sitting back in his chair with his hands in his pockets. John stared down at his hands and gave the appearance of someone completely absorbed in his nails. Ken furtively watched the movements of the teacher, his face strained and anxious.
At last the teacher came towards them, folded her arms and looked at them without a word and with nothing they could read on her face. Sam managed to stare defiantly, John blushed painfully and looked away, and Ken just could not raise his eyes.
"I think you know why I asked you to stay behind," she said.

No. 2 David eased the door back with just the faintest protest from the carpet pile and flatfooted towards the table.
"Funny," he thought, "I hadn't realised how quiet this room was." Suddenly his knee betrayed him with a sharp crack and he froze in sheer horror. Reason came to his rescue. "It's loud to me; but it wouldn't be heard outside this room." He listened intently between the frantic rushes of breath. "No, nothing!" With new confidence he stepped lightly to the table in the sitting room.
The catch lifted easily. In a moment the medal was in his hand. The blood drummed loudly in his ears, his forehead was suddenly cold, and with the rush of sick feeling came vivid memories of that moment when he had once fainted before an attack of 'flu. Some deep breaths. "Thank goodness for first aid lessons!" he thought—and he was right again.

He shut the case and with the medal in his pocket prepared for the journey back to the door and relative safety. But from behind him, in the recess of the alcove, there came a shattering crackle of fresh newspaper. In the still moment before his father spoke David berated himself in angry frustration: "Why *do* you always get into situations like this?"

"What are you doing, David?" The tone was quite expressionless. It could mean anything.

## Open Ender to a Given Theme

The following is an example of a completion exercise where the given theme is *Disappointment*.

*Instructions.* Complete the story in 100-150 words on a theme of *Disappointment*. Remember your work . . .

"I wonder why Mr. Williams asked me what books I liked? Of course he also asked Richard. Though he didn't really seem interested in what Richard said. I'm sure he wrote down something on that paper and put it in his pocket after he talked to me . . . but he didn't after talking to Richard.

A feeling of expectant pleasure radiated through him and he savoured it, watching and listening vaguely while one child after another mounted the steps, shook hands with the chairman and carried his book away.

From two rows in front, Sally turned suddenly, looked him straight in the eye, and winked. At once all his pleasure left him.

"Dad won the art prize in Form I. I simply must get it! Please God! Please remember I didn't eat that apple during the sermon after all . . .

"And now," continued the headmaster, smiling broadly, "I have great pleasure in awarding the Committee's special prize for art, to—er—yes, to Richard Maxwell."

## Writing under Pressure of Time

From trial and error experience, it was discovered that if the first draft of the "bounds" exercise is *scribbled* without any care to spelling and grammar, within *15 minutes,* the results are more satisfactory. This, of course, must be followed by time to make a finished copy, pupils being allowed to make as many drafts as they wish but required to keep all drafts and hand them in with the finished copy. This improves communication between teacher and pupil *in the event* that the pupil's work has flaws: it makes possible the retrieval of discarded, but significant, ideas; and where presentation of an idea offends the principle of probability in communication, it increases the likelihood of *teacher*-perception of its significance by making available the train of thought leading to it.

# *Appendix A*

## INSTRUMENTATION OF THE TAXONOMY OF EDUCATIONAL OBJECTIVES: COGNITIVE DOMAIN[1]

| | KEY WORDS | |
|---|---|---|
| **Taxonomy Classification** | **Examples of Infinitives** | **Examples of Direct Objects** |
| 1.00 Knowledge | | |
| 1.10 Knowledge of Specifics | | |
| 1.11 Knowledge of Terminology | to define, to distinguish, to acquire, to identify, to recall, to recognise | vocabulary, terms, terminology, meaning(s), definitions, referents, elements |
| 1.12 Knowledge of Specific Facts | to recall, to recognise, to acquire, to identify | facts, factual information, (sources), (names), (dates), (events), (persons), (places), (time periods), properties, examples, phenomena |
| 1.20 Knowledge of Ways and Means of Dealing with Specifics | | |
| 1.21 Knowledge of Conventions | to recall, to identify, to recognise, to acquire | form(s), conventions, uses, usage, rules, ways, devices, symbols, representations, style(s), format(s) |

[1] From R. J. Kibler *et al.*, *Behavioural Objectives and Instruction*, Allyn and Bacon, Inc., Boston, 1970, pp. 180-4.

## KEY WORDS

| Taxonomy Classification | Examples of Infinitives | Examples of Direct Objects |
|---|---|---|
| 1.22 Knowledge of Trends, Sequences | to recall, to recognise, to acquire, to identify | action(s), processes, movement(s), continuity, development(s), trend(s), sequence(s), causes, relationship(s), forces, influences |
| 1.23 Knowledge of Classifications and Categories | to recall, to recognise, to acquire, to identify | area(s), type(s), feature(s), class(es), set(s), division(s), arrangement(s), classification(s), category/categories |
| 1.24 Knowledge of Criteria | to recall, to recognise, to acquire, to identify | criteria, basics, elements |
| 1.25 Knowledge of Methodology | to recall, to recognise, to acquire, to identify | methods, techniques, approaches, uses, procedures, treatments |
| 1.30 Knowledge of the Universals and Abstractions in a Field | | |
| 1.31 Knowledge of Principles, Generalisations | to recall, to recognise, to acquire, to identify | principle(s), generalisation(s), proposition(s), fundamentals, laws, principal elements, implication(s) |
| 1.32 Knowledge of Theories and Structures | to recall, to recognise, to acquire, to identify | theories, bases, interrelations, structure(s), organisation(s), formulation(s) |
| 2.00 Comprehension | | |
| 2.10 Translation | to translate, to transform, to give in own words, to illustrate, to prepare, to read, to represent, to change, to rephrase, to restate | meaning(s), sample(s), definitions, abstractions, representations, words, phrases |

| | KEY WORDS | |
| Taxonomy Classification | Examples of Infinitives | Examples of Direct Objects |
| --- | --- | --- |
| 2.20 Interpretation | to interpret, to reorder, to rearrange, to differentiate, to distinguish, to make, to draw, to explain, to demonstrate | relevancies, relationships, essentials, aspects, new view(s), qualifications, conclusions, methods, theories, abstractions |
| 2.30 Extrapolation | to estimate, to infer, to conclude, to predict, to differentiate, to determine, to extend, to interpolate, to extrapolate, to fill in, to draw | consequences, implications, conclusions, factors, ramifications, meanings, corollaries, effects, probabilities |
| 3.00 Application | to apply, to generalise, to relate, to choose, to develop, to organise, to use, to employ, to transfer, to restructure, to classify | principles, laws, conclusions, effects, methods, theories, abstractions, situations, generalisations, processes, phenomena, procedures |
| 4.00 Analysis | | |
| 4.10 Analysis of Elements | to distinguish, to detect, to identify, to classify, to discriminate, to recognise, to categorise, to deduce | elements, hypothesis/ hypotheses, conclusions, assumptions, statements (of fact), statements (of intent), arguments, particulars |
| 4.20 Analysis of Relationships | to analyse, to contrast, to compare, to distinguish, to deduce | relationships, inter-relations, relevance, relevancies, themes, evidence, fallacies, arguments, cause-effect(s), consistency/consistencies, parts, ideas, assumptions |
| 4.30 Analysis of Organisational Principles | to analyse, to distinguish, to detect, to deduce | form(s), pattern(s), purpose(s), point(s) of view(s), techniques, bias(es), structure(s), theme(s), arrangement(s), organisation(s) |

## KEY WORDS

| Taxonomy Classification | Examples of Infinitives | Examples of Direct Objects |
|---|---|---|
| 5.00 Synthesis | | |
| 5.10 Production of a Unique Communication | to write, to tell, to relate, to produce, to constitute, to transmit, to originate, to modify, to document | structure(s), pattern(s), product(s), performance(s), design(s), work(s), communications, effort(s), specifics, composition(s) |
| 5.20 Production of a Plan, or Proposed Set of Operations | to propose, to plan, to produce, to design, to modify, to specify | plan(s), objectives, specification(s), schematic(s), operations, way(s), solution(s), means |
| 5.30 Derivation of a Set of Abstract Relations | to produce, to derive, to develop, to combine, to organise, to synthesise, to classify, to deduce, to develop, to formulate, to modify | phenomena, taxonomies, concept(s), scheme(s), theories, relationships, abstractions, generalisations, hypothesis/hypotheses, perceptions, ways, discoveries |
| 6.00 Evaluation | | |
| 6.10 Judgments in Terms of Internal Evidence | to judge, to argue, to validate, to assess, to decide | accuracy/accuracies, consistency/consistencies, fallacies, reliability, flaws, errors, precision, exactness |
| 6.20 Judgments in Terms of External Criteria | to judge, to argue, to consider, to compare, to contrast, to standardise, to appraise | ends, means, efficiency, economy/economies, utility, alternatives, courses of action, standards, theories, generalisations |

# *Appendix B*

## INSTRUMENTATION OF THE TAXONOMY OF EDUCATIONAL OBJECTIVES: AFFECTIVE DOMAIN[1]

| | **KEY WORDS** | |
|---|---|---|
| **Taxonomy Classification** | **Examples of Infinitives** | **Examples of Direct Objects** |
| 1.0 Receiving | | |
| 1.1 Awareness | to differentiate, to separate, to set apart, to share | sights, sounds, events, designs, arrangements |
| 1.2 Willingness to Receive | to accumulate, to select, to combine, to accept | models, examples, shapes, sizes, meters, cadences |
| 1.3 Controlled or Selected Attention | to select, to posturally respond to, to listen (for), to control | alternatives, answers, rhythms, nuances |
| 2.0 Responding | | |
| 2.1 Acquiescence in Responding | to comply (with), to follow, to commend, to approve | directions, instructions, laws, policies, demonstrations |
| 2.2 Willingness to Respond | to volunteer, to discuss, to practise, to play | instruments, games, dramatic works, charades, burlesques |
| 2.3 Satisfaction in Response | to applaud, to acclaim, to spend leisure time in, to augment | speeches, plays, presentations, writings |

[1] From R. J. Kibler *et al.*, *Behavioural Objectives and Instruction,* Allyn and Bacon Inc., Boston, 1970, pp. 186-7.

| Taxonomy Classification | KEY WORDS | |
| | Examples of Infinitives | Examples of Direct Objects |
| --- | --- | --- |
| 3.0 Valuing | | |
| 3.1 Acceptance of a Value | to increase measured proficiency in, to increase numbers of, to relinquish, to specify | group membership(s), artistic production(s), musical productions, personal friendships |
| 3.2 Preference for a Value | to assist, to subsidise, to help, to support | artists, projects, viewpoints, arguments |
| 3.3 Commitment | to deny, to protest, to debate, to argue | deceptions, irrelevancies, abdications, irrationalities |
| 4.0 Organisation | | |
| 4.1 Conceptualisation of a Value | to discuss, to theorise (on), to abstract, to compare | parameters, codes, standards, goals |
| 4.2 Organisation of a Value System | to balance, to organise, to define, to formulate | systems, approaches, criteria, limits |
| 5.0 Characterisation by Value or Value Complex | | |
| 5.1 Generalised Set | to revise, to change, to complete, to require | plans, behaviour, methods, effort(s) |
| 5.2 Characterisation | to be rated high by peers in, to be rated high by superiors in, to be rated high by subordinates in | humanitarianism, ethics, integrity, maturity |
| | and | |
| | to avoid, to manage, to resolve, to resist | extravagance(s), excesses, conflicts, exorbitancy/ exorbitancies |

# Appendix C

A. Depletion of natural resources in an insufficiently diversified economy has left the West Coast peculiarly vulnerable to changes in New Zealand's economy.

   I. Continued heavy dependence upon exhaustible natural resources rather than diversification of the economy has led to a substantial reduction in regional income following a decreased market for coal and timber.

      1. Easily-won income from the exploitation and export in an un- or little-processed state of originally valuable resources of gold, coal and timber provided little incentive for diversification which would have cushioned these reductions.

         (a) More easily-won returns from extractive industries on the West Coast and higher returns per unit of farm investment in other New Zealand regions were sufficiently competitive to discourage investment of capital in the extensive development of farming.

      2. The economic cushioning effects of farm development and the establishment of plants processing mineral and forest products have been greatly retarded due to unattractive or impractical investment prospects.

         (a) Substantial capital would be needed to extend the areas of highly productive farming because of the very serious drainage and fertility improvement problems involved in reclaiming the 'pakiki' flats, scattered in many pockets, thus also posing high transport cost problems.

         (b) Exploitation of mineral and forest resources has remained largely in the hands of outside business interests unwilling to process their products on the West Coast because such action would cause redundancies with their established plants elsewhere or, as with gas-making, prove economically impracticable.

   II. Changes in New Zealand's economy have enabled the utilisation of alternative sources of coal and timber, so lowering demand for the West Coast's chief products, thus depressing the economy.

---

[1] From D. W. F. Brown and J. U. Macaulay, *Topic Analysis in the Teaching of Geography, Proceedings of the Sixth New Zealand Geography Conference*, 1970, Vol. II, p. 85.

1. Competition, resulting from advancing technology, has led to the adoption of fuel sources other than coal, and high transport costs have favoured mining areas much closer to markets where the use of coal has been continued.

2. The much more rapid maturing of exotic forests has provided immense and far more accessible stands of single species of millable timber of a quality comparable with that of the West Coast's stands of mixed indigenous trees.

# *Appendix D*

## AN EXAMPLE OF PART II OF A TOPIC ANALYSIS FOR CORRECTION
## (GEOGRAPHY)

*An example of Part II of a Topic Analysis on Mixed Farming on the Canterbury Plains, New Zealand which needs correction. An outline of a correct version follows.*

A. Mixed farming on the Canterbury Plains exploits the need to renew pastures frequently.

   I. Pastures are renewed by utilising natural and seasonal resources in the adoption of a specific rotation system, through man's assessment and modification of the land.

      1. Extremes of climate and the light soils enforce the continual renewal of the pastures on the Canterbury Plains.

         a. Summer drought and winter harshness exhaust pastures and limit growth primarily to spring and autumn in most areas.

           i. In summer evaporation exceeds precipitation and the north-west (fohn) wind has an additional drying effect, therefore adaptions to counteract drought are necessary.

           ii. Winter growth is limited by the frequency of hard frosts and snow, hence the need for supplementary fodder crops.

           iii. Canterbury has one of the largest outputs of seed crops because the high sunshine hours are ideal for crop ripening and harvesting.

           iv. Effectiveness of temperature and precipitation in spring and autumn provide suitable conditions for planting and harvesting.

         b. Soils are a varying combination of loess and alluvium hence require careful conservation.

           i. The predominance of gravel restricts potential fertility, owing to the limited capacity for moisture retention.

           ii. Protection from erosion by north-west winds is provided by shelter belts.

           iii. The soils need continual application of fertilisers and a rotation involving nitrogenous crops to maintain their mineral content.

      2. Man has assessed and modified the Canterbury Plains by experimentation and the application of technological advances to develop mixed farming, hinging on economic demand.

a. The succession through progressive stages to mixed farming was aided by experimentation involving methods of increasing production, and technological improvements both overseas and in New Zealand.

   i. Experimentation with stock breeding, improvement of crop strains and sequences, fertilisers, pest control, drainage and irrigation in limited areas where finance is available has increased production per unit area.

   ii. World technological advances, especially in refrigeration, transportation and mechanisation have helped the evolution of the present farming pattern on the Canterbury Plains.

b. Mixed farming developed in an area of limited pasture growth involves animals, and cropping—not only for fodder but also for cash.

   i. Farming on the Canterbury Plains is dominated by livestock production for meat and wool.

   ii. Fodder crops are grown in considerable quantities to supplement pasture in the summer and winter non-growth periods.

   iii. Commercial grain crops fit naturally into the livestock programme in this area of considerable summer drought.

   iv. Pasture, the basis of this economy, is renewed in a sequence and animal grazing is rotated accordingly.

c. Economic factors have and always will determine the importance of the constituents of mixed farming on the Canterbury Plains.

   i. In order to maximise profits the farmer adjusts to the laws of supply and demand and concentrates on pastoralism, which provides greater returns than arable farming.

   ii. Meat may provide up to 50% of the total income, mainly from fat lambs.

   iii. Wool is a significant secondary product, hence is also significant in the economy.

   iv. The relative importance of cash cropping fluctuates according to returns from sheep farming.

*Outline of a correct version*

A. Man's assessment of the resources available on the Canterbury Plains has led to the development of mixed farming.

  I. Extremes of climate and the light soils enforce the continual renewal of the pastures.

   (a) Summer drought and winter harshness exhaust pastures.

   (b) Soils are a varying combination of loess and alluvium and hence require careful cultivation.

   (c) Growth is limited primarily to spring and autumn in most areas.

  II. Technological advances and controlled experimentation have combined to increase the yield of mixed farming.

   (a) Mixed farming can only be successful if it is a feasible economic proposition.

# Appendix E

*The example of Topic Analysis below illustrates typical difficulties in identifying and stating main ideas in an ordered manner. The annotations indicate the kind of dialogue which should follow this attempt.*

Topic Analysis:

A. Since a metal is able to be viewed as a +ive ion lattice with valence electrons freely permeating the structure, the relative ease with which the electrons may move through the structure, or under some conditions leave the structure, and the positive and negative forces acting in the lattice must determine the properties, both physical and chemical, of the metal. *Condense. Has main idea been identified*

  1. The addition of energy to the metallic lattice gives the electrons in it incentive to move more quickly in the direction of that added energy. *Confused of id*

    (a) Heat energy as well as electrical energy, since they both have this effect, are conducted through the lattice in this way.

*Not mentioned in A!?*

  2. The way the positive ions are packed together in the lattice which is determined by the resultant forces acting between them, and their size, decides other metal properties.

*Belongs to 1a ?,?*

    (a) Since displacement of the ions in the lattice relative to each other does not destroy the general attractive force which holds the lattice together, metals can be drawn out into long thin wires (Ductile) or hammered into thin sheets (Malleability). *(Insufficient explanation because*

    (b) Since each metal atom differs in size, the metal packing can be close or far apart causing each metal to have different densities.

  3. The ease with which electrons leave the lattice, leaving behind positive ions, which are then capable of joining up with ions of other elements determines the chemical reactivity of the metal.

*Overall :—*
*"A" too narrow.*

    (a) Reaction with air and water, important because it is to these elements most metals are subjected for most of the time, appears to designate most metals to a series of reactivity.

*Two main ideas should be made explicit.*

    (b) Acid reactivity is in agreement with the above pattern established.

*(needs re-classification of ideas. "(Hierarchy faulty)"*

# Bibliography

ADAMS, R. S. and BIDDLE, B. J., *Realities of Teaching*, Holt, Rinehart and Winston, New York, 1970.

ALLPORT, G. W., *Becoming*, Yale University Press, New Haven, 1955.

ALLPORT, G. W., "Crisis in Personality Development", in STROM, R. D. (Ed.), *Teachers and the Learning Process*, Prentice-Hall Inc., Englewood Cliffs, 1971.

AMIDON, E. and HUNTER, E., *Improving Teaching: The Analysis of Classroom Verbal Instruction*, Holt, Rinehart and Winston, New York, 1967.

AUSUBEL, D. P., *Ego Development and the Personality Disorders*, Grune and Stratton, New York, 1952.

AUSUBEL, D. P., *The Psychology of Meaningful Verbal Learning*, Grune and Stratton, New York, 1963.

AUSUBEL, D. P., "The Use of Advance Organizers in the Learning and Retention of Meaningful Verbal Material", *J. educ. Psych.* 1960, **51**, pp. 267-72.

AUSUBEL, D. P. and ROBINSON, F. G., *School Learning*, Holt, Rinehart and Winston, New York, 1969.

BARRETT, H. O., "Research", in *Education of the Gifted, The Fourteenth Yearbook of the Ontario School Inspectors' Association*, The Copp Clark Publishing Co. Ltd., Vancouver, 1958.

BARRON, F., "The Disposition Toward Originality", *J. abnorm. soc. Psychol.*, 1955, **51**, pp. 478-85.

BARRON, F., "Some Personality Correlates of Independence of Judgment", *J. Pers.*, 1953, **21**, pp. 287-97.

BARRON, F., "Complexity-simplicity as a Personality Dimension", *J. abnorm. soc. Psychol.*, 1953, **48**, pp. 163-72.

BARRON, F., "Originality in Relation to Personality and Intellect", *J. Pers.*, 1957, **25**, pp. 730-42.

BARTLETT, F. C., *Thinking*, Allen and Unwin, London, 1958.

BERLYNE, D. E., *Conflict, Arousal and Curiosity*, McGraw-Hill Book Co., New York, 1960.

BERLYNE, D. E., "Recent Developments in Piaget's Work", in HARPER, R. J. C. (Ed.), *Readings—The Cognitive Processes*, Prentice-Hall Inc., Englewood Cliffs, 1964.

BERNE, E., *Games People Play*, André Deutsch, London, 1966.

BERNSTEIN, B., "Social Structure, Language and Learning", *Educ. Res.*, June 1961, **III**, No. 3, pp. 163-76.

BIESTEK, F. P., *The Casework Relationship*, Unwin University Books, London, 1957.

BIGGE, M. L. and HUNT, M. P., *Psychological Foundations of Education*, Harper and Row, New York, 1962.

BLOOM, B. S. (Ed.) *et al.*, *Taxonomy of Educational Objectives—The Classification of Educational Goals, Handbook I: the Cognitive Domain*, David McKay, New York, 1956.

BLOOM, B. S., *Stability and Change in Human Characteristics*, John Wiley & Sons, New York, 1964.

BLOOM, B. S. *et al.*, *Handbook on Formative and Summative Evaluation of Student Learning*, McGraw-Hill Book Co., New York, 1971.

BOSSING, N. L., *Teaching in Secondary Schools*, Houghton Mifflin, Boston, 3rd ed., 1952.

BRALEY, L., "Strategy Selection and Negative Instances in Concept Learning", *J. educ. Psychol.*, 1963, **54**, pp. 154-9.

BROUDY, H. S. *et al.*, *Democracy and Excellence in American Secondary Education*, Rand McNally and Co., Chicago, 1964.

BROWN, D. W. F. and MACAULAY, J. U., *Topic Analysis in the Teaching of Geography, Proceedings of the Sixth New Zealand Geography Conference*, 1970, **II**, pp. 83-9.

BROWNELL, W. A., and HENDRICKSON, A., "How Children Learn Information, Concepts and Generalizations", *49th Yearbook, National Society for the Study of Education*, University of Chicago Press, Chicago, 1950.

BRUNER, J. S., "On Perceptual Readiness", *Psychol. Rev.*, 1957, **64**, pp. 123-52.

BRUNER, J. S., *The Process of Education*, Harvard University Press, Cambridge, 1961.

BRUNER, J. S., "On Going Beyond The Information Given", in HARPER, R. J. C. (Ed.), *Readings—The Cognitive Processes*, Prentice-Hall Inc., Englewood Cliffs, 1964.

BRUNER, J. S., "The Course of Cognitive Growth", *Am. Psychol.*, 1964, **19**, pp. 1-15.

BRUNER, J. S., *Toward A Theory of Instruction*, Harvard University Press, Cambridge, 1966.

BRUNER, J. S., GOODNOW, J. J., and AUSTIN, G. A., *A Study of Thinking*, John Wiley & Sons, New York, 1956.

BUSWELL, G., "Educational Theory and The Psychology of Learning", *J. educ. Psychol.*, 1956, **47**, pp. 175-84.

CALLAHAN, S. G., *Successful Teaching in Secondary Schools*, Scott Foresman, Glenview, 1966.

CANFIELD, R. G. "How Useful are Lessons on Listening?", *Elementary School Journal*, 1961, **62**, No. 3, pp. 147-51.

CARROLL, J. B., *Language and Thought*, Prentice-Hall Inc., Englewood Cliffs, 1964.

CARROLL, J. B., "Words, Meanings and Concepts", *Harvard Educational Review*, 1964, **34**, pp. 178-202.

CARTWRIGHT, D. and ZANDER, A., *Group Dynamics, Research and Theory*, Row, Peterson and Co., Evanston, 1962.

COLEMAN, J. S., *The Adolescent Society*, Free Press of Glencoe, New York, 1961.

CURRICULUM REVIEW GROUP, New Zealand Post-Primary Teachers' Association, *Education in Charge*, Longman Paul Ltd., Auckland, 1969.

DASHIELL, J. F., "A Survey and Synthesis of Learning Theories", *Psychol. Bull.*, 1935, **32**, pp. 261-75.

DE CECCO, J. P. (Ed.), *Educational Technology, Readings in Programmed Instruction*, Holt, Rinehart and Winston, New York, 1964.

DE CECCO, J. P., *The Psychology of Learning and Instruction: Educational Psychology*, Prentice-Hall Inc., Englewood Cliffs, 1968.

DE HAAN, R. F. and HAVIGHURST, R. J., *Educating Gifted Children*, University of Chicago Press, Chicago, Rev. ed., 1961.

DIENES, Z. P., *Concept Formation and Personality*, Leicester University Press, Leicester, 1959.

DIENES, Z. P., "The Growth of Mathematical Concepts in Children through Experience", *Educ. Res.*, 1959, **2**, pp. 9-28.

DINKMEYER, D. C., *Child Development: The Emerging Self*, Prentice-Hall Inc., Englewood Cliffs, 1965.

DOLLARD, J. and MILLER, N. E., *Personality and Psychotherapy*, McGraw-Hill Book Co., New York, 1950.

DUNCKER, K., "On Problem Solving", (trans. by L. S. LEES,) *Psychol. Monogr.*, 1945, **58**.

DUNHAM, J., "Appropriate Leadership Patterns", *Educ. Res.*, 1965, **7**, No. 2, pp. 115-26.

EELS, K. W. *et al.*, *Intelligence and Cultural Differences*, University of Chicago Press, Chicago, 1951.

EISNER, E. W., "Instructional and Expressive Objectives", in POPHAM, W. *et al.*, *Instructional Objectives*, Rand McNally and Co., Chicago, 1969.

ERICKSON, E. H., *Childhood and Society*, Norton and Co., New York, 1950.

ESTES, W. K. *et al.*, *Modern Learning Theory*, Appleton-Century-Crofts, New York, 1954.

EYSENCK, H. J., *Dimensions of Personality*, Routledge and Kegan Paul, London, 1947.

FESTINGER, L., *A Theory of Cognitive Dissonance*, Row, Peterson and Co., Evanston, 1957.

FESTINGER, L., and CARLSMITH, J. M., "Cognitive Consequences of Forced Compliance", *J. abnorm. soc. Psychol.*, 1959, **58**, pp. 203-10.

FLANDERS, N. A., "Teacher Influence, Pupil Attitudes and Achievement Studies in Interaction Analysis", *University of Minnesota Final Report, Co-operative Research Project No. 397*, Office of Education, Department of Health, Education and Welfare, 1960.

FLAVELL, J. H., *The Developmental Psychology of Jean Piaget*, Van Nostrand, Princeton, 1963.

FRENCH, J. R. P., and RAVEN, B., "The Bases of Social Power in Studies", in CARTWRIGHT, D. (Ed.), *Social Power*, Institute for Social Research, Ann Arbor, 1959.

FROMM, E., *The Art of Loving*, Harper and Row, New York, 1956.

GAGNÉ, R. M., *The Conditions of Learning*, Holt, Rinehart and Winston, New York, 1965; 2nd ed., 1970.

GAGNÉ, R. M., "The Acquisition of Knowledge", *Psychol. Rev.*, 1962, **69**, pp. 355-65.

GALLAGHER, J. J., *Teaching the Gifted Child*, Allyn and Bacon, Boston, 1964.

GERLACH, V. S. and ELY, D. P., *Teaching and Media: A Systematic Approach*, Prentice-Hall Inc., Englewood Cliffs, 1971.

GLASER, R., *Teaching Machines and Programmed Learning II*, Department of Audio Visual Instruction, National Educational Association of the U.S.A., Washington, 1965.

GORDON, W. J. J., *Synectics: The Development of Creative Capacity*, Harper and Row, New York, 1961.

GUILFORD, J. P., "Creativity", *Am. Psychol.*, 1950, **V**, pp. 444-54.

S

GUILFORD, J. P., "A System of the Psychomotor Abilities", *Am. J. Psychol.*, 1958, **71**, pp. 164-74.

GUILFORD, J. P. "Three Faces of Intellect", *Am. Psychol.*, 1959, **14**, pp. 469-79.

GUILFORD, J. P., *The Nature of Human Intelligence*, McGraw-Hill Book Co., New York, 1967.

HANS, MARCIE, "Fueled, in *Save Me a Slice of Moon,* Harcourt Brace Jovanovich, Inc., New York, 1965.

HARLOW, H. F., "The Formation of Learning Sets", *Psychol. Rev.*, 1949, **56**, pp. 51-65.

HARRÉ, R., *An Introduction to the Logic of the Sciences*, Macmillan, London, 1960.

HARTSHORNE, H. and MAY, M., "Studies in the Organization of Character", in KUHLEN, R. and THOMPSON, G. (Eds.), *Psychological Studies of Human Development*, Appleton-Century-Crofts, New York, 2nd ed., 1963.

HAVIGHURST, R. J., and TABA, H. *et al.*, *Adolescent Character and Personality*, John Wiley & Sons, New York, 1949.

HAVIGHURST, R. J. *et al.*, *Studies of Children and Society in New Zealand*, Department of Education, Canterbury University College, Canterbury, 1954.

HAVIGHURST, R. J., STIVERS, E. and DE HAAN, R. F., "A Survey of the Education of Gifted Children", *Supplementary Educational Monograph*, No. 85, University of Chicago Press, Chicago, 1955.

HEBB, D. O., *The Organization of Behaviour*, John Wiley & Sons, New York, 1949.

HIERONYMUS, A. N., "A Study in Social Class Motivation", *J. educ. Psychol.*, 1951, **42**, pp. 193-205.

HIGHET, G., *The Art of Teaching*, Methuen and Co., London, 1963.

HILGARD, E. R., *Theories of Learning*, Appleton-Century-Crofts, New York, 1956.

HOLT, J. C., *How Children Fail*, Pitman and Sons, London, 1964.

HUNT, J. McV., *Intelligence and Experience*, The Ronald Press, New York, 1961.

HURD, P. D., *New Directions in Teaching Secondary School Science*, Rand McNally and Co., Chicago, 1969.

HYMAN, R. T., *Ways of Teaching*, J. P. Lippincott, Philadelphia, 1970.

INHELDER, B., and PIAGET, J., *The Growth of Logical Thinking*, Routledge and Kegan Paul, London, 1958.

JACKSON, P. W., *Life in Classrooms*, Holt, Rinehart and Winston, New York, 1968.

JONES, H. E. "Environmental Influences on Mental Development", in CARMICHAEL, L. (Ed.), *Manual of Child Psychology*, John Wiley & Sons, New York, 1946.

JONES, V., "Character Development in Children", in CARMICHAEL, L. (Ed.), *Manual of Child Psychology*, John Wiley and Sons, New York, 1946.

JOURARD, S. M., *The Transparent Self*, Van Nostrand, Princeton, 1964.

KAHN, R. L. and CANNELL, C. F., *The Dynamics of Interviewing*, John Wiley & Sons, New York, 1957.

KENNAN, G. F., "Democracy and the Student Left", *Dialogue*, 1968, **2**, No. 2, U.S. Information Service, p. 16.

KERSH, B. Y., "The Motivating Effect of Learning by Directed Discovery", *J. educ. Psychol.*, 1962, **53**, pp. 93-100.

KERSH, B. Y., "Programmed Classroom Instruction", in GLASER, R. (Ed.), *Teaching Machines and Programmed Learning II: Data and Directions*,

Department of Audio Visual Instruction, National Education Association, 1965, pp. 321-68.

KIBLER, R. J. et al., Behavioural Objectives and Instruction, Allyn and Bacon, Boston, 1970.

KINGSLEY, H. L. and GARRY, R., The Nature and Conditions of Learning, Prentice-Hall Inc., Englewood Cliffs, 1957.

KRATHWOHL, D. R. et al., Taxonomy of Educational Objectives—The Classification of Educational Goals, Handbook II: the Affective Domain, David McKay, New York, 1964.

KRUMBOLTZ, J. D. and THORESEN, C. E., Behavioural Counselling: Cases and Techniques, Holt, Rinehart and Winston, New York, 1969.

LAWRENCE, P. J., "The Significance of Method in Intellectual Tasks". Unpublished Ph.D. Thesis in Education, Canterbury University College, Christchurch, 1955.

LEWIN, K., Field Theory in Social Sciences, Harper and Row, New York, 1951.

LEWIN, K., LIPPITT, R. and WHITE, R. K., "Patterns of Aggressive Behaviour in Experimentally Created Social Climates", J. soc. Psychol., 1939, 10, pp. 271-99.

LEWIN, K. et al., "Levels of Aspiration", in HUNT, J. McV. (Ed.), Personality and the Behaviour Disorders, The Ronald Press, New York, 1944.

LIGON, M. G., and McDANIEL, S. W., The Teacher's Role in Counselling, Prentice-Hall Inc., Englewood Cliffs, 1970.

LEMBO, J. M., The Psychology of Effective Classroom Instruction, Charles E. Merrill, Columbus, 1969.

LOVELL, K., "A Study of the Problem of Intellectual Deterioration in Adolescents and Young Adults", Br. J. Psychol., 1955, 46, pp. 199-210.

LOVELL, K., "A Follow-up Study of Some Aspects of the Work of Piaget and Inhelder on the Child's Conception of Space", Br. J. educ. Psychol., 1959, 29, pp. 104-17.

LOVELL, K., The Growth of Basic Mathematical and Scientific Concepts in Children, University of London Press, London, 1961.

LOVELL, K., MITCHELL, B., and EVERETT, I. R., "An Experimental Study of the Growth of Some Logical Structures", Br. J. Psychol., 1962, 53, No. 2, pp. 175-88.

LUNDY, R. M., and BERKOWITZ, L., "Cognitive Complexity and Assimilative Projection in Attitude Change", J. abnorm. soc. Psychol., July 1957, 55, pp. 34-37.

LURIA, A. R. and JUDOVICH, F. I., Speech and the Development of Mental Processes, Staples Press, London, 1959.

McASHAN, H. H., Writing Behavioural Objectives, Harper and Row, New York, 1970.

McCLELLAND, D. et al., The Achievement Motive, Appleton-Century-Crofts, New York, 1953.

McCLOSKEY, M. G., Teaching Strategies and Classroom Realities, Prentice-Hall Inc., Englewood Cliffs, 1971.

MAGER, R. F., Preparing Instructional Objectives, Fearon Publishers, Palo Alto, 1962.

MASLOW, A. H., "Deprivation, Threat and Frustration", Psychol. Rev., 1941, 48, pp. 364-6.

MASLOW, A. H., Motivation and Personality, Harper and Brothers, New York, 1954.

MEDNICK, S. A., Learning, Prentice-Hall Inc., Englewood Cliffs, 1964.

MEILI-DWORETZKI, G., "The Development of Perception in the Rorschach", in KLOPFER, Bruno *et al.*, *Developments in the Rorschach Technique*, **II**, G. Harrap & Co., London, n.d.

MILGRAM, S., "Behavioural Study of Obedience", *J. abnorm soc. Psychol.*, 1963, **67**, No. 4, pp. 371-8.

MORRIS, B., "The Personal Foundations of Education", *Education*, New Zealand Department of Education, 1960, **9**, No. 6, pp. 162-4.

MOWRER, O. H., *Learning Theory and Personality Dynamics*, The Ronald Press, New York, 1950.

MURPHY, G., *Human Potentialities*, Basic Books, New York, 1958.

MURRAY, H., *Explorations in Personality*, Oxford University Press, New York, 1938.

NAGEL, E., *The Structure of Science*, Routledge and Kegan Paul, London, 1961.

Nebraska Symposium on Motivation, *Current Theory and Research in Motivation*, **I**, University of Nebraska Press, 1953.

New Zealand Educational Institute, "Progress in Professional Promotion and Protection—A Summary", in *National Education Journal of the N.Z.E.I.*, Wellington, 1970, p. 256.

NORTHROP, E. S. C., *The Logic of the Sciences and the Humanities*, Meridian Books, Cleveland, 1959.

OSGOOD, C. E., *Method and Theory in Experimental Psychology*, Oxford University Press, New York, 1953.

PECK, R. F. and HAVIGHURST, R. J. *et al.*, *The Psychology of Character Development*, John Wiley & Sons, New York, 1960.

PEEL, E. A., *The Psychological Basis of Education*, Oliver and Boyd, Edinburgh, 1958.

PEEL, E. A., *The Pupil's Thinking*, Oldbourne Book Co., London, 1960.

PIAGET, J., *Judgement and Reasoning in the Child*, Kegan Paul, Trench, Trubner and Co., London, 1928.

PIAGET, J., *Moral Judgement of the Child*, Harcourt Brace and World, New York, 1932.

PIAGET, J., *The Psychology of Intelligence*, Routledge and Kegan Paul, London, 1950.

PIAGET, J., *The Child's Conception of Number*, Routledge and Kegan Paul, London, 1952.

PIAGET, J., *The Origin of Intelligence in the Child*, Routledge and Kegan Paul, London, 1953.

PIAGET, J., *The Construction of Reality in the Child*, Routledge and Kegan Paul, London, 1954.

PIAGET, J., and INHELDER, B., *The Child's Conception of Space*, Routledge and Kegan Paul, London, 1956.

POLLACK, O., "Treatment of Character Disorders: A Dilemma in Casework Culture", in YOUNGHUSBAND, E., (Ed.) *Social Work and Social Values: Readings in Social Work*, Allen and Unwin, London, 1967, **III**, pp. 121-41.

POPHAM, W. J. *et al.*, *Instructional Objectives*, Rand McNally and Co., Chicago, 1969.

POPHAM, W. J. and BAKER, E. I., *Systematic Instruction*, Prentice-Hall Inc., Englewood Cliffs, 1970.

POSTMAN, L., BRUNER, J. S., and McGINNIES, A., "Personal Values as Selective Factors in Perception", *J. abnorm. soc. Psychol.*, 1948, **43**, pp. 142-54.

ROGERS, C. R., *Client-Centred Therapy*, Houghton Mifflin, Boston, 1951.

ROGERS, C. R., *Counselling and Psychotherapy*, Houghton Mifflin, Boston, 1942.

ROGERS, C. R. *On Becoming a Person*, Houghton Mifflin, Boston, 1961.

ROGERS, C. R., *Encounter Groups*, Harper and Row, New York, 1970.

SANDERS, N. M., *Classroom Questions: What Kinds?*, Harper and Row, New York, 1966.

SCHMUCK, R. A. and SCHMUCK, P. A., *Group Processes in the Classroom*, W. C. Brown Co., Dubuque, 1971.

SEARLES, H. L., *Logic and Scientific Methods*, The Ronald Press, New York, 2nd ed., 1956.

SEARS, P. S., "Levels of Aspiration in Academically Successful and Unsuccessful Children", *J. abnorm. soc. Psychol.*, 1940, **35**, pp. 498-536.

SEARS, P. S. and HILGARD, E. R., "The Teacher's Role in the Motivation of the Learner", *The Sixty-third Yearbook of the National Society for the Study of Education, Part I*, University of Chicago Press, Chicago, 1964.

SEARS, R. R. *et al.*, *Patterns of Child Rearing*, Row, Peterson and Co., Evanston, 1957.

SHAFTEL, F. R. and SHAFTEL, G., *Role Playing for Social Values*, Prentice-Hall Inc., Englewood Cliffs, 1967.

SHERIF, M. and CANTRIL, H., *The Psychology of Ego-involvements*, John Wiley & Sons, New York, 1948.

SHERIF, M. and SHERIF, C. W., *Groups in Harmony and Tension*, Harper Brothers, New York, 1953.

SIEGEL, S., "Levels of Aspiration and Decision Making", *Psychol. Rev.*, July 1957, **64**, pp. 253-62.

SILBERMAN, C. E., *Crisis in the Classroom*, Random House, New York, 1970.

SKINNER, B. F., "Are Theories of Learning Necessary?", *Psychol. Rev.*, 1950, **57**, pp. 211-20.

SKINNER, B. F., *Science and Human Behaviour*, Macmillan, New York, 1953.

SKINNER, B. F., *Verbal Behaviour*, Appleton-Century-Crofts, New York, 1957.

SKINNER, B. F., "Reflections on a Decade of Teaching Machines", in GLASER, R., *Teaching Machines and Programmed Learning II*, Department of Audio Visual Instruction, National Education Association of U.S.A., 1965.

SKINNER, B. F., *The Technology of Teaching*, Appleton-Century-Crofts, New York, 1968.

SMITH, B. O., "A Concept of Teaching", *Teachers' College Record*, 1960, **61**, pp. 229-41.

SMITH, K. Y. and SMITH, M. F., *Cybernetic Principles of Learning and Educaitonal Design*, Holt, Rinehart and Winston, New York, 1966.

STOLUROW, L. and PAHEL, K., "Letter to the Editor", *Harvard Educational Review*, Summer 1963, **33**, pp. 383-5.

STROM, R. D. (Ed.), *Teachers and the Learning Process*, Prentice-Hall Inc., Englewood Cliffs, 1971.

TABA, H. and FREEMAN, F. Elzey, "Teaching Strategies and Thought Processes", *Teachers' College Record*, 1964, **65**, pp. 524-34.

TANNENBAUM, R. and SCHMIDT, W. H., "How to Choose a Leadership Pattern", in SUTERMEISTER, R. A., *People and Productivity*, McGraw-Hill Book Co., New York, 1963.

TAYLOR, C. W., *Creativity, Progress and Potential*, McGraw-Hill Book Co., New York, 1964.

THOMPSON, I. G. and HUNNICUTT, C., "The Effects of Repeated Praise and Blame on the Work Achievement on Introverts and Extroverts", *J. educ. Psychol.*, 1944, **35**, pp. 257-66.

TRAVERS, J. F., *Learning: Analysis and Application*, David McKay, New York, 1965.

TROW, W. C., *Psychology in Teaching and Learning*, Houghton Mifflin, Boston, 1960.

URIS, A., "How Good a Leader Are You?", in SUTERMEISTER, R. A., *People and Productivity*, McGraw-Hill Book Co., New York, 1963.

VERNON, M. D., "The Development of Imaginative Construction in Children", *Br. J. Psychol.*, 1948, **39**, pp. 102-11.

VERNON, P. E., *The Structure of Human Abilities*, Methuen, London, 1950.

VERNON, P. E., "Education and the Psychology of Individual Differences", *Harvard Educational Review*, 1958, **28**, pp. 91-104.

VINACKE, W. E., *The Psychology of Thinking*, McGraw-Hill Book Co., New York, 1952.

WALLACH, M. A. *et al.*, "Diffusion of Responsibility and Level of Risk Taking in Groups", *J. abnorm. soc. Psychol.*, 1964, **68**, pp. 263-74.

WALLER, W., *The Sociology of Teaching*, John Wiley and Sons, New York, 1932.

WARTERS, J., *Techniques of Counselling*, McGraw-Hill Book Co., New York, 1954.

Webster's *New Twentieth Century Dictionary*, World Publishing Co., Columbus, 2nd ed., 1963.

WERTHEIMER, M., *Productive Thinking*, Harper Brothers, London, 1945.

WHEELER, L., *Interpersonal Influence*, Allyn and Bacon, Boston, 1970.

WHITEHEAD, A. N., *Adventures of Ideas*, Cambridge University Press, Cambridge, 1920.

WHITEHEAD, A. N., *The Aims of Education and Other Essays*, Williams and Norgate, London, 1932.

WILLIAMS, J. D., "Teaching Problem Solving", *Educ. Res.*, November, 1960, **III**, No. 1, pp. 12-36.

WILLIAMS, J. D., "Teaching Arithmetic by Concrete Analogy—I. Miming Devices", *Educ. Res.*, Feb.-June 1961, **III**, pp. 112-25 and pp. 195-213.

WITHALL, J. and LEWIS, W. W., "Social Interaction in the Classroom", in GAGE, N. L. (Ed.), *Handbook of Research on Teaching*, Rand McNally and Co., Chicago, 1963.

WITKINS, H. A. *et al.*, *Personality Through Perception*, Harper and Brothers, New York, 1954.

# Index